ULTIMATE ILLUSTI
GUIDE TO SEWING CLOTHES

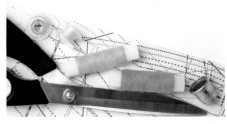

Ultimate Illustrated Guide to Sewing Clothes

Landauer Publishing, www.landauerpub.com, is an imprint of Fox Chapel Publishing Company, Inc.

This book is a collection of new and previously published material. Portions of this book have been reproduced from: *Garment Construction* (ISBN 978-1-56523-509-0), *Tailoring* (ISBN 978-1-56523-511-3), and *Couture Techniques* (ISBN 978-1-56523-534-2).

Project Team
Acquisition editor: Amelia Johanson
Editors: Leslie T. (O'Neill) Galliano and Colleen Dorsey
Designer: Mary Ann Kahn
Proofreader and indexer: Jean Bissell

ISBN 978-1-947163-74-4 (paperback)
ISBN 978-1-63981-015-4 (spiral)

Library of Congress Control Number: 2021945613

We are always looking for talented authors. To submit an idea, please send a brief inquiry to acquisitions@foxchapelpublishing.com.

Printed in China

ULTIMATE ILLUSTRATED GUIDE TO SEWING CLOTHES

A COMPLETE COURSE ON MAKING CLOTHING FOR FIT AND FASHION

Joi Mahon

CONTENTS

59

250

38

267

245

203

215

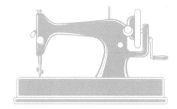

INTRODUCTION

I have always loved sewing! I remember the first time I read a sewing catalog, the first sewing magazine I purchased, and especially my very first sewing project. Like many of you, I was young when the sewing bug hit. I fully admit, the clothes I created in the early years were not necessarily blue ribbon–worthy, but I loved them nonetheless.

Many people learn sewing out of necessity, but I learned out of the love for sewing. I enjoyed the whole process of creating something from the design and pattern phase to the finished product. It was all hand sewing in my early years before I started to use a machine. Today, people are rediscovering home sewing with the advent of DIY television, reality fashion contests, and limitless YouTube videos. But now, it is more about modern design and less about sewing to save money. The idea of creating unique designs and personally fitted clothing appeals to many. It is not uncommon for people who have not sewn for several decades to return to fashion sewing as well as for those wanting to learn for the first time getting started.

Now more than ever, with the advances in sewing machine technology, fabrics, threads, and notions, we have access to everything we need to achieve our sewing goals. New home tailors can create classy, fun, and unique Pinterest-worthy garments. The inspiration and options are limitless.

We will begin our journey together through chapters "Sewing Basics," "Selecting and Preparing Fabrics," and "Achieving the Right Fit." Then you will learn how to build the foundation for your own designer wardrobe in "Sewing Classic Garments." When we are finished, you will have the fundamental skills to sew almost anything.

As a self-taught sewer, I encourage my students to love sewing first, then focus on mastery, because developing skills takes time. The more you sew, the more you grow. Keeping that principle in mind, I would like to share a story that left a major impression on me.

During my senior year of high school, I was determined to win the Fashion Review Trophy, which was going to be a big challenge because they selected only one winner out of many participants. I spent the entire summer sewing an ensemble that included every design element possible: plaid wool fabric with perfect pleats and a blind-faced hem, buttons and buttonholes, and a silk blouse with perfectly hand-rolled narrow hems on the ruffles, interfacing in the collar, front facing with buttonholes, cuffs, and more. I had a difficult time lining up the plaid skirt and remember crying at the frustration. My dad calmed me down and helped me rip out the mistakes at the seam and encouraged me to try again. I worked until I had a beautiful and perfect outfit that would be hard to beat. At the fashion show I was awarded the Grand Champion! This was my very last sewing event before going to college and the one achievement I aspired to. Success!

However, when the fashion show was over, the superintendent came running up to me and told me they said the wrong name. I was actually the runner-up. They took the trophy from my hands and left me in tears! Why did I cry? Honestly, I wanted the darn trophy! I lost perspective. People can take your trophy or your joy (forgive me!), but it does not define who you are or take away your experience, learning, skills, and satisfaction. Furthermore, you simply cannot win them all.

Sewing is a journey that makes many stories—you are writing your future sewing story today! I hope you will learn from the lessons in this book and remember to embrace your successes and learn from your failures. There is always something new to try and a new garment to design. I am so glad I get to share that journey with you.

—Designer Joi

This jar is full of notions and sewing tools that I played with in my grandma's attic at their farm when I was growing up. These were some of my first sewing memories.

CHAPTER 1

SEWING BASICS

Success in any craft begins with a solid foundation of basic skills. Mastery comes with time and practice. Each time you practice a basic skill, you grow your abilities and improve. By practicing and experimenting with the techniques in this book, you will continue to develop your foundational sewing skills as well as learn new techniques. When that happens, you have truly made those skills your own. Before you know it, you will be a confident and masterful sewist!

If you are new to sewing, start by learning about both machine and hand sewing. In addition, you should understand the different tools that are available while also learning basic skills such as ironing and how to sew a basic seam. If you are returning to sewing after a long absence, you might feel your skills are a little rusty or need updating with modern sewing techniques and technology. A refresher course may be exactly what you need to feel inspired again.

Regardless of your level of sewing abilities, you are bound to learn a new tip or technique that is different or more useful than your standard method. Once you have a solid foundation in the sewing basics, you will be ready to choose a pattern and get underway with more creative projects and sewing success.

A Note about Step-by-Step Numbering

In this book, step-by-step instructions are broken down into small, bite-sized chunks for each phase of a project. Photos are given for some essential steps, but not all steps. Photos are almost always right next to the step text or mini section with which they correspond. If they're not, they have an extra caption clarifying what they're showing. So don't be confused if you see more than one step 1 on a page!

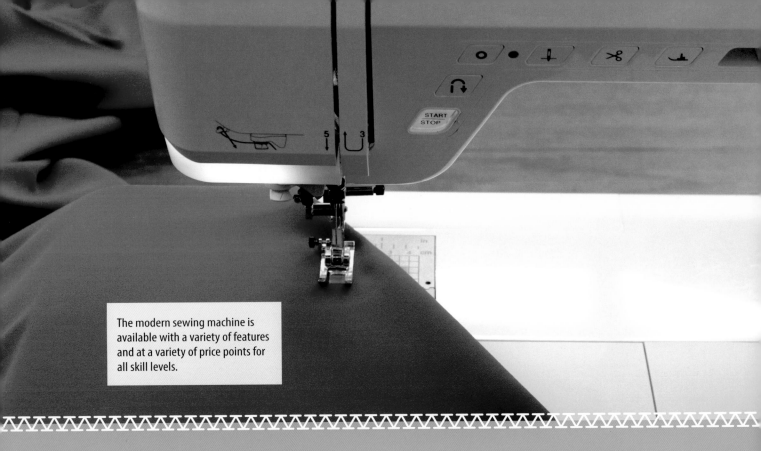

The modern sewing machine is available with a variety of features and at a variety of price points for all skill levels.

MACHINE SEWING TECHNIQUES
SELECTING A SEWING MACHINE

If you do not yet own a sewing machine, you will find the marketplace packed with options. It makes sense to purchase a machine that you can grow into as sewists often find that they become interested in more complex projects as their skill sets improve. First, evaluate your overall sewing goals to guide you in choosing the machine best suited for your needs. Two primary factors to consider are what you want to sew and how often you will be using the machine. Sewing heavier textiles will require different tools than basic fabrics for everyday clothing. You may also want to invest in a higher quality machine if you plan to use it for a variety of types of sewing or if you consider yourself more than just a casual sewist.

Many brands and styles of machines are available and can be purchased new or used. They range anywhere from $99 for a basic, electric straight stitch and zigzag model to several thousand dollars for a top-of-the-line computerized model with embroidery capabilities. (Don't worry—you don't need a machine that costs thousands of dollars to make great clothes!) Your first machine may be basic, but it should include features for garment sewing such as variable stitch lengths and styles, buttonhole stitching, and a zipper foot. For a machine with these features, you can expect to spend between $180 and $350. If you are interested in advanced or modern design techniques, you can find machines that embroider, monogram, or create intricate quilting stitches with state-of-the-art computerized screens and scanning capabilities, just to name a few.

Avoid purchasing the cheapest machine available from a big box store. Buying a mid-range machine from a reputable dealer will provide customer support, warranty, and often complementary classes on how to use your new machine. You will also be more likely to receive personalized customer service from someone with experience and knowledge in using the machines.

Machines have lots of options and features, notions are available in all kinds of styles, and threads and fabrics come in thousands of colors and patterns. Fashion sewing has never been more engaging for the modern sewist.

MACHINE SETUP

Regardless of the brand or functions, certain fundamentals concerning needles, thread, and stitching apply to all sewing machines.

- The standard size 12–14 needle is suitable for all medium-weight fabrics except knits.
- Knits are best sewn with a size 14 ballpoint needle.
- The standard thread is a 50 weight all-purpose polyester thread or mercerized cotton.
- Set the machine to sew regular seams at 12 stitches per inch (2.5cm).
- Unless your machine makes stitches designed for knits, knit fabrics require special procedures (page 17).

For specific instructions on setting up, threading, and operating your sewing machine, see the manual that came with the machine. Note that the most common sewing machine abuses are simply failing to maintain the machine after purchase. Keep up on general maintenance with your sewing machine. See your user guide for instructions.

TIP *Your machine is designed for you to only turn the handwheel toward you. Never force the machine wheel to turn in reverse. This may damage the sewing mechanisms.*

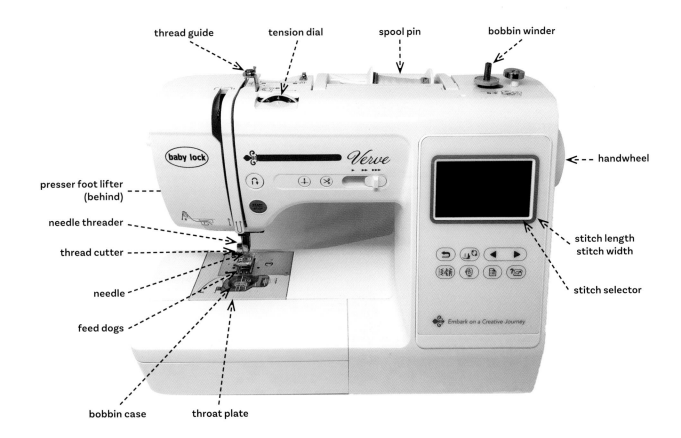

SEWING A BASIC SEAM: THE FOUNDATION OF ANY SEWING PROJECT

1. For a permanent seam, lower the needle into the fabric ¼" (0.5cm) from the beginning edge of the seam. Sew two to three stitches forward and stop.
2. Push reverse and sew two to three stitches back and stop. (This is backstitching.)
3. Sew forward to complete the seam and stop. Let the machine feed the fabric under the needle by itself; do not pull or push it. Use your hands only to guide and control the fabric along the stitching line.
4. Push reverse and sew two to three stitches back from the edge. Sew forward two to three stitches to reinforce.
5. Lift the needle and foot, remove the fabric, and cut the thread. This basic seam is the foundation for any sewing project.

TIP

What is a basting stitch and when do you use it? Basting is a temporary stitch used to test a seam, anchor a seam, or check the fit before sewing the actual seam. Basting stitches are longer and fewer per inch and often are removed. Do not backstitch basting.

A regular seam has approximately 12 stitches per inch (2.5cm). This may vary slightly based on the size of your thread, needle, and fabric selection.

A balanced seam will look the same on the top and bottom. If you see loops on one side or the other, adjust your tension by tightening. If it looks like the thread is pulling too tight into the fabric, you may need to loosen the tension. If this does not help, reference your machine manual for troubleshooting. The correct thread and needle for your fabric may also affect the seam appearance.

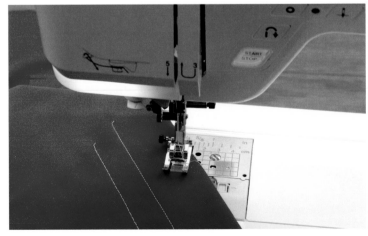

A basting stitch will have approximately 6 stitches per inch (2.5cm), but may vary based on the stitch selection and your machine settings.

SEWING AROUND A CORNER

You may encounter corners in many garment projects such as on collars, pockets, waistbands, and mitered edges.

1. To get around a right-angled corner, sew to the point of the angle and set your needle down (through the fabric) in this precise spot.
2. Raise the presser foot. With the needle holding it in place, you can now pivot your fabric without it shifting. Rotate the fabric 90°. Drop the presser foot and continue to sew along the new line.

TIP
Marking your angle with a chalk roller is a useful guide and will ensure you create precise stitching.

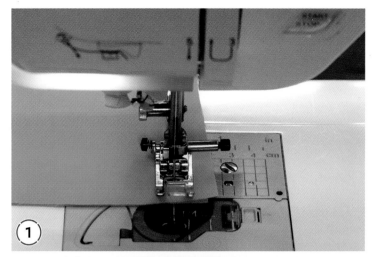

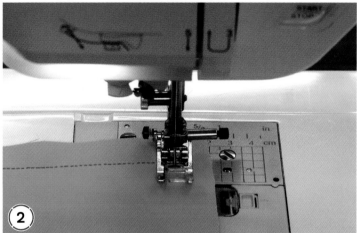

SEWING ACUTE ANGLES

An acute angle is common in some shirt collars and notched jacket lapels. The process is the same as sewing right angles, only the key is to insert a single straight stitch as a transition from one side of the angle to the other. This additional stitch will allow for the fabric to relax and the point will look flawless from the outside of the garment. If you omit this extra stitch, it will be difficult to achieve a sharp point on the outside of the fabric.

Sew to within one stitch of the point. With the needle down, raise the presser foot and pivot halfway. Lower the presser foot and make a single stich by turning the machine handwheel. Keep the needle down. Pivot again and sew to the other side.

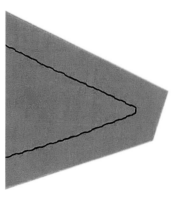

The acute angle occurs frequently in stylized clothing such as collars and cuff edges. The stitches are sewn to a point and with the needle in the fabric and presser foot lifted, the garment is rotated to an angle that does not form a right angle.

SEWING AROUND CURVES

Many areas feature curves such as necklines, waistlines, arm openings, and the crotch curve of pants. When a pattern piece that features a curve is cut out, you stitch a row of stitches just inside the width of the seam allowance that will be sewn; this is called stay-stitching. This will help reinforce the curved edge, prevent stretching or distortion of the edge, and prevent clipping through into the seam.

Curves in garment construction might be gradual and easy to sew or dramatic and require more control. When stitching around a curved seam, use a shorter stitch length such as 17 stitches per inch (2.5cm) and guide the fabric carefully around the curve with your hands. Marking the stitching line with a sewing chalk or pencil will help with precise sewing placement, and sewing slowly will also help control the shape of the curve.

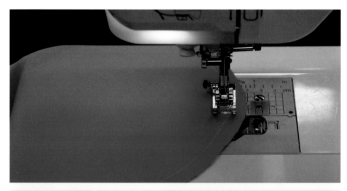

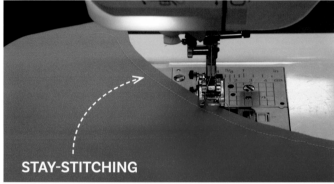

STAY-STITCHING

Before sewing some fabric edges it is necessary to stitch a line of stitches called stay-stitching. Often this is used when the seam line will be clipped. The stay-stitches reinforce the edge, prevent stretching, and are a guide for not clipping too deep into the seam. The seam may be straight, curved, or any angle.

SEWING EASED SEAMS

In your sewing projects, you may encounter the need to ease a seam when one side of the seam is longer than the other. Sometimes the difference is a slight amount, while other times it is significantly more. A few examples of easing include sewing the inseam of pants, the underarm of the sleeve, and joining a sleeve to the arm opening of the bodice.

To join the seams, one option is to cinch up and gather the longer edge and distribute the excess fabric evenly on the shorter corresponding edge. Or you may strategically place the excess in a specific area. This works best for seams that are very different in length.

Most often the desired effect is to make either side of the seam look the same length with no visible gathering, tucks, or pleats. The pattern piece of the longer edge has a little excess to allow for movement in the pattern. One way to achieve this is to distribute the longer piece evenly against the shorter. Pin in several places and stitch slowly with control over how the fabric goes through the machine. By providing some tension on the shorter piece you can ease in the excess beautifully.

EDGE STITCHING

Sewing a straight, even row of decorative stitches close to the edge of the fabric is called "edge stitching." One of the most common uses is sewing around a pocket or shirt collar. The stitch placement is approximately ⅛" (3mm) from the edge of the fabric. By using the markings on your presser foot, you can easily achieve consistent placement.

To turn the corner, stop with the needle in the fabric at the exact pivot point. Raise the presser foot and rotate your project. Put the presser foot down and continue sewing.

Edge stitching pockets is easier than a collar because the pocket is sewn flat on a larger pattern piece. Because the stitching is so close to the edge on a collar, for example, you may need to use an awl or tip of the seam ripper to help ease the point or edge through the pressure foot as you continue sewing.

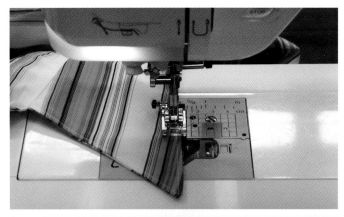

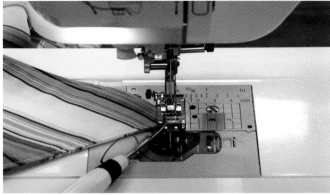

You may need to use an awl or tip of the seam ripper to help ease the point or edge through the pressure foot as you continue sewing.

TOPSTITCHING

Topstitching is meant to be seen from the top edge of a garment and is usually decorative. It is commonly used on necklines, pockets, and hems. Functionally, it can also be used to make flat-fell, the folded over and topstitched jeans seams, for example; however, its main focus is for decorative effect.

Many beautiful decorative threads further enhance the embellished characteristics of a seam. To achieve a professional look, the stitches should lay perfectly parallel to the edge of the fabric unless there is a design reason not to do so.

Topstitching can have a longer or shorter stitch length based on the thread selection and fabric combinations. A topstitched denim pocket may have fewer stitches per inch when using a heavy or bulkier thread, while a topstitched collar on a silk blouse may utilize smaller stitches and fine thread weight.

Press your seams or areas of topstitching prior to sewing. This will reduce bulk and provide a smooth sewing surface. To guide the topstitching, you may first stitch a row of edge stitching next to the edge of the project. Line up with the first row of edge stitching. It is helpful to use the throat plate of your sewing machine to sew perfect parallel stitches.

BASIC ZIPPER SEWING

There are many styles of zippers, such as separating, jeans/trouser, invisible, and regular lapped. Read the pattern envelope to determine the type of zipper needed for your specific garment, because each of these requires different steps in assembly. Before you tackle a fly front, you want to master the basic lapped zipper application.

When sewing on a zipper by machine, use the special one-toed zipper foot. This has a groove on each side. To prevent the zipper teeth from interfering with the stitching, move the foot to the left or right of the needle position based on the edge of the zipper you are sewing.

1. Sew the seam of your garment, leaving open the area where the zipper will be attached. Press the zipper seam allowance to the inside.

2. With the right side of the zipper facing up, pin the left edge of the zipper opening to the zipper tape next to the teeth of the zipper. Place the zipper foot to the left of the needle and stitch.

3. Lay the right edge of the fabric on top of the zipper, lining up the folded edge of the fabric. Pin in place. Place the zipper foot to the left of the needle. Starting at the bottom, stitch across the bottom edge of the zipper. Pivot, then stitch up the fabric, catching the zipper tape underneath. This row of stitching will be approximately ⅝" (1.6cm) from the center of the seam opening.

TIP

Sometimes the zipper tab is difficult to sew around when nearing the top of the right zipper side. Stitch up as far as you can. Make sure the needle is in the fabric, lift the presser foot, and unzip the zipper so the tab is where you have already sewn. Put the presser foot down and stitch the last portion of the upper edge.

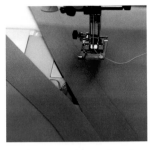

TIP

Insert a zipper longer than the opening for a seamless result. The zipper will extend beyond the top edge of the garment. Insert the zipper. Once it is sewn, pull the zipper pull down into the garment. Place a safety pin on the zipper to prevent accidentally pulling off the zipper pull. Trim off the excess at the top and place a new zipper stop at the top by squeezing it with pliers.

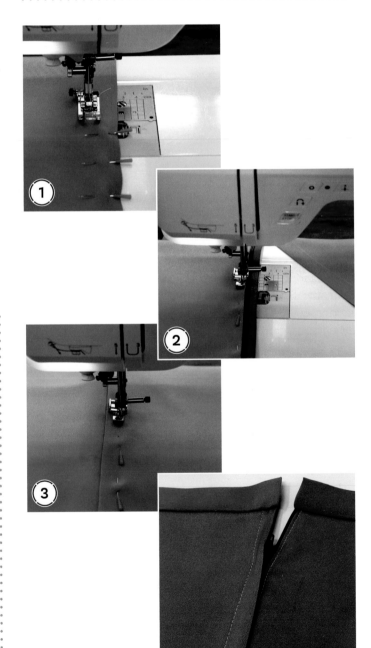

SEWING KNIT FABRICS

If your sewing machine is well maintained, you should easily be able to sew knit fabrics. The new technology in sewing machines does make knit sewing easier. If you have an older machine that has not been used in a while, it is imperative that you have it serviced and oiled to ensure that it is in good working order. New or old, a machine that is not working well will cause issues when sewing, especially knit fabrics.

The biggest difference in sewing a knit compared to other fabrics is the type of needle you need to use. Sewing machine needles use the needle system HAX1SP, which is a standard needle length and size for fitting the needle into the machine. The difference among needles is the tips; you select the needle type based on the requirements for your specific project. Knit fabrics require either a ballpoint, stretch, jersey, or Microtex needle (Microtex is used for fine delicate knits).

A common issue with knit sewing is skipped stitches, which most often occur when the wrong needle is used or the machine is out of service. Holes in the fabric, or running, also occur when the incorrect needle has been used on the fabric. These issues can easily be corrected by selecting the proper needle.

Sewing Knits Formula

Once you have selected your fabric, use an easy formula for determining the stitches needed for your specific project. Lighter weight and delicate fabrics require less bulky seams, whereas a heavy fabric may need a thicker thread and a bigger stitch to ensure it holds the two edges of the seam together. Use the below formula for setting up your machine. Remember, you can always create a test sample if you are not sure of your choices. If you like the results, attach your sample to a notecard and save for the next time you sew that fabric. Stitch samples are a great idea even on non-knit fabrics.

1. Select the stitch
2. Select the stitch width
3. Select the length
4. Select the thread
   Evaluate:
   - Do the stitches hug the fabric evenly?
   - Is the stitch too heavy, too light, or appropriate for the fabric and garment?
   - Most importantly, is the stitch durable for its function?

Special needles are required to sew sturdy knit or stretch garments.

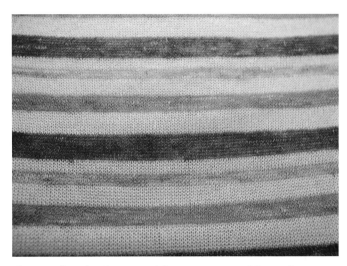

This stripe linen knit has a very delicate open weave. A heavy, dense stitch would not form well on this fabric. Instead, use a lighter, more open stitch. If serging, use a 3-thread overlock instead of a 4-thread overlock.

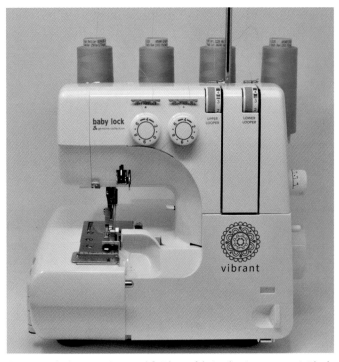

A serger, which sews, trims, and finishes a fabric edge in one pass, is ideal for sewing knits. A serger is a specialty machine that uses three or more threads at a time, and provides a professional seam finish.

Machine sewing is not a replacement for all hand sewing—some work is best done by hand.

HAND SEWING TECHNIQUES

No matter how sophisticated your sewing machine, there will always be a time and place for hand stitches—not only temporary basting and marking stitching, but the permanent finishing stitches that can make the difference between an amateur and a professional look.

Skilled hand work has many benefits and is necessary in those difficult places machines cannot readily reach. It provides more precision and control and can create stitches that are more elegant and less likely to harm delicate fabrics than machine stitches. The quality of hand stitching will always be apparent wherever you choose to apply these techniques, even though the stitches are often invisible and the seams are hidden.

NEEDLE AND THREAD

Needles are available in many sizes. In hand sewing needles, the higher the size number, the smaller the needle. A size 7 or 8 is used with polyester or cotton thread, while a size 8 or 9 is used for silk. (In machine needles, it's the opposite: The lower the size number, the smaller the needle.) When selecting the needle size, remember that the eye must be large enough for thread to pass through freely, and the shank must be heavy enough not to bend, but the point must be fine enough to pierce the fabric without marring. You should use the shortest needle possible and measure your thread approximately the length of your arm—18"–24" (45.7–61cm). If the thread is cut any longer, it will be more likely to tangle.

Readily available mercerized cotton and all-purpose polyester are the most common threads. They are used to sew cotton, linen, rayon, and cotton-synthetic blends. Silk thread is superior for sewing silk, wool, wool-silk blends, and synthetics, because it is elastic and leaves no lint. However, there are other specialty threads, such as pre-waxed Silamide, which is used in tailoring, Sereflex, which is used for superior elongation and stretch, and buttonhole twist, which is used for decorative buttonholes and bar tacks. Thread color should match that of fabric or be slightly darker if an exact match is not possible.

THIMBLES

A thimble can be an asset to your hand sewing to improve speed and accuracy, although they are not as widely used as in the past. Thimbles are made of plastic, wood, porcelain, silicone, or metal. Avoid collectible or craft thimbles as they may be difficult to use. In traditional tailoring, the thimble has an open top (see page 39). Your thimble should be lightweight and fit snugly on your middle finger. Contrary to how a thimble is often portrayed, the correct way to use a thimble is pushing the needle side-to-side with a bent finger while pinching the needle between your thumb and forefinger, rather than in an up-and-down motion.

KNOTTING THE THREAD

1. To prepare to tie the knot in the end of the thread, loop the end of the thread once around the tip of your index finger. For a thicker knot that will hold on heavy fabric, loop the thread around your finger two or three times.
2. Roll the loop of thread off your fingertip, keeping the thread taut.
3. With the loop of thread pinched between your thumb and finger, draw it down into a knot.
4. Some stitches do not require a knot. The formation of the stitch and overlap will anchor the stitch.

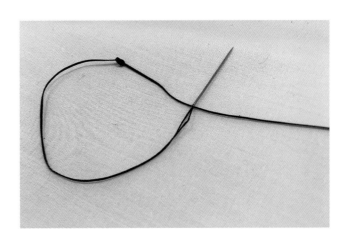

TIP

If you are left-handed, follow the stitch samples beginning from left to right.

THE BASTING STITCH: FOR MARKINGS AND TEMPORARY SEWING

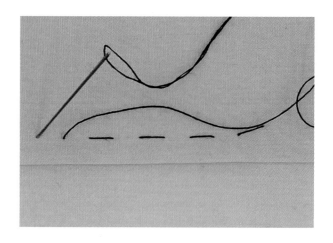

Sew basting stitches with a single strand of thread. When basting to mark a stitching line (marking), sew directly on the seam line markings. When basting for a fitting, sew the garment pieces together a fraction inside or outside the seam line so that the stitches will leave no visible trace. On knit fabrics, begin and end basting stitches with a loose fastening stitch and use a shorter stitch length. It is necessary for the seam to utilize a stretch thread for flexibility. Hold the fabric with your left hand and push the needle with your right.

1. Using a knotted thread, take a stitch down and up through all the fabric thicknesses, bringing the point of the needle out just in front of your left index finger. Push the needle all the way through the fabric with the front side of your thimble and pull the thread through.

2. Continue the process using another ½"–1" (1.5–2.5cm) length stitch spaced ½" (1.5cm) apart. Pull the thread through firmly, yet loosely enough not to pucker the fabric. Continue the process. You will develop your own techniques, so your lengths may vary. The objective is to practice consistency.

3. When completed, a finished row of ½" (1.5cm) basting stitches will appear on both sides of the fabric. Secure the end of the line of stitches with a fastening stitch (page 26). In the case of markings, leave a 4" (10cm) loose thread tail.

4. To remove the basting stitches, first snip the stitch next to the knot. Next, snip the fastening stitches and continue to snip at 5" (12.7cm) intervals. Remove the threads. Never pull knots through fabric.

TIP

When basting fabrics that may shift, interrupt the basting stitches at various intervals with short fastening (backstitches) stitches to create a stronger fit.

THE TAILOR TACK:
FOR TRANSFERRING PATTERN
MARKINGS TO FABRIC

The tailor tack stitch is used to transfer pattern markings to both sides of one or more layers of fabrics. It enables you to mark quickly and precisely and will not remain on the fabric permanently, as chalk might.

1. Using a double strand of unknotted mark-stitching thread, take a ½" (1.5cm) stitch from right to left on the outside and at the far-right edge of the line to be marked. Adjust the threads so that they are even, then stitch through the paper pattern and both fabric layers.

2. Pull the threads through, leaving a 2" (5cm) loose end. Then take a 1" (2.5cm) long stitch at least ½" (1.5cm) to the left of the previous stitch. Push the needle all the way through the fabric with the front part of the thimble as in step 1 of the basting stitch. Pull the thread through gently, leaving a 2" (5cm) loop on top of the pattern piece. Continue the process, ending the row of tailor tacks with at least 2" (5cm) of loose thread so that the thread does not pull through.

3. If marking only one point, such as the tip of a dart, take a ¼" (0.5cm) long stitch, leaving 2" (5cm) long loose ends. Then take another stitch through the same point and pull the thread through, leaving a 2" (5cm) loop on top of the pattern piece. End with at least 2" (5cm) of loose thread.

4. Similarly mark all pattern markings. Do not stitch around corners, but after marking one line, begin another at a right angle to the first.

5. Remove all pins and clip through the loops of thread on the top of the pattern. Then separate the pattern piece from the fabric layers. Carefully pull back the top layer of fabric and clip through the exposed threads with the tip of a pair of sharp scissors.

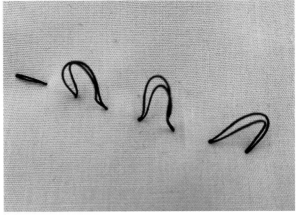

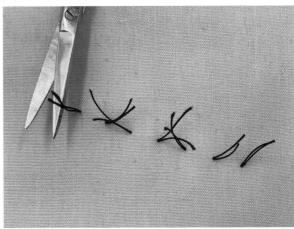

THE PICK STITCH: FOR TOPSTITCHING AND PLACING ZIPPERS

The pick stitch is a tiny hand stitch used for decorative purposes or for attaching a zipper on a delicate garment or in a hard-to-reach area where, due to bulk or placement, it's difficult to position under a sewing machine. It is often featured in couture or high-end sewing.

1. Using a knotted thread, draw the needle up from the underneath piece of fabric to the top about ¹⁄₁₆" (2mm) from the right edge and pull it through.

2. Insert the needle to the right three or four threads and bring it out ¼" (0.5cm) to ⅜" (1cm) to the left of the stitch made in step 1.

3. Continue the process, smoothing the fabric every few stitches.

4. End with a fastening stitch (page 26), catching only the underneath piece of the fabric.

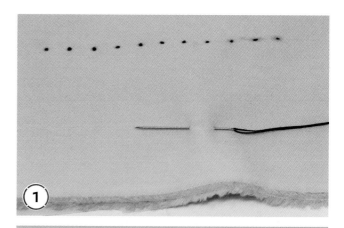

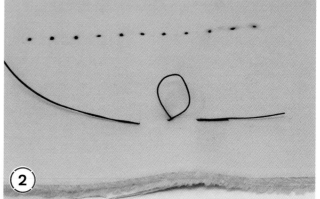

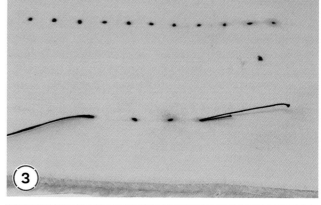

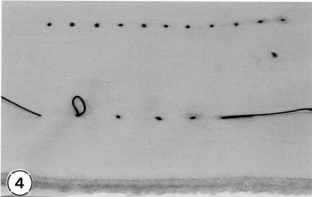

THE PADDING STITCH: TO ADD BODY AND HOLD INTERFACING IN PLACE

The padding stitch is part of the tailor's repertoire of permanent hand stitches and is concealed within the layers of collars and lapels, helping to give them body and shape.

1. Place the garment section to be padded in your lap. Thread the needle with knotted cotton thread and begin by bringing out the needle. Pull the needle through the interfacing and the upper layer of fabric at the top right of the area to be padded.

2. Bring the needle down at least ¼" (0.5cm). The distance should be equal to the length desired for the diagonal padding stitch. Keeping the thread to the right of the needle, take a horizontal stitch from right to left so that the needle emerges directly below the point where the thread first emerged. The stitch should be equal to half the length of the diagonal stitch.

3. Push the needle through with the front of the thimble.

4. Bring the needle down the same distance as in step 2 and, keeping the thread to the right of the needle, take another horizontal stitch from right to left directly under the previous stitch.

5. After taking the last stitch at the end of the row, insert the needle back where it last emerged. To begin the next parallel row, which will be to the left of the original row, take another stitch from right to left. You will now be ready to work from bottom to top.

6. Bring the needle up so that it is just short of the top of the corresponding diagonal stitch on the previous row and take a stitch from right to left directly above the previous stitch. Continue the process.

7. At the top of the row, repeat step 5. This will start the next row. Bring the needle down and take a horizontal stitch from right to left, directly below the previous stitch as in step 2. Secure the end of the thread with a fastening stitch (page 26). Start again with a new thread length by embedding its knot between the layers as in step 1.

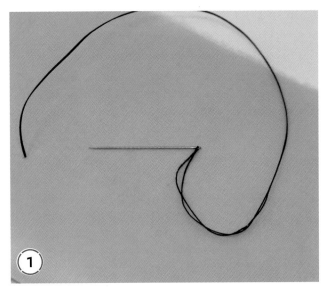

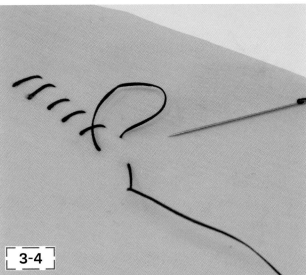

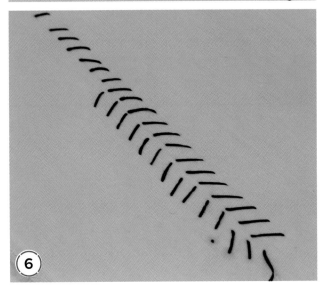

THE CHAIN STITCH: TO REINFORCE AN AREA UNDER STRESS

The chain stitch features several stitches in a row that have a loop or chain look. A popular embellishment in fashion, this stitch is usually decorative, can float on the top of a single layer of fabric, and can be enhanced by adding beads or decorative threads in various thread weights.

1. Using knotted, coarse-weight thread or buttonhole twist, bring the needle out from underneath the top layer if lined or from the underside if a single layer. This will embed the knot between the fabric layers. Pull the thread through.

2. Insert the needle ⅛" (3mm) above the point where the thread emerged. Holding the long strand of thread to the left and above the stitch with your thumb, bring the needle out ¼" (0.5cm) to the left of the first stitch. Push the needle through the fabric with the front of the thimble.

3. To complete the first chain, pull the thread through the loop that formed in the previous step.

4. Again, holding the thread above and to the left of your stitches with your thumb, insert the needle inside the previous chain, and bring it out ¼" (0.5cm) to the left, pull it through as in step 3 to complete the second chain.

5. Continue the process across the row, ending by inserting the needle down outside the last loop so it emerges on the wrong side of the fabric.

6. Secure the stitches with a small fastening stitch (page 26) on the wrong side.

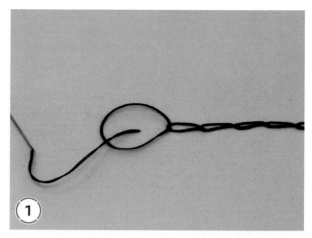

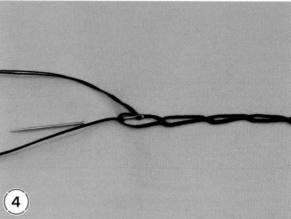

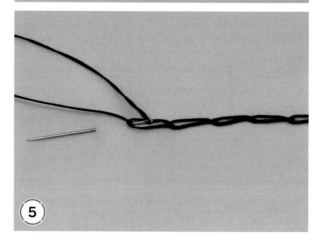

THE BAR TACK: TO REINFORCE THE ENDS OF POCKETS AND BUTTONHOLES

The hand-stitched bar tack is used to reinforce an area of a garment that may have additional stress through the course of wearing. The bar tack is most recognized on the top edge of a pocket opening and the bottom of the zipper fly, but it may also be used on the collar or top of a detail such as a pleat.

1. To make the thread bar part of the bar tack, use a double thread or one strand of buttonhole twist knotted at the end and bring the needle up from the wrong side of the fabric.

2. Insert it back ½" (1.3cm) or however long you want the bar tack to be. Bring out the needle where the thread first emerged.

3. Repeat this fastening stitch two or three times through the same points on the fabric to complete the thread bar.

4. Insert the needle under the thread bar at its left edge and pull it through, tightening the stitch as close to the edge as possible.

5. Continue across the bar, tightening the thread as close to the previous stitch as possible. At the end of the row, insert the needle down to the wrong side of the fabric and secure with a fastening stitch (page 26).

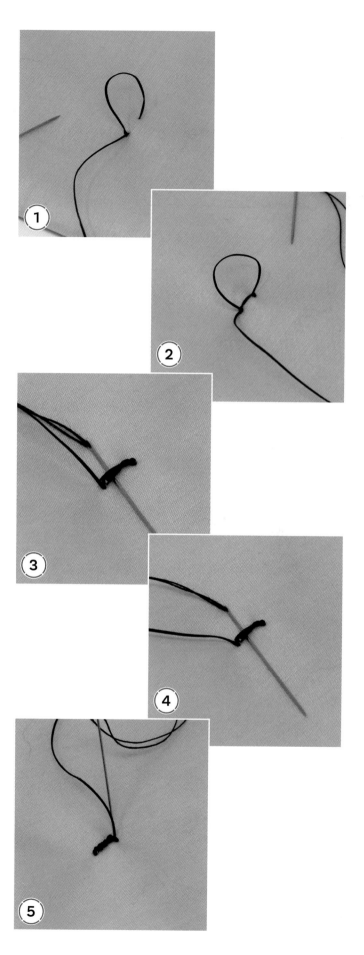

THE FRENCH TACK: TO CONNECT A HEMMED LINING TO A GARMENT

The French tack is used to hold layers of fabric together from the underside, such as the lining next to the hem of the garment or in layers of fabrics such as in bridalwear. The idea is that you do not see the tack from the right side of the garment, and it prevents the fabric from shifting out of place. The tack configuration may be an actual chain stitch or may be similar to a bar tack with a few vertical rows of threads.

1. At each vertical seam, make a thread bar (see bar tack, steps 1 and 2) between the lining and the garment hem. Begin by taking a stitch in the middle of the lining hem, then pick up a few threads of the under layer of the garment hem. Repeat these two or three times in the same place and end with a fastening stitch (page 26) on the hem of the garment.

2. Make the chain part of the French tack by inserting the needle through the loops of thread as in the buttonhole stitch (page 31).

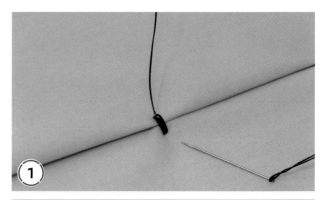

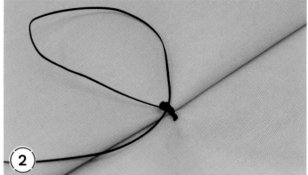

THE FASTENING STITCH: TO ANCHOR THREAD

When hand sewing, it may be necessary to anchor the beginning and end of a row of stitches. By creating a few stitches either on top of each other or right next to each other, you will reinforce the seam with a fastening stitch.

To end a row with a fastening stitch, insert the needle back ¼" (0.5cm) and bring it out at the point at which the thread last emerged. Make another stitch through these same points for extra firmness.

To begin a row with a fastening stitch, leave a 4" (10cm) loose end and make the initial stitch the same way as an ending stitch.

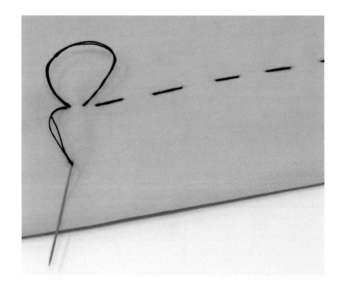

THE RUNNING STITCH:
TO MARK OR BASTE SMALL AREAS
AND TOPSTITCH

The running stitch has several functions in apparel
sewing such as being used to create a seam quickly,
basting to mark or hold a seam together temporarily, or
to gather an edge of fabric. By training your hands to
weave the needle in and out of the fabric multiple times
in one motion, your stitching will become faster and
more fluid. The length of the stitch is modified based on
how the stitch is being used.

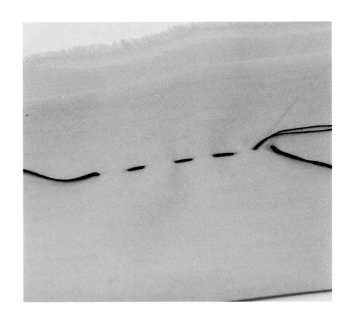

1. Insert the needle, with knotted thread, from the
   wrong side of the fabric and weave the needle in
   and out of the fabric several times in ⅛" (3mm)
   evenly spaced stitches. Pull the thread through.
2. Continue across, making several stitches at a time,
   and end with a fastening stitch. When basting,
   make longer, evenly spaced stitches.

THE CATCH STITCH: TO HEM KNITS
AND HEAVY FABRIC

A beautiful stitch that is not only functional but
decorative when finishing a garment is the catch stitch.
Used to hold two fabric edges together, it also adds a
finish with thread wrapping around the raw edge of
the fabric. The catch stitch adds a nice touch to any
garment hem and can be created with very fine thread
for delicate fabrics or more coarse thread for heavier
fabrics. In knits, the catch stitch adds flexibility with
its zigzag formation. Other areas for the catch stitch
include attaching collar felt in tailoring, attaching a
lining to the top edge of a bodice, stitching a seam
allowance to the lining on the inside of the garment,
and anywhere you want a decorative yet stable stitch.

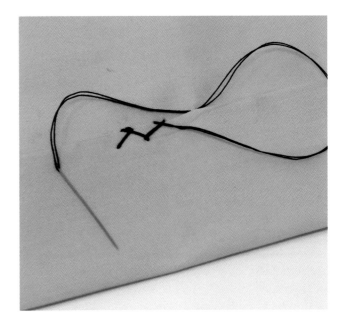

1. Working from left to right, anchor the first stitch
   with a knot inside the hem ¼" (0.5cm) down from
   the edge.
2. Point the needle to the left and pick up one or two
   threads on the garment directly above the hem,
   then pull the thread through.
3. Take a small stitch in the hem only (not in the
   garment), ¼" (0.5cm) down from the edge and
   ¼" (0.5cm) to the right of the previous stitch. End
   with a fastening stitch (page 26).

THE SLIP STITCH: TO CLOSE AN OPENING

Also known as the ladder stitch, the slip stitch is used to invisibly stitch an area closed. The stitch length can be very short or longer based on the weight of the fabric. On a hem, you may only be stitching the hem down, but you can stitch between two edges of a garment to close it shut. For example, if a seam splits open, you can slip stitch back and forth, pulling the edges together to close the opening. When lining a garment that is turned inside out through a small opening in the lining, the slip stitch is used to close the opening, making it invisible.

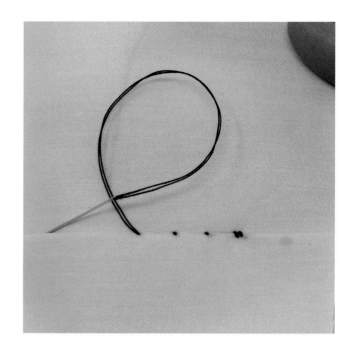

1. Fold under the hem edge and anchor the first stitch with a knot inside the fold.
2. Point the needle to the left. Pick up one or two threads of the garment fabric close to the hem edge, directly below the first stitch, and slide the needle horizontally through the folded edge of the hem ⅛" (3mm) to the left of the previous stitch. End with a fastening stitch (page 26).

THE HEMMING STITCH: TO FINISH A GARMENT EDGE

Used to finish the edge of garment, the hemming stitch is a simple stitch used to pick up a single thread and hold the folded edge under. It is very unique to the individual sewer and may take on the look of a few other stitches. It may be short like a pick stitch or angled like half of a catch stitch. However your hemming stitch is formed, it is not to show through the outside of the garment. This stitch provides a lot of control in hemming and avoiding the unsightly show-through that can happen when using a machine-formed blind stitch.

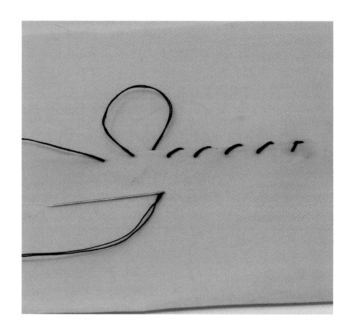

1. Anchor the first stitch with a knot inside the hem.
2. Pointing the needle up and to the left, pick up one or two threads of the garment fabric close to the hem. Push the needle up through the hem ⅛" (3mm) above the edge and pull the thread through.
3. Continue picking up one or two threads and making ⅛" (3mm) stitches in the hem at intervals of ¼" (0.5cm). End with a fastening stitch (page 26).

THE OVERCAST STITCH: TO PREVENT UNRAVELING

An edge of fabric may need a finish to prevent unraveling or fraying of threads, so an overcast stitch may be used. If a bulky or decorative thread is used, then the stitch becomes not only functional, but decorative. An example would be the edge of netting or a very fine, narrow hand-rolled hem. If two edges of fabric need to be joined together with a stitch that wraps over the edge horizontally rather than parallel to the edge like when sewing a seam, then an overcast is used. This mimics the blanket stitch that is popular on heavy blanket coats. The overcast stitches can be placed right next to each other or spaced apart based on the weight of the fabric and intended use.

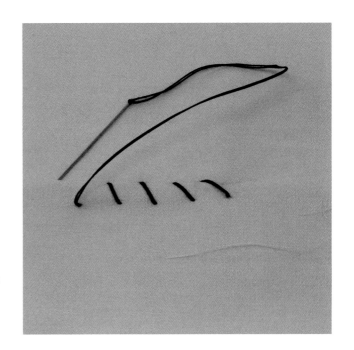

1. Draw the needle, with knotted thread, through from the wrong side of the fabric ⅛" (3mm) to ¼" (0.5cm) down from the top edge.
2. With the thread to the right, insert the needle under the fabric from the wrong side ⅛" (3mm) to ¼" (0.5cm) to the left of the first stitch.
3. Continue to make evenly spaced stitches over the fabric edge and end with a fastening stitch (page 26).

THE DIAGONAL BASTING STITCH: TO STABILIZE FABRIC

When cutting out a garment from a fabric that may move around or stretch, a diagonal basting stitch helps to stabilize the seam line. Unlike a straight basting stitch that will stretch with the direction of the fabric, the diagonal stitch helps to create some support at a different angle to the seam. It can also be used to hold two layers of fabric flat when sewing so one does not shift out of place.

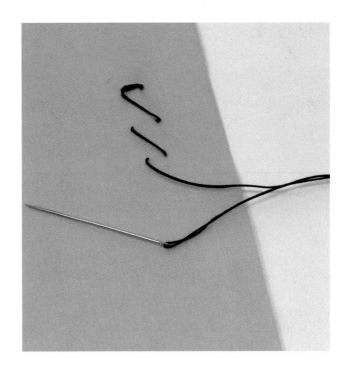

1. Anchor the basting with a fastening stitch (page 26) through all fabric layers. Keeping the thread to the right of the needle, make a ⅜" (1cm) stitch from right to left, 1" (2.5cm) directly below the fastening stitch.
2. Continue making diagonal stitches, ending with a backstitch if the basting is to be left in or with a 4" (10cm) long loose end if it is to be removed.

THE BLIND HEMMING STITCH: TO CREATE AN INVISIBLE FINISH

A blind hem or invisible hem is very desirable in many fashion garments. The classic trouser or jacket hem are two common uses for a blind hem where the goal is a professional finish with no stitches visible on the outside of the garment. When forming the stitch, the thread and stitch falls in between the folded-under edge of the hem and the layer of fabric that is visible on the outside of the garment. Unlike a sewing machine, which cannot feel the characteristics of the fabric, a blind hem formed by hand provides ultimate control for how deep the stitch is taken into the garment for the best finish possible. The depth of the stitch in blind hemming is called the bite.

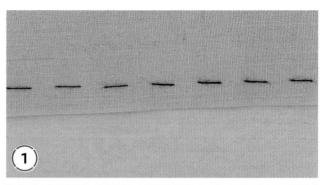

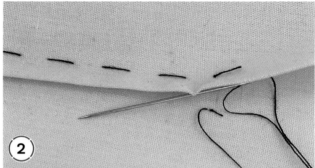

1. Baste the prepared hem into the garment ¼" (0.5cm) from the edge of the hem. Fold the hem along the basting so that the hem lies underneath the garment and the unstitched edge projects above the garment.
2. Using knotted thread, insert the needle through one or two threads of the garment just below the fold and pull the thread through.
3. Pick up one or two threads just above the fold and ½" (1.5cm) to the left of the previous stitch. Pull the thread through.
4. Continue with similar stitches, ending with a fastening stitch (page 26) on the hem.

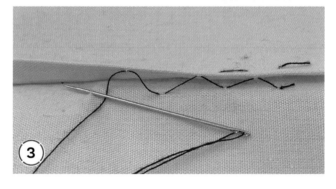

THE HERRINGBONE STITCH: TO EMBELLISH

The herringbone pattern is a popular and timeless pattern in fashion fabrics and hand sewing. The angled stitches sewn in rows add eye-catching embellishment to any garment. By incorporating contrasting threads, even more interest is added to a garment. The collar edge, sleeve, hem, and even over a seamline are areas that may feature the herringbone stitch.

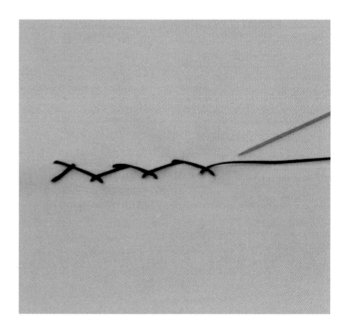

1. Working from left to right, anchor the first stitch with a knot inside the hem ¼" (0.5cm) down from the edge. Point the needle to the left and pick up one or two threads on the garment directly above the hem, then pull the thread through.
2. Take a small stitch in the hem only (not in the garment), ¼" (0.5cm) down from the edge and ¼" (0.5cm) to the right of the previous stitch. End with a fastening stitch (page 26).

THE BUTTONHOLE STITCH: FOR BINDING BUTTONHOLES

Hand-sewn buttonholes are often associated with high-end sewing, but they are easy for anyone to create. The hand-sewn buttonhole stitch uses some of the skills similar to the blanket stitch, but it simply is wrapping thread around the cut edge of the buttonhole, knotting the thread, and placing the stitches close together to create the buttonhole. Hand buttonholes allow more control in hard-to-sew areas or allow for a larger button opening that a sewing machine may not be able to create.

1. With a light pencil or wash-away marking pen, draw the stitching guideline for your hand buttonhole approximately ⅛" (3mm) longer than your button and ¼" (0.5cm) wide. Back with a layer of adhesive wash-away stabilizer. If the fabric is a looser weave, work a tight straight stitch directly on top of the rectangular tracing line and tie off. **Note:** If the fabric can be washed, you can also draw the buttonhole guideline directly on your stabilizer, apply to the front of your garment, and stitch directly through it, and then wash away.

2. Cut down the center of your rectangle from one vertical end to the other. It's very important that you do a test buttonhole to determine size, as once you cut your opening it can't be changed.

3. Using a single knotted thread, draw the needle up from the wrong side of the fabric at the lower left corner of your buttonhole guide and pierce back down through the center opening just to the left of your exit point. Loop the thread around behind the eye of the needle in a counterclockwise circle, continuing behind the point of the needle where it emerged.

4. Draw the needle through, pulling it straight up toward the cut edge of the fabric and using your nail to push the tiny loop created to the top (cut edge).

5. Repeat the stitching process from steps 3 and 4, working to the left of the first stitch to make very close stitches of even depth and creating a ridge along the cut opening.

6. When you reach the end of your guideline, stitch a bar tack (see page 25) over the vertical end line,

7. Flip your work, work buttonhole stitch to the opposite end, and finish with a second bar tack.

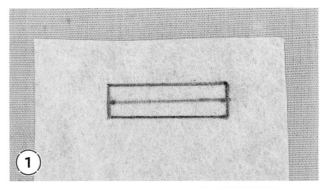

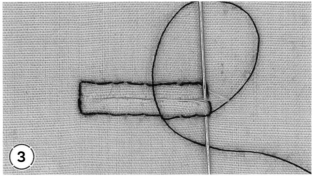

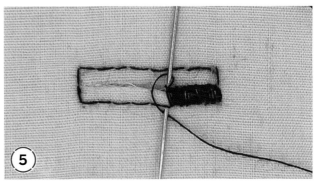

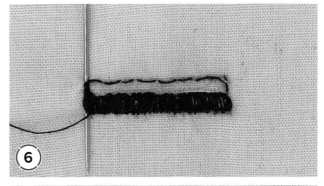

Finished buttonhole

THE ROLLED HEMSTITCH: FOR LIGHTWEIGHT FABRICS

The rolled hemstitch is best suited for delicate to lightweight fabrics. To form the hem, the edge of the fabric is rolled to prevent fraying and to enclose the edge of the hem. The stitch is then sewn around the edge to secure in place. This stitch is often seen on chiffon, netting, and bridal fabrics, but it is also appropriate for linen and knits.

1. Turn the edge of the fabric over ⅛" (3mm). Using a knotted thread and pointing the needle to the left, make a horizontal stitch ¼" (0.5cm) long at the top corner of the fold.

2. Pick up one or two threads on the main fabric, below and on a line with the stitch made in step 1.

3. Take another horizontal stitch in the fold, 1⁄16" (2mm) to the left of the stitch made in step 1.

4. Repeat steps 2 and 3 for approximately 1" (2.5cm). Holding the sewn section of fabric securely and gently, firmly pull the thread taut with your other hand. The material will roll over on itself and the stitches will disappear.

5. Continue the rolled hemstitches, pulling the thread taut every 1" (2.5cm) and ending with a fastening stitch (page 26) hidden in the fold.

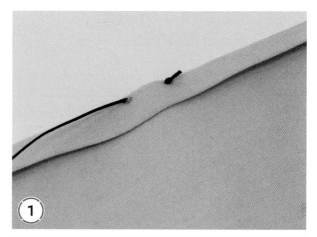

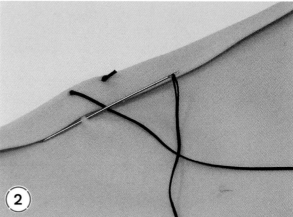

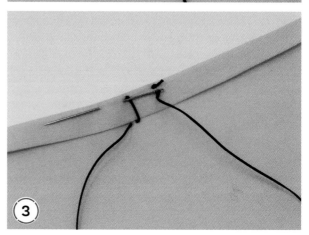

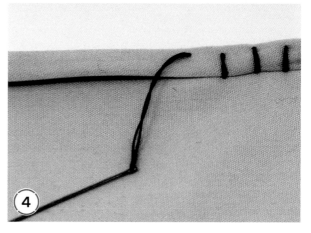

THE BLANKET STITCH: FOR DECORATIVE FABRIC EDGES

The blanket stitch is often associated with finishing bulky and heavy fabrics, such as wool and fleece, but this decorative and functional stitch is a lovely finish on many garments. The vertical stitches add interest that is visible on both sides while joining edges or finishing off the edge. Additional interest is added when contrasting or decorative thread is used. Try this on a sleeve hem, pocket edge, or pant hem.

1. Draw a guideline with chalk ¼" (0.5cm) above the edge to be sewn. Using a knotted thread, insert the needle from the bottom piece of fabric to the top, at the far-left edge of the line.

2. Holding the thread with your left thumb, insert the needle ¼" (0.5cm) to the right of the stitch made in step 1. Keep the thread behind the needle and pull the needle through the loop.

3. Continue the process, ending with a fastening stitch (page 26) on the underneath piece of the fabric.

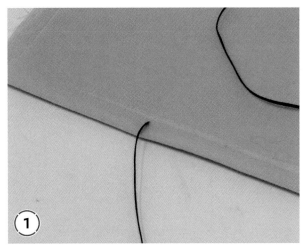

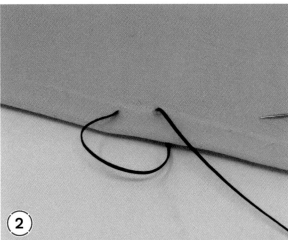

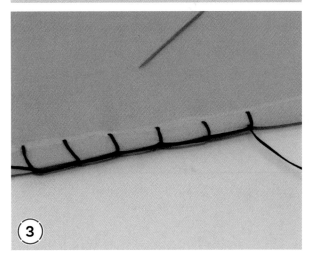

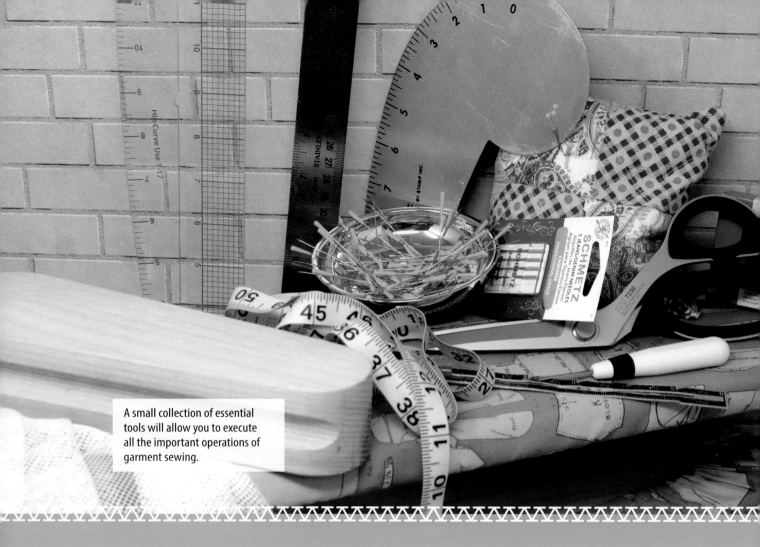

A small collection of essential tools will allow you to execute all the important operations of garment sewing.

SEWING EQUIPMENT, TOOLS, AND NOTIONS

Whether you are sewing a simple skirt or a tailored dress, the craft of sewing requires an assortment of tools that have remained unchanged for years. The modern sewist's basic tools still include:

- Sewing machine
- Needles
- Thread
- Pins
- Pincushion
- Chalk
- Hem gauge
- Seam ripper
- Sewing scissors
- Thimble
- Steam iron

Many other countless items crowd your local craft or fabric store, but most are needed only for special tasks. However, the following tools are fairly standard, and many sewers find them useful:

- A 60" (1.52m) tape measure with numbers on both sides is best for body measurements as well as for gauging curved stitching lines and aligning pattern pieces on the fabrics. A glass-fiber model is superior to cloth or plastic because it will not fray or stretch. Look for a tape measure with metal tips at each end.
- A transparent ruler, called a French curve, is also handy because it enables you to trace smooth curves instead of drawing them freehand.
- A 2" x 18" (5 x 45.7cm) transparent plastic ruler should be available for short measurements like buttonholes and for assuring accuracy when placing pattern pieces on fabric. You could also use a 6" (15.2cm) or 12" (30.5cm) wooden ruler with a metal strip at one edge.
- Keep a yardstick (hardwood if possible) for longer measurements. They are best for checking fabric grain lines and measuring fabric yardage.
- Pressing cloths (fabrics used on top of a piece being ironed to protect it) of both the sheer and thick cotton varieties are necessary as well as a sleeve board (used for easily ironing sleeves) and a pressing clapper (a hand-sized wooden tool used to press and remove heat quickly).

- An emery bag is a small pincushion that contains abrasives like those used for sharpening knives. Pins and needles are quickly sharpened when thrust in and out of it.
- A pair of pointed, 4" (10.2cm) or 3" (7.6cm) scissors is perfect for cutting buttonholes, snipping thread, and trimming other small jobs and hard-to-reach areas.

Beyond the tools, you'll always need plenty of notions for any project. Notions are any items such as buttons, hooks, and zippers that are needed to finish the garment. Buttons are measured in units called lines; 40 lines equal 1" (2.5cm). Use 24-line buttons on sleeves, vests, and the back trouser pockets, 30-line buttons on single-breasted jackets, 34-line buttons on double-breasted jackets, 27-line suspender buttons on the pant waistband, and small fly buttons on a button-up fly front trouser. For a trouser waistband, select a strong hook and eye and use a sturdy fly zipper with metal teeth. Use nylon zippers only with synthetics or for lightweight women's pants.

There are many creative options for storing your sewing tools and notions, including large clear plastic boxes, baskets, fancy trays, or simply the drawers of your sewing table. Make sure you protect the tips of your scissors and seam ripper by using a scissor protector or cloth wrap.

Following is more detail about some of the essential tools as well as information about some specialized tools that you might find useful for particular projects.

SCISSORS

Three basic scissors will see you through every step of making most garments. Cut out the pattern pieces from fabric with 8" (20.3cm) or 10" (25.4cm) bent-handled dressmakers' shears (also called tailors' shears). These have long, heavy blades and a handle that bends upward so that the bottom blade can rest firmly on the cutting table. If the shears become stiff, put a drop of sewing machine oil on the bolt. Do not use the shears to cut paper; this will dull the blades.

Clip curves and small areas with 6" (15.3cm) or smaller scissors. Finish raw seam edges by trimming with pinking shears, which have zigzag teeth (if not using a serger or other edge finish).

For long, straight cuts, a rotary cutter is useful. Shaped like a pizza cutter, the sharpened wheel slices through single and double layers of fabric quickly and easily. To ensure straight lines, use a plastic ruler as a cutting guide. To avoid dulling the blade, always cut on a plastic mat designed for use with a rotary cutter.

Sewing baskets or drawers are usually full of our favorite tools. To prevent fabric snags, grabbing the pointed tip or dulling the blade, store your scissors in the box they came in, in a separate drawer, or with a point guard.

Cutting Straight Lines

Open the shears wide and take in fabric the whole length of the blades. Cut with one long steady closure for a smooth edge.

Clipping

Clip into curves and small details with the tips of 6" (15.3cm) scissors. Do not open them all the way; you can more easily see how far to clip if you use only the tips.

Cutting Curves

Open the shears halfway and never quite close them as you cut around a curve. This will make an arc instead of a series of jagged lines.

Pinking

Finish seam edges on any fabric but knits by pinking them; open the shears wide and close them smoothly.

Cutting Right Angles

Cut two intersecting straight lines by cutting along one marked line, then pulling the shears out and cutting along the second line at the point at which the two intersect. This produces a crisp, true angle instead of a swivel.

Using a Rotary Cutter

Place a cutting mat on your work surface, marked side up. Lay the fabric on the mat, aligning two sides with two intersecting lines of the mat. Place a plastic ruler on the fabric, aligning it with either pattern pieces or guidelines on the mat, and hold it in place with one hand. Using the other hand, push the trigger on the rotary cutter, set it against the ruler, and press firmly while rolling the cutter along the ruler edge. Start and end your cut on the mat, off the edge of the fabric.

You will need (from left) at minimum a pair of dressmakers' shears, a pair of small scissors, and pinking shears. A rotary cutter (right) may also be helpful.

PINS

Pins come in many different styles, weights, and thicknesses, and each has a specific use. Like machine needles, straight pins need to be replaced frequently to avoid holes, prevent snags, and eliminate marks and stains on your final project.

Use New Pins

Use new pins to protect your fabrics and fashion garments—this is especially important with delicate fabrics. Use a different pincushion for each style of pins, which will help you stay organized and prevent you from having to rummage through a messy pincushion to find the exact pin needed for your project or seam. For example, you might use medium length and weight pins for a long seam on a coat, appliqué pins to mark the zipper, and silk pins to mark a lining hem.

It is not necessary to have hundreds of pins for use on most garments. Most seams require few pins, so having a large quantity is not the same as having good quality.

Clean Your Pins

Have you ever placed a pin in your blouse or wrist pincushion? Pins get dusty and dirty. To avoid this problem, clean your pins. It may not be the best idea to stick pins in your blouse, especially if you forget they are there! Try placing them in a scrap piece of cloth or pincushion, because it does help to remove the dirt. Even a new pin pushed through a fashion fabric carries the tiny risk of making a mark on your project. Taking a few minutes to prep your pins is a great, professional step to use in the sewing room.

Separating your pins into various types helps you use the best pin for your project. Some pins are perfect for pinning multiple layers of fabric, some for pinning small details, and some for pinning delicate silk or lining fabric.

TIP

Once a pin hits the floor, throw it away! It is probably now dirty or bent with rough or blunt edges.

PIN 911 SPOTS

Not realizing pins are the culprit, occasionally a mysterious flaw will appear on a garment and you are left figuring out what went wrong, where it came from, and how to remove it. Pins are inexpensive, so toss those old, tiny daggers, and get some new pins for your fabric and project. However, when accidents do happen, you can use a Q-tip and carefully dot on a tiny bit of water or spot remover to swipe across the spot.

THREAD

No sewing project is possible without thread, and high-quality threads are a requirement for every sewing application. Avoid skimping on your threads, because not all threads are created equal. Cheaper quality threads often lack durability and strength, and the lint will clog the mechanics of your sewing machine. It is also tempting to use old or inherited thread, but a little-known fact is that thread expires or wears out. Save old thread for a decoration or craft. Look for a reputable brand with high strength, excellent smoothness, and quality materials that will ensure the time you spend on your sewing projects will result in ease of sewing and professional results.

Threads come in a variety of weights, such as 28, 40, 50, and 60, and they may vary from type of thread and brand. A smaller number means a heavier weight or thicker thread. Threads also come in a variety of spool sizes or length per spool. Some examples are 55 yards (50m), 164 yards (150m), and 547 yards (500m). These too may vary from brand to brand.

Different threads and a wide range of colors provide everything that you need for sewing, quilting, embroidery, and overlocking. You might even find that you use different threads in a single project, such as basic sewing for assembly, cone thread for serging, silk thread for hand sewing, and waxed thread for attaching buttons. Specialty threads are available in a diverse range of colors, surface finishes, looks, and effects. Some threads you may consider using include:

- **Polyester all-purpose thread:** for most garment applications with excellent colorfastness
- **100% quilting cotton thread:** can be used on any garment. The cotton is appropriate for cotton fabrics and garments needing natural fibers and a more matte finish
- **Variegated multi-colored thread:** when you want a whimsical color-shifting effect and blending when a fabric has a variety of colors
- **Embroidery thread:** for machine embroidery and decorative stitching with a highly reflective surface
- **Silk thread and buttonhole twist:** for sewing finer weight fabrics, decorative sewing, and hand sewing
- **Cone thread:** for overlock serging when multiple spools are used
- **Stretch and elastic thread:** for knitted fabrics and when flexibility in a seam is needed
- **Denim thread:** a stronger thread for use in sewing sturdy denim
- **Bobbin thread:** for fine and delicate fabrics, ideal as a bobbin thread
- **Nylon transparent thread:** for invisible stitching
- **Metallic thread:** for added bling
- **Glow-in-the-dark thread:** for a fun effect
- **Waxed thread:** used in tailoring and hand sewing hems and linings, this thread comes flat rather than on a spool with a waxed coating. It prevents the thread from knotting as you hand sew

Thread comes in a huge variety of colors, allowing you to match to most fabrics quite precisely.

MACHINE NEEDLES

The needle was one of humankind's first tools. Over the centuries it developed from a simple craft item into a precision tool for modern sewing machines, constantly adapted for new industrial applications and requirements. Choose your needle size based on the type and weight of thread that is being used as well as the fabric that is being sewn. The goal is to have the needle slide easily through the fabric without damaging the fibers or creating too large of a hole and to carry the thread smoothly without damaging it while sewing.

Needles come in a wide range of sizes, designated by numbers: low-numbered needles are longer and thicker, whereas high-numbered ones are shorter and thinner. You will need an assortment of long to medium-length round-eyed needles called Sharps, and some short, stubby needles called Betweens. Sharps are used for most hand-sewing tasks; use size 3 for sewing through many thicknesses, size 3 or 4 for marking stitches such as tailor tacks, size 5 or 6 for basting, padding stitches on interfacing, and on medium-weight lapels, sizes 5–8 for sewing garment fabric or linings, and size 8 or 9 for fine details such as hemming and padding stitches on lightweight lapels. Betweens, being stronger, are for sewing extra-thick fabrics; use size 4 for basting, sizes 5 and 6 for sewing on buttons, sizes 6 and 7 for hand-working buttonholes, and sizes 6–9 for fine hand sewing, such as padding stitches.

Important points to remember:

- Needles do not last forever; they should be replaced approximately every eight hours of sewing.
- The eye of the needle should be 40 percent larger than the diameter of the thread.
- When going to a larger size of thread, a larger needle should be used.
- Use the appropriate needle for the type of fabric being sewn.

Turn the page for a detailed breakdown of needle structure and types.

TAILOR'S CHALK

These are flat squares made of wax, stone, or clay that are used to transfer pattern markings or adjustments onto fabric. For marking wool or other natural fibers, use wax chalk in a contrasting color; the wax can be easily removed by pressing lightly with a steam iron. For pattern pieces and interfacings, black wax shows up best. On synthetic fabrics or blends, use stone or clay chalk; when the marks are no longer needed, simply brush them off.

TAILOR'S THIMBLE

This is a special thimble that, together with the distinctive sewing technique used with it, allows the needlecrafter to push through heavy fabrics and interfacings. The thimble, made from sturdy metal and open at the top for comfort, should be worn on the middle finger of the hand that holds the needle. Choose a thimble in a size that covers your finger down to the first joint, but leaves the fingertip exposed. When sewing, use only the fingernail side of the thimble, and push the needle through all layers of fabric in a long, smooth motion, using the whole arm.

GIMP

Gimp is a heavy cord made of silk, cotton, or wool strands threaded with metal wire. It is used to reinforce hand-worked buttonholes. Use buttonhole twist if gimp is not available, or if you simply want a softer buttonhole.

Tailor's chalk makes marking (and removing marks) a breeze.

SCHMETZ is internationally known as the finest sewing machine needle manufacturer in the world. Sewers everywhere count on the quality of their products. Your choice of high quality sewing machine needles can result in the same high quality of maintaining smooth, even stitches in your work. (Thank you to SCHMETZ for providing this expert needle information.)

SCHMETZ NEEDLE GUIDE

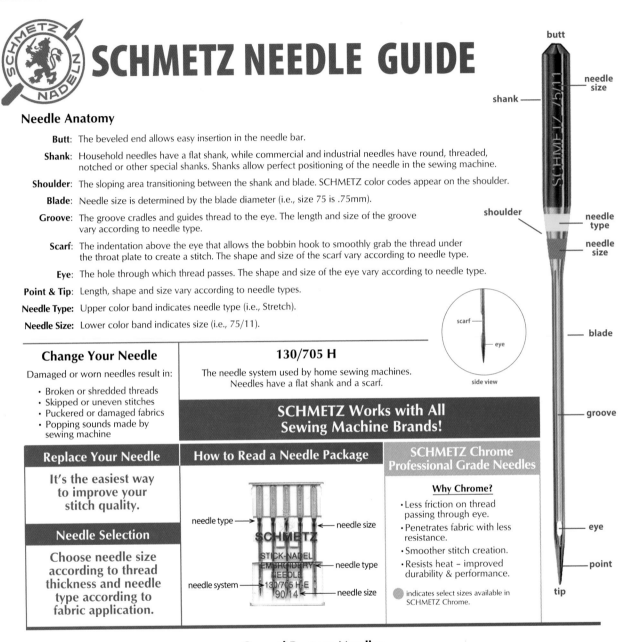

Needle Anatomy

Butt: The beveled end allows easy insertion in the needle bar.

Shank: Household needles have a flat shank, while commercial and industrial needles have round, threaded, notched or other special shanks. Shanks allow perfect positioning of the needle in the sewing machine.

Shoulder: The sloping area transitioning between the shank and blade. SCHMETZ color codes appear on the shoulder.

Blade: Needle size is determined by the blade diameter (i.e., size 75 is .75mm).

Groove: The groove cradles and guides thread to the eye. The length and size of the groove vary according to needle type.

Scarf: The indentation above the eye that allows the bobbin hook to smoothly grab the thread under the throat plate to create a stitch. The shape and size of the scarf vary according to needle type.

Eye: The hole through which thread passes. The shape and size of the eye vary according to needle type.

Point & Tip: Length, shape and size vary according to needle types.

Needle Type: Upper color band indicates needle type (i.e., Stretch).

Needle Size: Lower color band indicates size (i.e., 75/11).

Change Your Needle

Damaged or worn needles result in:

- Broken or shredded threads
- Skipped or uneven stitches
- Puckered or damaged fabrics
- Popping sounds made by sewing machine

130/705 H

The needle system used by home sewing machines. Needles have a flat shank and a scarf.

SCHMETZ Works with All Sewing Machine Brands!

Replace Your Needle

It's the easiest way to improve your stitch quality.

Needle Selection

Choose needle size according to thread thickness and needle type according to fabric application.

How to Read a Needle Package

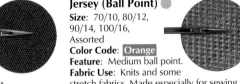

SCHMETZ Chrome Professional Grade Needles

Why Chrome?

- Less friction on thread passing through eye.
- Penetrates fabric with less resistance.
- Smoother stitch creation.
- Resists heat – improved durability & performance.

● indicates select sizes available in SCHMETZ Chrome.

General Purpose Needles

Universal ●
Size: 60/8, 65/9, 70/10, 75/11, 80/12, 90/14, 100/16, 110/18, 120/19, Assorted, Twin, Triple
Color Code: None
Feature: Slightly rounded point.
Fabric Use: Numerous - woven and knits. A great general purpose needle.

Jersey (Ball Point) ●
Size: 70/10, 80/12, 90/14, 100/16, Assorted
Color Code: Orange
Feature: Medium ball point.
Fabric Use: Knits and some stretch fabrics. Made especially for sewing on knits. The medium ball point does not damage or break knit fibers.

Stretch ●
Size: 65/9, 75/11, 90/14, Twin
Color Code: Yellow
Feature: Medium ball point, special eye and scarf.
Fabric Use: Elastic materials and highly elastic knitwear. The medium ball point, specially designed eye and scarf prevent skipped stitches.

Specialty Needles

Jeans
Size: 70/10, 80/12, 90/14, 100/16, 110/18, Assorted, Twin
Color Code: Blue
Feature: Modified medium ball point and reinforced blade.
Fabric Use: Denim and similar fabrics. Advanced point design is a SCHMETZ exclusive. For penetrating extra thick woven fabrics, denims, or quilts with minimum needle deflection, reduced risk of needle breakage and skipped stitches.

Quilting
Size: 75/11, 90/14, Assorted
Color Code: Green
Feature: Special taper to the slightly rounded point.
Fabric Use: Made especially for piecing and machine quilting. The special tapered design allows easier fabric penetration and helps eliminate skipped stitches.

Leather
Size: 70/10, 80/12, 90/14, 100/16, 110/18, Assorted
Color Code: Brown
Feature: Cutting point.
Fabric Use: Leather, artificial leather, heavy non-woven synthetics. Do not use on knit or woven fabrics.

Quick Threading
Size: 80/12, 90/14
Color Code: None
Feature: Universal needle with a slip-in threading slot in the eye.
Fabric Use: Numerous — woven and knits. A general purpose needle for effortless threading.

Microtex (Sharp)
Size: 60/8, 70/10, 80/12, 90/14, 100/16, 110/18, Assorted
Color Code: Purple
Feature: Very slim acute point.
Fabric Use: Micro fibers, polyester, silk, foils, artificial leather, coated materials. Very thin acute point creates beautiful topstitching and perfectly straight stitches for quilt piecing when precision is paramount.

Embroidery
Size: 75/11, 90/14, Assorted, Twin
Color Code: Red
Feature: Light ball point, wide eye and groove.
Fabric Use: Use with rayon, polyester and other specialty embroidery threads. The special scarf, widened groove and enlarged eye protect fragile threads and guard against excess friction allowing trouble-free embroidery and decorative stitching.

Gold Embroidery
Size: 75/11, 90/14
Color Code: None
Feature: Titanium Nitride coating, slightly rounded point and enlarged eye.
Fabric Use: Coarse and densely woven materials. Slightly rounded point and enlarged eye are perfect for embroidery on most fabrics and with the most fragile specialty threads. Titanium coating resists adhesives, improves needle wear and penetration of coarse and densely woven fabrics.

Metallic
Size: 80/12, 90/14, Twin
Color Code: Pink
Feature: Elongated eye.
Fabric Use: Metallic and other specialty threads. A "must have" for sewing with sensitive metallic threads. The elongated eye prevents shredding and breaking of metallic threads.

Topstitch
Size: 80/12, 90/14, 100/16
Color Code: Lt. Green
Feature: Extra long eye.
Fabric Use: Topstitch, heavy, multiple or poor quality threads. Achieve perfectly straight stitch lines and even stitches when using a straight

www.SCHMETZneedles.com

Super NonStick
Size: 70/10, 80/12, 90/14, 100/16
Feature: Anti-adhesive coating (NIT), extra large eye, distinctive scarf, and reinforced blade prevent skipped stitches and provides a residue-free needle.
Fabric Use: Use when sewing with embroidery stabilizer, temporary spray adhesive, or self-adhesive hook & loop tape.

Hemstitch
Size: 100, 120, Twin
Color Code: None
Feature: A wing on each side of the needle.
Fabric Use: Light or medium weight loosely woven fabrics. Popular for heirloom sewing and to create decorative cutwork.

Double Eye
Size: 80/12
Color Code: None
Feature: Universal needle with two eyes.
Fabric Use: Numerous — woven and knits. Use two different threads for shading and texturing effects for embroidery and topstitching.

Multiple Needles

Twin
Double needles are actually two needles mounted on one shaft used to create two rows of stitches simultaneously. Use two spools of thread and one bobbin thread.

Universal Twin
Sizes: 1.6/70, 1.6/80, 2.0/80, 2.5/80, 3.0/90, 4.0/80, 4.0/90, 4.0/100, 6.0/100, 8.0/100, Assorted

Double Hemstitch
Size: 2.5/100
A hemstitch needle and a universal needle with a 2.5 mm separation.

Embroidery Twin
Size: 2.0/75, 3.0/75

Metallic Twin
Size: 2.5/80, 3.0/90

Jeans Twin
Size: 4.0/100

Stretch Twin
Size: 2.5/75, 4.0/75

Universal Triple
Size: 2.5/80, 3.0/80

SEWING MACHINE NEEDLE TROUBLESHOOTING GUIDE

PROBLEMS	CAUSES	SOLUTIONS
Upper Thread Breaks	Incorrect threading	Rethread machine properly
	Knots or twists in thread	Replace thread
	Tension too tight	Reset bobbin and top thread tension
	Damaged/old needle	Replace needle
	Needle too small	Use correct needle for thread and application
Bobbin Thread Breaks	Bobbin case incorrectly threaded	Remove bobbin and re-thread with bobbin turning clockwise
	Bobbin case incorrectly inserted	Remove and re-insert bobbin case
	Bobbin does not turn smoothly in bobbin case	Check that bobbin case and bobbin are in "round"; replace if necessary
	Lint in bobbin case	Clean bobbin case and surrounding machine area
	Bobbin tension too tight	Check and reset bobbin tension
Skipped Stitches	Thread tension too tight	Reset top and bobbin tension
	Needle damaged	Replace needle
	Needle wrong size	Use correct needle size
	Sewing machine out of adjustment	Have sewing machine adjusted for timing; hook to needle clearance; needle bar height
Frayed Stitches	Needle too small	Increase needle size
	Tension too tight	Reset tension
	Damaged thread	Replace thread
Thread Loops on Bottom	Thread not in top tension	Rethread machine with presser foot up
	Machine incorrectly threaded	Rethread machine incorporating takeup lever
	Top tension too loose	Reset top tension
	Burr on hook mechanism	Remove burr
Irregular Stitches or Malformed Stitches	Wrong needle size	Ensure correct needle for fabric & thread
	Incorrect threading	Un-thread machine and carefully rethread
	Upper tension too loose	Reset lower and upper thread tension
	Operator pulling fabric	Check presser foot pressure
	Bobbin wound unevenly	Re-wind bobbin
Fabric Puckers	Excessive stitch length	Decrease stitch length
	Needle point is blunt	Change needle more often
	Excessive thread tension	Check bobbin and upper tension
	Fabric is too soft	Use stabilizer
	Thread displacement—too much thread in a small area	Decrease field density; scale embroidery designs; increase stitch length
	Fabric not feeding	Check presser foot, needle plate, feed dogs

IRONING
AND
PRESSING

A skilled sewist or tailor puts as much artistry into wielding a hot iron as she gives to plying a needle. Factory sewing often eliminates pressing after each step; however, in custom and couture sewing, as soon as you finish a seam, it is pressed flat. At virtually every stage of garment assembly, the fabric is carefully molded with a pressing technique.

Select an iron temperature that matches your fabric. Natural fibers such as cotton and wool can withstand high temperatures, but synthetic fibers can easily scorch. Steam and moisture may be used depending on the fabric and garment.

Ironing is a lost art. I have learned a lot about garment care because my mom irons every day, including pillowcases, sheets, shirts, and all the family clothing.

IRONING

Use the iron as soon as you begin a project in order to smooth the material and pattern. The secret of perfect ironing is to use a long, gliding motion. Do not push when you move the iron forward. Try not to move backward so that you do not put wrinkles back in the material.

PRESSING

Pressing is a quite different technique from ironing. Pressing is used to flatten details such as pleats or seams as soon as they are permanently sewn. The trick here is to set the iron straight down vertically, directly on the spot to be pressed, add heat and pressure, and then lift straight up.

DETAIL PRESSING

It is easier to press a seam during the sewing process than it is to wait until later when the iron must be wiggled into the corners of the completed garment. With your free hand, open the angles and folds in the fabric. Use only the point of the iron to press the confined spaces. Pressing tools such as a mini-iron or point presser are perfect to press these hard-to-reach areas.

FINISHING

Final ironing and pressing are done on the right side of the fabric, the side that is visible in the completed garment. Place a cloth over the material to protect it from scorching or developing a shine. Use a silicone cloth for heavy fabrics and silk organza or cotton for lightweight materials. To get the right ironing temperature, experiment with a swatch of extra material.

Of course, the most essential pressing tools are a first-rate steam iron and an ironing board with a scorch-resistant cover. Some people use an adjustable board and others may like a flat surface or table mat. In addition, specialized pressing boards and forms allow the sewist to do the extra-fine shaping and molding that help give a tailored garment its distinctive look.

Back row (left to right): velvet board, pressing ham, pressing sleeve; front row: pressing clapper, mesh pressing cloth, pressing mit, iron, spray stiffener; underneath: sleeve board

PRESSING EQUIPMENT AND HOW TO USE IT

Sleeve Board

This is a miniature ironing board for pressing small areas such as sleeve and neck seams that will not fit over the end of a regular ironing board. The sleeve board may also be used when pressing straight darts and when shrinking out puckers along the armhole seams. The best sleeve boards for tailoring rest on a sturdy wooden platform. They should be well padded and covered with a firmly woven twilled cotton fabric called cotton drill cloth. Wash the cloth cover before using it to remove all sizing or starch, which would otherwise cause the iron to stick and would also adhere to the garment fabric.

Pressing Cloth

When pressing, you should place this piece of fabric, preferably cotton drill cloth, between the iron and the garment. For all pressing operations while the garment is being made, use a dry cloth; enough steam from your iron will pass through the cloth to shape the fabric. For final pressing, use a damp cloth to remove any gloss or shine the fabric has picked up during construction. Wash all new pressing cloths before using to remove the sizing. If cotton drill cloth is not available, substitute white paper towels.

Tailor's Ham

This oval, ham-shaped cushion has built-in curves that conform to the general contours of the body. Use the ham when pressing areas that require shaping, such as the curved darts on the jacket front and the seams at the bust, chest, shoulder, and hip. The ham is also a convenient aid for pressing collars into shape, for sculpting the roll line of lapels, for pressing open the armhole seam, and for shrinking out fullness at the armhole. Select a ham that is firmly stuffed, smoothly rounded, and with a surface free of lumps. One half should be covered with cotton drill cloth, to be used when pressing most fabrics. The other half should be covered with soft, lightweight wool, which must always be used when pressing woolen fabric to prevent shine.

Press Mitt

A soft, padded, thumbless mitten that fits over the entire hand, this item is used to give a light pressing to small, curved areas, such as sleeve caps, that do not fit over the tailor's ham or the regular ironing board. It may also be slipped over the narrow end of the sleeve board to provide extra padding. As in the tailor's ham, one side of the mitt should be covered with cotton drill cloth and the other side with soft, lightweight wool.

Point Presser

A point presser is a narrow, hardwood board mounted on its side and shaped into a fine point at one end; it's also called a seam board or tailor's board. It is used for pressing open small seams in narrow or hard-to-reach places such as collars, lapel peaks or points, and waistbands. Since the point presser is bare wood, not covered by padding or drill cloth, it also provides a firm, hard surface for pressing open regular seams on hard fabrics that do not flatten easily. Before using, make sure that the hardwood surface and edges of the presser are completely smooth, with no nicks or splinters that could cause damage to the fabric. Point pressers and clappers (see below) are frequently combined into a single piece of equipment.

Tailor's Sleeve Cushion

This is a long, flat pad with a sleeve-like silhouette that is sometimes inserted into a completed sleeve to prevent wrinkling the underside or forming undesired creases when pressing. Since sleeve cushions are not generally available outside tailor's specialty shops, you may have to make do with an ordinary ironing board. Simply lay the sleeve on the ironing board and press it down the center, being careful not to crease the edges. Then roll the sleeve slightly and again run the iron down the center. Continue in this manner until the entire sleeve is pressed.

Sponge

For dampening a pressing cloth—or the fabric itself if you need extra moisture to flatten a stubborn seam—a sponge is perfect. The sponge is also handy to wipe up water spillage from an overfull steam iron. Keep the sponge clean and let it dry out frequently to avoid mildewing; never store it near metal tools or you run the risk of rusting them.

Tailor's Clapper

A tailor's clapper is an oblong or rectangular piece of hardwood; it's also called a beater, striker, or pounding block. As these names imply, the clapper is wielded like a paddle to slap parts of the garment in order to shape them. Typically, it is used to flatten the edges of collars, hems, and lapels, to form trouser creases and pleats, or in any other areas where a crisp, sharp edge is desired. When working with very heavy fabrics, use a clapper to smooth and reduce the bulk of seams. Before using a clapper, cover the fabric to be shaped with a press cloth and apply steam from the iron until the fabric is thoroughly moistened. Remove the cloth and pound the area until the fabric is dry and the desired edge has become distinct. Because a clapper (like a point presser, above) has no cloth covering, make sure that the surface and the edges are smooth and splinter-free.

CHAPTER 2

SELECTING AND PREPARING FABRICS

One of the greatest joys of sewing your own clothes is selecting the fabrics and creatively pairing them with different pattern styles. Not only is it enjoyable, but it is also beneficial in the long run to spend a little time choosing the best piece of material for your project and properly preparing it for the sewing process. It is important to consider all the design elements of your project, and most pattern envelopes include fabric suggestions. You will find that your finished garments are more flattering when the weight and type of fabric coordinate with the pattern. A medium-weight twill or gabardine makes up into a nice skirt or pants, while a softer and silky cotton is better for a blouse and a jersey knit drapes nicely for a dress. Chose fabrics that work well for your body type by selecting colors and designs that will complement your figure and complexion.

Once you have made your fabric purchase, the next step is to prepare your fabric prior to cutting it. You may need to wash and pre-shrink the fabric unless the label indicates it is already pre-shrunk. Take it to a dry cleaner if the material is non-washable, such as wool.

Straightening the fabric is another important preparatory step. Sometimes fabric is stretched out of shape prior to being placed on the bolt or if it was not cut on the true grain—that is, with the lengthwise and crosswise threads at right angles to each other. In general, natural fibers are more easily cut on the true grain than synthetics and are also easier to adjust, even if they are slightly off. Synthetic fabrics, and those that are a mixture, may need more straightening; however, both can be adjusted by following the instructions within this chapter for aligning the crosswise, lengthwise, or selvage, edges. These straightening techniques can help correct issues that may keep the finished garment from fitting properly or hanging evenly.

The selection of a fabric is partly based on personal preference, but also on the characteristics of the fabric, which are created by the fibers within.

FABRIC CHARACTERISTICS

The characteristics of fibers directly affect the properties of the fabric they are woven into. A 100 percent pure cotton fabric feels luxurious. However, it is also important to know when to choose a blended fabric and how they can support the overall look, feel, and wear of a garment. For example, one reason polyester is blended with cotton is to eliminate shrinkage and to compensate for the weaker cotton fibers, increasing durability and improving fit. Acrylic fibers are used in faux fur because their properties closely mimic those of wool and fur, and an untrained eye may not be able to tell them apart. If you would like to create an elegant and expensive-looking dress but are not able to afford silk, consider using rayon instead—it is known as "artificial silk." With some basic knowledge, the average sewer can make educated decisions on what fibers and fabrics are best for their next sewing project.

A fiber can be described as any substance, natural or manufactured, that is suitable for being processed into a fabric. Fiber properties include length (staple or filament), size, and surface contour. Some key factors that affect the end use of fabric include serviceability, aesthetics, durability, comfort, appearance retention, and care. To create a fabric, fibers are first spun into yarns and then woven or knit into the fabric.

TYPES OF FIBERS

There are four types of fibers: natural, manufactured, synthetic, and other minor miscellaneous types.

Naturally occurring fibers include cotton, linen, flax, wool (including any form of animal hair, even human hair, not just from sheep), and various other minor novelty fibers like hemp and spun corn. You can pick up natural fibers and spin them right into a yarn.

Manufactured fibers, such as rayon and acetate, are derived from cellulose and protein. Many people consider rayon a natural fiber, but it is not. Rayon was the first manufactured fiber in the United States; it was developed in 1911 to mimic the costly silk fabrics of the time. It is spun from naturally occurring polymers to replicate a natural fiber.

Synthetic, or man-made, fibers could take up a whole book alone and include many types and varieties. New fibers are being developed all the time. Some well-known and often-used synthetics are polyester, acrylic, and nylon. This category includes microfibers, which are "everything fibers" that are blends of other synthetics.

Special use fibers are less common, but people may be surprised to learn that they may encounter them daily. Fibers like rubber are used where Spandex can be used. Metal, such as stainless steel, is used in carpets. Other metals, such as silver and gold, are woven into fabrics. New and innovative uses for fibers are being developed every day.

Cotton fibers used to create 100% mercerized cotton threads or cotton fabric and fabric blends are created by using the natural fibers of the cotton plant.

The Mettler 100% Cotton Thread is an example of a high quality thread that provides dependable results in garment sewing with high strength and no shrink mercerized cotton.

When looking closer at a bundle of threads, the individual fibers are more visible and may give insight into its quality and characteristics.

FIBER PROPERTIES

Reading a fabric bolt label is like reading a food label. Often the consumer does not understand the ingredients, why some cost more than others, or what exactly they do. Similarly, understanding the makeup of a fabric helps to answer important questions such as why you should choose a synthetic when a natural fiber seems better or why a fabric was made into a blend. There are many answers to these questions. One reason fabric is made into blends is because they are cheaper to produce. Often, they are created to produce a specific look or texture. Or there can be technical design considerations, like creating a stronger yarn for fabric production since pure cotton is weaker and the blended fabric enables the garment to last longer. Fibers are like vitamins in the sense that you are considering individual components and how they combine to support the desired result in your fabric. Understanding how the characteristics of fibers affect fabric will help you to make better fabric selections.

Some basic fiber properties, pros, and cons that are applicable to the home sewing consumer include:

Natural cellulose fibers: Cotton and flax are examples of natural cellulose fibers. They have good absorbency and are a good conductor of heat. Both wrinkle easily and pack tightly. They are heavy, very flammable, and easy to print or dye.

Natural protein fibers: These fibers, such as wool and silk, have an animal origin. They resist wrinkling. They are hygroscopic, absorbing moisture, and comfortable in a cool, damp climate, but weaker when wet because they shrink. Natural protein fibers are harmed by dry heat. They are flame resistant and dye well.

Synthetic fibers: These are fibers made from chemicals, are heat sensitive, and melt easily. They are resistant to moths, fungi, and abrasions and have a low absorbency. Synthetic fibers are strong and easy to care for, less expensive, and readily available.

Rolls and bolts of fabric are labeled with their fiber content, which is important for selecting the right fabric for your project. Understanding how the characteristics of fibers affect fabric will help you to make better choices. Can it be ironed or washed? Should it be dry-cleaned? Will it stretch? These are all things to determine before you buy.

IDENTIFYING FABRIC QUALITY IN NATURAL FIBERS AND FABRICS

Often sewers from beginning to advanced skill levels do not understand what factors contribute to the differences in fabric quality. The wrong fiber, fabric, characteristic, or quality can ruin a project and discourage any sewer. Even selecting a simple cotton muslin includes a variety of factors, such as thread count, weight, grain, and weave, that determine if a bolt is more suitable for a particular project than another. In addition, the dyes and pigments used to create color and prints also vary in quality. These are some characteristics of basic natural fabrics that can impact a garment's end use.

Linen: Linen is the classic material for summer dresses, blouses, skirts, and suits. It is strong, smooth, and long-lasting. It is a good conductor of heat, allowing warmth to pass quickly from the body, and it absorbs and releases moisture rapidly to create a crisp, dry feeling.

Wool: Warm, soft, and resilient, wool has a springiness that allows wrinkles to quickly hang out. It is an excellent insulator against cold and will absorb up to 30 percent of its weight in moisture without feeling damp. That absorbency makes wool a good summer fabric in its lighter weights and allows it to accept and hold a wide range of dye colors. Soft, fuzzy woolens and smooth, strong worsteds lend themselves especially well to knit fabrics. Wool jerseys and double-knits are extraordinarily supple and formfitting, and virtually wrinkle-proof.

Cotton: Coolness and shape-retention are the best-known qualities of cotton. It is admirably light, absorbent, comfortable, and cool. Cotton is approximately 10 percent stronger when wet, which allows it to be laundered, bleached, and put through many finishing processes.

Silk: Silk is lighter and strong than other fibers, which permits the weaving of very thin fabrics. It is treasured for the deep natural luster of its fibers, which can be woven and dyed or printed in brilliant colors of great clarity, producing rich, durable fabrics that range from crisp, watermarked moirés to glossy, ribbed faille, raw shantung, shining satins, and lustrous crepes.

Fabrics may be purchased off of a bolt or roll. Evaluate the fabric for damage, spots, or shop wear prior to purchase.

FABRIC THREAD COUNT

Thread count refers to the number of warp and filling yarns per square inch (more about this on page 60). It is listed with warp first, such as 80 x 76, or as a total, such as 156. Sewists may encounter this with higher quality cottons or suiting materials. The higher the number, the more threads per square inch, indicating the fabric is sturdier and more expensive.

Higher thread count fabrics are firm, strong, have good body, are wind and water repellent, and may have less raveling of edges. Lower count fabrics are flexible, permeable, pliable, have a higher shrinkage rate, ravel more, and drape well. Considering these characteristics may help to determine what fabric is better for a certain project. You may select a high-count cotton for durability in a pair of pants, but a lesser count for a pliable, softly flowing blouse. If you were tackling a three-piece suit, you would want to make sure a higher thread count suiting is selected for good tailorability and longevity.

A close-up view of your fabric will help you determine the thread count in the crosswise and lengthwise grain.

FABRIC WEIGHT

Common words describing the weight of a fabric include "light," "medium," and "heavyweight." A pattern may call for a lightweight fabric for a blouse with a cowl neckline or a heavyweight fabric for an outerwear garment. Lightweight fabrics include cotton or rayon broadcloth and percale. Medium-weight fabrics include gabardine, suiting, and flannels. Heavyweight fabrics include some denims, most wool twills, and suiting. While most sewists recognize this concept, it should be mentioned when helping a novice understand the importance of fabric weight. A winter coat cut in a soft baby flannel or a bustier constructed from a tartan plaid wool will not turn out like the picture on the pattern envelope!

The lighter-weight silk in the bodice drapes and hangs softer in contrast to the wool shorts that hold a beautiful pleat and waistband. Selecting the right weight fabric for your garment will help your results be more successful.

DYING VS. PRINTS

How color and designs get onto our fabric is another characteristic to consider when selecting yardage for a project. Yarns that are dyed before weaving make a fabric that is more colorfast and of a higher quality than fabrics that are batch dyed or printed. How do you tell the difference?

A printed fabric is the easiest to recognize. Simply look at the front and back of the fabric, as the technical front will have the color, design, or pattern in more vivid colors and more defined edges, and the back will be plainer, less vivid, and less defined. This is common and easy to recognize in quilting cottons.

Batch, or piece-dyed fabrics, start as a grey goods, which is plain cloth that is dyed solid after the fabric is woven. These are a little more difficult to recognize, but it is important to learn how to do so. Imagine pulling a significantly faded red garment out of the laundry, the color bleeding over all the other clothing. If you wash it a few more times, the color is almost gone. There is a wide range of quality in batch or piece-dyed fabrics, so you need to be sure to pre-wash and test a sample before creating your whole project.

Yarn-dyed fabrics are the best for colorfastness and are generally higher in quality and price. Fabrics like jacquards, tapestry, and damask are obviously yarn dyed as the designs and patterns are created during the weaving process. Fabrics that are yarn dyed will have the pattern on the front and back, thus creating a more colorfast fabric. When you unravel several yarns, each yarn may be a different color. With a print, several colors will be on the same yarn. Think about a suiting fabric with pinstripes or tweed—these are examples of yarn-dyed fabrics. Others include ginghams and chambrays, which look batch dyed; however, if you look closely, one yarn is white or a different color, as in iridescent chambrays.

There are different reasons and uses for the various methods of dying and printing fabric, but each can affect the end use and durability of a design. Manufactured fibers can be colored when still in the solvent stage before being spun into fiber. These are colorfast and have minimal, if any, fading. However, this process is not often used for fashion goods because the high fashion colors change so quickly.

Silk fibers absorb dye extremely well. This silk velvet fabric illustrates the vibrant colors and how new color patterns and effects result when adding fabric dye.

CHARACTERISTICS OF CLOTH

The contribution made by the following four basic characteristics of cloth may be subtle, but they all weigh significantly in the appearance and wearability of a finished garment. Fine quality cloth can be distinguished from average by these characteristics within each major fiber group.

Hand: the character of a particular fabric as communicated through the sense of touch. For example, a summer worsted wool feels smooth, cool, and substantial. A good linen feels crisp and cool, while a cotton broadcloth should be smoother and thinner and feel just as cool.

Drape: the way a fabric falls naturally when it is hung. A slightly stiff medium-weight linen may be right for a formal, tailored dress, while a wool crepe may have the hugging ability to move with the body for a cocktail dress.

Texture: the surface appearance of fabric. A country woolen looks richer and warmer if it has the soft, fuzzy nap of an unfinished worsted. This would be quite out of character on a cocktail dress—but the dress, on the other hand, would gain allure from the smoothness and luster of silk satin or spun rayon.

Color: the dyes and pigments used for textiles. Silks and rayons can blaze with brilliant hues, while woolens take dyes less flamboyantly, producing prized subtleties in depth and richness of shading.

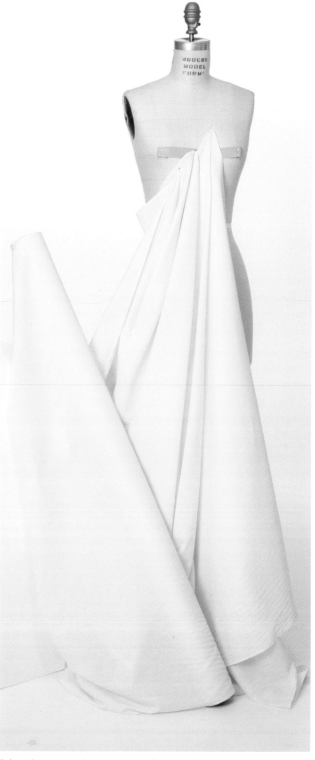

Fabric draping is when you take a fabric and let it hang or mold around a body or dress form. Draping helps to visualize three-dimensionally how a fabric will react to a garment style or on a body. This bolt of cotton muslin is a great tool for testing your design.

HANDLING AND CARING FOR FASHION FABRICS

In the chart on pages 56–57 are procedures recommended for handling a variety of fashion fabrics. Most of those that tend to shrink have been pre-shrunk by the manufacturer; for any that have not, follow the pre-shrinking instructions provided.

Before working with knitted fabrics, let them lie flat on the floor, or a bed, overnight to allow the yarns to assume their natural shape; place them, as well as crêpes, on a working surface large enough so that none of the fabric hangs over the edge. To hold silks and other slippery fabrics, cover the work surface with a sheet or a piece of felt.

When machine-stitching knitted fabrics, test a folded swatch first, adjusting the needle and bobbin thread tensions until a balanced stitch is obtained. When stitching the garment, stretch the knitted fabric slightly by applying firm tension with your fingers behind and in front of the needle. Fabrics like crêpes ought to be handled the same way, but they should be held taut rather than stretched.

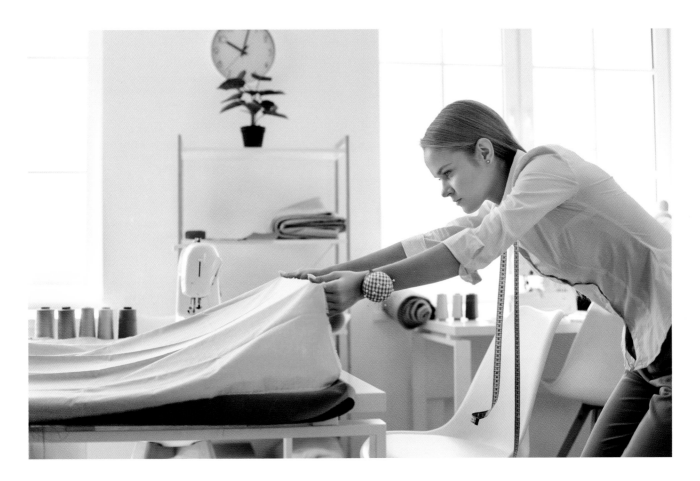

FABRIC	PREPARING THE FABRIC	MARKING, CUTTING, AND BASTING
Cotton (dressweight)	If not pre-shrunk, wash the fabric in lukewarm water, squeeze, and hang to drip dry. Press out creases (last column).	Attach the pattern with steel pins; mark with a tooth-edged tracing wheel. Baste with a size 7 needle and mercerized cotton thread (No. 50) or polyester thread.
Linen (dressweight)	If not pre-shrunk, dry clean, or soak in lukewarm water, squeeze, and hang to dry (soak colored linens to set the dye). Before cutting, press out creases (last column).	Attach the pattern with steel pins; mark with a tooth-edged tracing wheel. Baste with a size 7 needle and mercerized cotton (No. 50) or polyester thread.
Nylon Jersey Knit	Pre-shrinking is not required. Before cutting, press out any creases (last column).	Attach the pattern with steel pins, using a "nap layout." Transfer markings with a smooth tracing wheel. Baste with a fine ballpoint needle and polyester thread.
Nylon Spandex	Pre-shrinking is not required. Before cutting, press out any creases (last column).	Attach the pattern following a "nap layout," using steel pins. Transfer markings with a smooth-edged tracing wheel. Baste with a size 7 needle and polyester thread.
Rayon (dressweight)	If not pre-shrunk, dry clean the fabric, or soak in lukewarm water, squeeze gently, and hang up to drip dry. Before cutting, press out any creases (last column).	Attach the pattern with steel pins; transfer markings with a tooth-edged tracing wheel. Baste with a size 7 needle and mercerized cotton (No. 50) or polyester thread.
Rayon Polyester Knits	If not pre-shrunk, dry clean the fabric. Before cutting, press out any creases (last column).	Attach the pattern with steel pins; mark with a smooth-edged tracing wheel. Baste with a fine ballpoint needle and mercerized cotton (No. 50) or polyester thread.
Lace (various styles)	Pre-shrinking is not required. Before cutting, press out any creases (last column). Determine lace placement on pattern prior to cutting.	Attach pattern pieces with steel pins at 2" (5cm) intervals to prevent slipping; transfer markings with tailor's tacks. Baste with a size 8 needle and silk or polyester thread.
Silk Organza	Pre-shrinking is not required. Before cutting, press out any creases (last column).	Attach pattern pieces with steel pins; transfer markings with tailor's tacks. Baste with a size 8 needle and silk or polyester thread.
Silk Satin	Pre-shrinking is not required. Before cutting, press out any creases (last column).	Attach pattern pieces with steel pins, following the guide for "nap layout." Transfer markings with tailor's tacks. Baste with a size 8 needle and silk or polyester thread.
Silk Shantung	Pre-shrinking is not required. Before cutting, press out any creases (last column).	Attach pattern pieces with steel pins; transfer markings with tailor's tacks. Baste with a size 8 needle and silk or polyester thread.
Wool Crêpe	If not pre-shrunk, dry clean the fabric. Before cutting, press out any creases (last column).	Attach pattern pieces with steel pins; transfer markings with tailor's tacks. Baste with a size 7 needle and mercerized cotton thread (No. 50) or polyester thread.
Wool Jersey	If not pre-shrunk, dry clean the fabric. Before cutting, press out any creases (last column).	Attach the pattern with steel pins, following the "nap layout." Mark with a smooth tracing wheel. Baste with a fine ballpoint needle and polyester thread.
Wool Gabardine	If not pre-shrunk, dry clean the fabric, or soak in cold water, squeeze gently, and hang up to drip dry. Before cutting, press out any creases (last column).	Attach the pattern with steel pins, following a "nap layout." Transfer markings with a tooth-edged tracing wheel. Baste with a size 7 needle and polyester thread.
Faux Fur	Pre-shrinking is not required. Do not iron.	Trace the pattern to the back of the fabric following a "nap layout" using chalk. Cut taking short snips only through the backing to prevent trimming the fur. Baste with a fine ballpoint needle and polyester thread.

MACHINE SEWING	FINISHING	CLEANING AND PRESSING
Use a size 14 needle and mercerized cotton thread (No. 50) or polyester thread, setting the machine at 10 to 12 stitches per inch.	Line or underline, depending on the style of the garment (pages 273–280).	Machine or hand-wash in lukewarm water and mild soap. Squeeze, hang to drip dry. Press on the wrong side while damp, with iron set for "cotton" and "steam".
Use a size 14 needle and mercerized cotton thread (No. 50) or polyester thread, setting the machine at 10 to 12 stitches per inch.	To prevent fraying, finish seams with machine zigzag stitching or hand or machine overcasting. Line or underline, depending on the style of the garment (pages 273–280).	Dry clean, or hand-wash in lukewarm water and mild soap. Squeeze, hang to drip dry. Press on the wrong side while damp, with the iron set for "linen" and "steam."
Use a size 11 ballpoint needle and thread, setting the machine at 12 to 14 stitches per inch. Adjust machine tensions and select a stretch stitch as you sew.	Avoid underlining, which constricts the fabric flexibility; use a separate lining if desired. Knitted fabrics stretch, so hang the garment overnight before hemming.	Hand- or machine-wash in warm water (100°F) with detergent; tumble dry at the "warm" setting. Press on the wrong side, setting the iron for "nylon."
Use a size 11 needle and polyester thread, setting the machine at 10 to 12 stitches per inch. Adjust machine tensions and select a stretch stitch as you sew.	Finish seams with machine zigzag, hand, or machine overlock. To prevent puckering, avoid underlining; use a separate lining if desired.	Hand- or machine-wash in warm water (100°F). Press on the wrong side, with iron set for "nylon" and "steam," with brown paper under the seams. Air dry only.
Use a size 14 needle and mercerized cotton thread (No. 50) or polyester thread, setting the machine at 10 to 12 stitches per inch.	To prevent fraying, finish seams with machine zigzag stitching or hand overcasting. Line or underline, depending on the style of the garment (pages 273–280).	Dry clean, or hand-wash in lukewarm water and mild soap. Squeeze, hang to drip dry. Press on the wrong side while damp with iron set for "rayon" and "steam."
Use a size 12 needle and polyester thread, setting the machine at 10 to 12 stitches per inch. Test a swatch; adjust machine tensions and use a stretch or flexible stitch as you sew.	To prevent fraying, finish seams with machine zigzag stitching or hand or machine overcasting. Line or underline, depending on the style of the garment (pages 273–280).	Hand wash warm or dry clean only. Press the fabric on the wrong side, setting the iron for "rayon."
Use a size 11 needle and silk or polyester thread, setting the machine at 10 to 12 stitches per inch (12 to 15 for light crêpe). Adjust tensions and keep fabric taut. May require all hand sewing.	To prevent fraying, finish seams with machine zigzag stitching or hand overcasting. Hang the garment overnight before hemming.	Hand wash warm or dry clean only. Place press cloth on the wrong side, using a press cloth covered by damp muslin; set the iron for "silk" and "dry." Place brown paper under seams to avoid marks.
Use a size 11 needle and silk thread or polyester thread, setting the machine at 10 to 12 stitches per inch. Test a swatch; adjust tensions and keep the fabric taut.	To prevent fraying, finish seams with machine zigzag stitching or hand or machine overcasting. Line or underline, depending on the style of the garment (pages 273–280).	Dry clean. Press on the wrong side using a press cloth covered by damp muslin; set the iron for "silk" and "dry." Place press cloth under seams to avoid marks.
Use a size 11 needle and silk or polyester thread, setting the machine at 10 to 12 stitches per inch. Adjust tensions and keep the fabric taut as you stitch.	To prevent fraying, finish seams with machine zigzag stitching or hand or machine overcasting. Line or underline, depending on the style of the garment (pages 273–280).	Dry clean only. Press the fabric on the wrong side, setting the iron for "silk" and "dry."
Use a size 11 needle and silk or polyester thread, setting the machine at 10 to 12 stitches per inch.	To prevent fraying, finish seams with machine zigzag stitching or hand or machine overcasting. Line or underline, depending on the style of the garment (pages 273–280).	Dry clean only. Press on the wrong side, using a press cloth covered by damp muslin and setting the iron for "silk" and "dry."
Use a size 14 needle and mercerized cotton (No. 50) or polyester thread, setting the machine at 10 to 12 stitches per inch. Adjust tensions and keep the fabric taut.	Line or underline, depending on the style of the garment (pages 273–280). Because crêpe tends to stretch, hang up the garment overnight before hemming.	Dry clean only. Press gently on the wrong side, setting the iron for "wool."
Use a size 14 ballpoint needle and polyester thread, setting the machine at 10 to 12 stitches per inch. Adjust tensions and stretch the fabric slightly as you sew or use a stretch stitch.	Avoid underlining, which constricts fabric flexibility; use a separate lining if desired. Knitted fabrics tend to stretch, so hang the garment up overnight before hemming.	Dry clean only. Press the fabric on the wrong side, setting the iron for "wool" and "steam."
Use a size 14 needle and mercerized cotton thread (No. 50) or polyester thread, setting the machine at 10 to 12 stitches per inch.	Use an underlining suitable to the weight of the fabric (pages 273–280).	Dry clean only. Press on the wrong side; set the iron for "wool" and "steam." Place press cloth under seams to avoid press marks.
Use a size 14 ballpoint needle and polyester thread, setting the machine at 10 to 12 stitches per inch. Adjust tensions, and smooth fur fibers away from the seam.	Avoid underlining, which constricts fabric flexibility; use a separate lining if desired. Knitted fabrics tend to stretch, so hang the garment up overnight before hemming.	Follow fabric bolt recommendations. Most fur may be hand-washed and rinsed in cool water. Lay on a towel to dry. Do not iron.

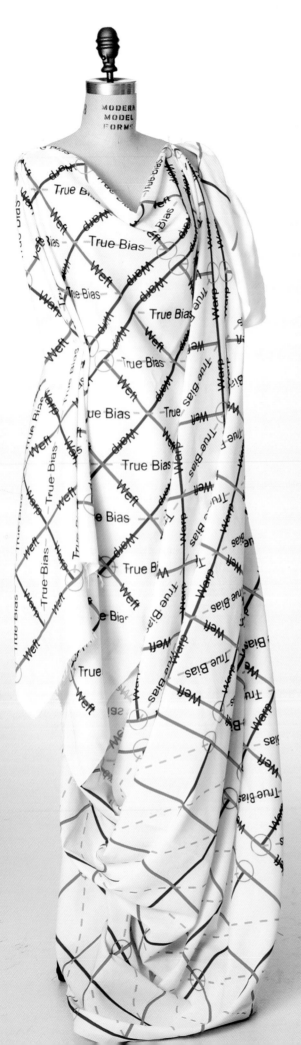

TECHNICAL FABRIC

UNDERSTANDING GRAIN AND BIAS

To understand fabric, you must understand the characteristics of grain. Fabrics are created by first laying the warp—the lengthwise—yarns and then filling in with the weft—the crosswise—yarns. The warp runs vertically up and down parallel to the selvage (the tightly bound edge); these are the strongest, stable yarns of the fabric with little to no give and what you match the grain line to on the pattern. Weft yarns are not as close together, thus have a little give. True bias is at a 45° angle, and anything off-grain or off-warp is on the bias. It's important to understand that bias is part of a woven fabric. How you cut a garment in relation to the warp and weft will affect its fit, comfort, and stretch.

When sewing knits, the quality of your fabric is key for successful results. Good quality does not necessarily mean expensive, but sometimes paying just a little more will help you avoid common pitfalls such as skewed or off-grain fabric structure, skipped stitches, and twisting. Avoid the bargain bin at the big box store. Look at and evaluate the fabric for quality—it will last longer and will be worth your investment and time.

This technical fabric is used to illustrate the types of grain and how the grain is placed on the body when making patterns. The true grain, crossgrain, and true bias are clearly marked and provide a clear reference to the designer.

YARNS: WEFT AND WARP

Fabrics, unless bonded or knits, are woven together using weft and warp yarns. Remember that "weft" rhymes with "left," meaning they are the yarns that go back and forth. Warp yarns are the up and down yarns parallel to the selvage. These yarns form the structure for any kind of weave or pattern in a fabric.

If a fabric is cut off-grain, there are two additional terms to understand. "Skew" is when the weft yarns are not at a 90° angle to the warp, and it is common in printed fabrics before finishing. "Bow" is when the weft yarns dip or curve in the center of the fabric. Both skew and bow occur during processing, but these problems are increasingly less common because computers correct grain problems during weaving or finishing.

Off-grain weft and warp yarns can directly affect any sewing project. An off-grain print may look fine at first glance, but, after straightening the grain (see page 63), the design becomes distorted. Think about trying to hem an off-grain chiffon gown with a bowed fabric—yikes! That is every sewist's nightmare. While cost does not always reflect quality, there is usually a difference in grain, bow, and thread count between the discount fabric store and the better fabric retailer. When making an educated fabric selection, take a close look at the yarns and how they are woven.

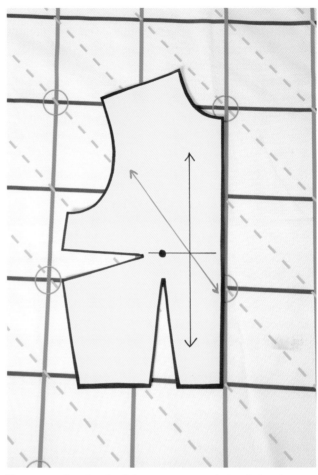

The warp and weft grain of the pattern are marked and placed to the corresponding grain lines of the fabric. When you mark your pattern, it gives you a more accurate layout of where a pattern is more stable or where it may have more stretch. Knowledge of this helps you to utilize these properties and modify your pattern for better fit and styling.

TIP

To check the grain alignment of the fabric, fold the fabric lengthwise. If the raw edges do not match each other and the corners do not form right angles, the grain is off.

FINDING THE TRUE BIAS

Place the fabric on a flat surface and fold it diagonally so that one selvage is parallel to the crossways edge and perpendicular to the other selvage. The diagonally folded edge is the true bias. Any degree off the straight of the grain is utilizing bias, but the 90° angle is the true bias.

WEAVE

Weaving is done on a loom, and all the weaves done in the present day have been done for thousands of years. While looms have changed, the basics are still the same. Warp yarns are held taut, and weft (filling) yarns are inserted to make a cloth.

"Balance" refers to the ratio of warp yarns to weft yarns. A balanced fabric has approximately one warp for every weft or filling yarn. An unbalanced fabric has more of one yarn then another. A typical unbalanced fabric is broadcloth. An example of one weight of broadcloth would have a count of 144 x 76 and a ratio of 2:1. This means that there are 144 warp yarns per inch and 76 filling yarns per inch. In other words, there are twice as many warp yarns as filling yarns. Balance is important in recognizing and naming fabrics and in distinguishing the warp and direction of a fabric.

Often fabrics take on the name of a weave, which can be confusing to sewers and retail consumers. A bride will ask for a satin gown, likely thinking of a smooth satiny fabric; but what she is actually requesting is satin weave, not realizing that she may select silk satin, polyester satin, acetate, or rayon satin. Similarly, twill is also a fabric called by the name of the weave. Walk into any fabric store and you may run across a section with beautiful twill suiting; however, these nameless fabrics are created with a twill weave. Try this experiment: the next time you wear jeans, ask someone if they like your "stonewashed twill pants," because denim is a twill weave. You might get a funny look, but denim, or jeans, is an example of a weave that has taken on a more recognizable name.

Sewists frequently ask how to determine the front from the back of a fabric. Understanding the following weave characteristics can help to identify the correct side.

Basic Weaves

The list of weaves is lengthy, and every educated sewist might find it interesting to look at a book with diagrams of the many common variations. Whether you know them by name or not, what is important to recognize are the key visual characteristics that determine how the fabric will work for the end use. Following are a few examples of the most common three weaves.

Plain weaves: The most common, plain weaves are basic over-and-under patterns that are easy to recognize. This weave is best for printed fabrics. It accepts finishes well, wrinkles the most, and is the least absorbent. There is no technical front or back of the weave unless printed on. Common balanced plain weaves include muslin and quilting cottons.

This close-up illustration shows how a fabric is created with yarns running up and down as well as back and forth to create a fabric. Variations in how the yarns are laid out is called the weave, and different weaves can create fabrics with different characteristics such as more shiny, softer, more abrasion resistant, or more flexible. When the weave is combined with the thread and fiber characteristics, unique fabrics are created.

Plain weave

Twill weave: Characterized by a diagonal line created by yarns in one direction floating over two or more yarns in the other direction, twills includes denim, houndstooth, herringbone, and gabardine. Twill may have a front and back; however, it is rarely printed on. It has better wrinkle recovery than other weaves and can be right- or left-handed or at different angles. Twill is typically more expensive due to the higher yarn count.

Satin weave: These weaves use tightly packed yarns with long floats (the yarn resting on top of the other fibers) to create a smooth, lustrous looking surface. Satin fabric snags easily due to the long floats and tends to unravel more. Common fabrics include satin, sateen, and crepe-back satin using a crepe yarn. A silk satin is always higher quality then a cotton satin because of the long, smooth silk fibers. The small staple fibers in cotton will eventually look fuzzy on a cotton satin garment.

Fancy Weaves

Fancy weaves usually create a specific design or characteristic in a fabric due to specialty yarns, extra yarns creating slack in the tension, or other structural factors. Two fancy fabrics are dotted Swiss (swivel-dot weave) and pique (pique weave ribs). Well-known Jacquard weaves include damask with satin floats on satin, brocade with satin floats on plain background, and tapestry with a dominant design on the front. Specialty fabrics, such as double cloth and some velvet, are cut in half in the center. Seersucker is a warp, slack-tension weave that creates the bubbly effect. Common unbalanced plain weaves that use ribs in the weave include broadcloth, taffeta, shantung, poplin, and faille.

Fabric structure plays an integral part in how a fabric will perform during sewing and in everyday use. The idea is not to focus so much on the technical details, but to understand why or how a weave or grain will affect a project. A tightly woven fabric may need an extra sharp needle to prevent snags, an off-grain cotton may have uneven shrinkage, and an open weave tweed may require interfacing to stabilize the fabric for tailoring. With some basic fiber and fabric knowledge, the average sewist can make educated decisions on what fibers and fabrics are best for their next project.

TIP

A bit of trivia: paper is considered a non-woven fabric!

Twill weave

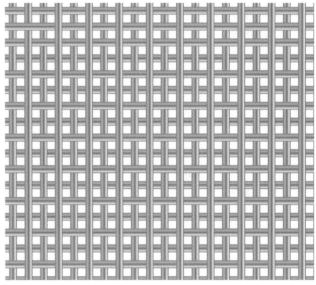

Satin weave

Dotted Swiss

Jacquard

Seersucker

Velvet

Taffeta

Shantung

Faille

THE DIFFERENCE BETWEEN WARP AND FILLING

- Selvage always runs lengthwise (warp) in fabric.
- Most fabrics have less elongation (stretch) in the warp.
- Warp yarns lay straighter and more parallel in fabric due to loom tension.
- Fancy and specialty yarns are usually in the weft or filling.
- Specific fabric characteristics may indicate warp and filling direction.
- Warp yarns are smaller and higher in twist to withstand loom tension.

Straightening fabric grain is an essential step before cutting your pattern pieces.

STRAIGHTENING FABRIC GRAIN

When placing a sewing pattern on the fabric, you will line up the grain line of the pattern with the grain of the fabric. It´s important to check the fabric to make sure the grain is straight prior to cutting. Sometimes the yarns shift in production or from being rolled on the fabric bolt. This can be corrected by cutting it straight when cutting from the bolt, by clipping and pulling a single thread, or by manually pulling the fabric on the bias to straighten out the fabric. Once the edges line up evenly, you will know you have done it correctly and are ready to cut.

STRAIGHTENING THE CROSSWISE EDGES

Before beginning, iron the fabric on the wrong side to remove wrinkles and any lines made by folding. Spread the fabric wrong side up on a flat surface. Align the selvage against one edge of the table and the raw crosswise edge against the other. If the raw edges do not match evenly and the corners do not form right angles, the fabric is off grain and needs straightening.

If your fabric is woven:

1. Snip into the selvage (lengthwise) edge near one end at a point where a single thread runs the entire width of the material. Using a pin, snag a crosswise thread from the snipped edge.
2. Pull gently on the thread, easing it along as though you were gathering the fabric. The pulled thread will show up as a puckered line.
3. If the pulled thread breaks as you pull it, cut along the pulled line to the point of the break and pick up the same or nearest crosswise thread. Continue to pull the thread.
4. Cut along the pulled line from one selvage through to the other; this is the true crosswise grain.
5. Repeat steps 1–4 at the opposite end of the fabric.

If your fabric is knit:

1. Place an L-shaped square near one crosswise edge of the fabric. Align one side of the square with a selvage edge.
2. Draw a chalk line along the crosswise grain of the fabric at a right angle to the selvage.
3. Cut along the chalk line from one selvage to the other.
4. Repeat steps 1–3 at the opposite end of the fabric.

Woven step 1

Knit step 1

PRESHRINKING AND STRAIGHTENING THE FABRIC

1. If the fabric is not washable, send it to a dry cleaner to be pre-shrunk by steam pressing. Then recheck the alignment of the edges. If the fabric still needs straightening, repeat the steps on page 64.

2. If the fabric is washable, pre-shrink it by folding it in deep folds and immersing it in cold or lukewarm water for about an hour. Then gently squeeze out the water, but do not wring. Lay the fabric on a flat surface until it is only slightly damp.

3. To straighten the damp fabric, grasp one corner and a point as far along the diagonally opposite selvage edge as you can reach. Pull hard. Move both hands down along the selvage edges and repeat. Continue to pull diagonally at intervals until you have stretched the entire piece of fabric.

4. Fold the fabric in half lengthwise wrong side out and pin it together along the selvage and crosswise edges at 5" (12.7cm) intervals, using rustproof pins. As you pin, smooth the fabric toward the fold with your hands.

5. Using a steam iron, start ironing at the pinned selvage edges and move toward the fold. Continue moving in parallel paths until you have ironed the entire length of the fabric.

When preshrinking fabrics that cannot be machine washed, the preshrinking may be done by holding the iron just above the surface of the fabric and using heavy steam. Any fibers that may react to the heat will shrink, simulating shrinkage from machine washing.

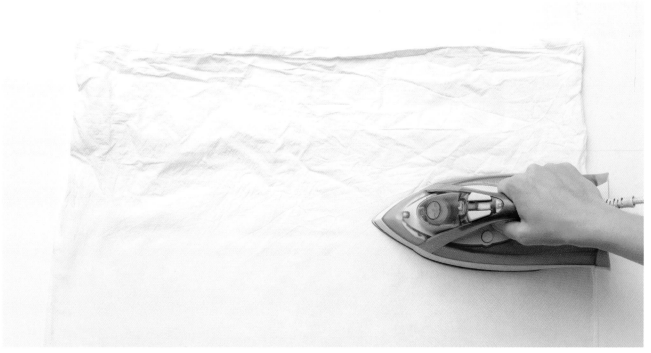

Fabrics that wrinkle during the pre-shrinking or pre-washing process may require a preliminary press prior to straightening the grain. Lightly iron the fabric in a lengthwise fashion to remove wrinkles, but avoid stretching throughout the surface of the fabric. Once the wrinkles have been removed, the fabric can then be straightened according to step 3. The fabric can then be further pressed after straightening.

FOLDING SOLID FABRIC

Once your fabric has been straightened and pre-shrunk, you are ready to fold it in half, and even line up fabric patterns and cut out your pattern pieces.

1. For most patterns, fold your fabric in half lengthwise so that it is wrong side out. This layout conserves fabric and enables you to position all at once as many pattern pieces as you need. Pin the selvages together at 1" to 2" (2.5 to 5cm) intervals.

2. For pattern pieces that are too wide to be cut on fabric folded lengthwise, fold the fabric in half crosswise so that it is wrong side out.

3. If your cutting guide requires some pieces to be cut from a double thickness of fabric and some from a single thickness, fold all the fabric as shown in step 1 or 2, depending on the cutting guide instructions, and cut out all the pieces requiring double thicknesses. Then spread the rest of the material out in a single thickness, wrong side down.

FOLDING STRIPED OR CHECKED FABRIC

1. If the fabric has stripes or checks of similar size, fold it so that the fold line falls exactly halfway through a stripe or check.
2. Starting near the fold and working to the selvages, stick pins through the top layer of fabric where check lines intersect or at the edge of stripe lines.
3. Fold back the top layer and make sure that the pins bring together the two layers at points where the pattern matches exactly. If the pattern does not match, adjust the fabric.
4. Catch the point of the pin to hold the layers together. Continue inserting pins in this manner at several points. Then pin the fabric together at the edges.

This designer fabric features an array of bold yet natural-looking colors, patterns, and textures. Fabrics that have more natural coloring, rather than a neon color for example, are more timeless and will last longer in your wardrobe. They also tend to look more attractive on various shapes, sizes, and skin tones.

CONSIDERING COLORS AND PRINTS

The color and weight of a fabric can make the wearer look larger or smaller, depending on the tone and whether the fabric drapes against the body or stands away from it. Pattern—whether large, small, regular, or random—is of course also vital. Regardless of whether you select the garment pattern first or the fashion fabric first, the pattern of the fabric itself is often the garment's most eye-catching element. Although small prints can often be treated almost like solids, bold patterns restrict the choice of style, calling for a simple design with a minimum of darts and seams. Prints demand special care in cutting and stitching, and a garment that in a plain material could be made by elementary methods calls for additional special attention when material is boldly patterned. At the end of Chapter 3 (page 123) we will cover actual fabric layout for patterns, stripes, and prints, but in the meantime, consider the following general guidelines when it comes to colors and prints.

Warm colors: Warm colors, such as red and orange, tend to exaggerate the size of the body and can make even a slender person appear more voluptuous—especially when the color is used lavishly in a long garment. The enlarging effect diminishes, however, in a short dress, and becomes so minimal in a bikini that it could safely be worn on an ample figure.

Cool colors: Cool colors, such as blue and green, minimize the dimensions of a figure so that they produce a soft, even fragile, effect on a slim body. On a large person, they can create the impression that the figure is closer to ideal proportions. As with warm colors, cool ones become more effective as the quantity of fabric increases.

Vertical stripes: Vertical stripes generally make the wearer look taller and slimmer. In a simple dress, wide stripes give a dramatic illusion of greater height. However, in a more detailed dress, such as one with a waistband, yoke, or collar, the same wide stripes become a detriment by making the garment appear too busy. In contrast, a detailed dress made in narrow stripes recaptures the impression of slimness. Vertical stripes also give a tailored appearance.

Horizontal stripes: Horizontal stripes appear to make the wearer look broader and shorter. The illusion is most marked when the stripes are both wide and warm in color. This effect of breadth can be minimized by using the stripe in a cool color, or a narrow stripe of any color.

Patterns: Patterns can draw bold attention to a figure, in either a positive or negative way. Large-scale prints can make a body appear larger, as can small prints in bright colors. Geometric prints that run vertically can, like stripes, make the wearer appear taller. Circular patterns create a softer, more fluid look than stripes or other geometric shapes.

Plaids and checks: Plaids and checks pose few figure problems if the patterns are small and cut so they run vertically and horizontally. Bold plaid can make the body look larger; cutting them on the diagonal minimizes this effect.

Textures: Textures differ so dramatically that they create a variety of effects even when made in identical styles. Soft, clinging knits give an alluring look, while a crisp fabric like cotton duck looks sporty. Mohair, having more nap, can make the wearer's figure seem fuller.

CHAPTER 3

ACHIEVING THE RIGHT FIT

Your custom body shape + flattering fabric combined with the right pattern fitted to scale and proportion = fitting success.

The key to making clothing that fits well begins with choosing pattern lines, fabric color, weight, and texture all properly proportioned to one another to complement the scale of your figure. The fabric should correspond to the style of pattern you are sewing. Instead of using the standard pattern size, you might need to make few custom modifications so that the pattern will match your custom body contours.

Visualizing how a silhouette will look on your own figure can be difficult. We all have our favorite garments that make us feel and look great, which is an ideal place to start to look for ideas when sewing your own clothes. Choose a pattern that emphasizes your good features while drawing attention away from any problem areas. For example, an empire waistline nicely accentuates a small bust and trim shoulders, but it also can help conceal a prominent bottom. Pleated and gathered skirts can pad out hips that are slim, but they make heavy hips even more noticeable; instead, choose a sleek A-line silhouette.

Once you choose a style, buy the pattern that most closely matches your measurements. The ideal is to measure the fullest part of the bust for upper body designs and the full hip for the lower body. Your ordinary dress size is not a reliable guide to the correct pattern size, because women's sewing patterns are not reflective of ready-to-wear clothing sizes. By following some basic instructions illustrating how to custom fit the pattern to your body (page 74) and create a fit sample (page 91), you will ensure that your finished garment is as comfortable and flattering as possible.

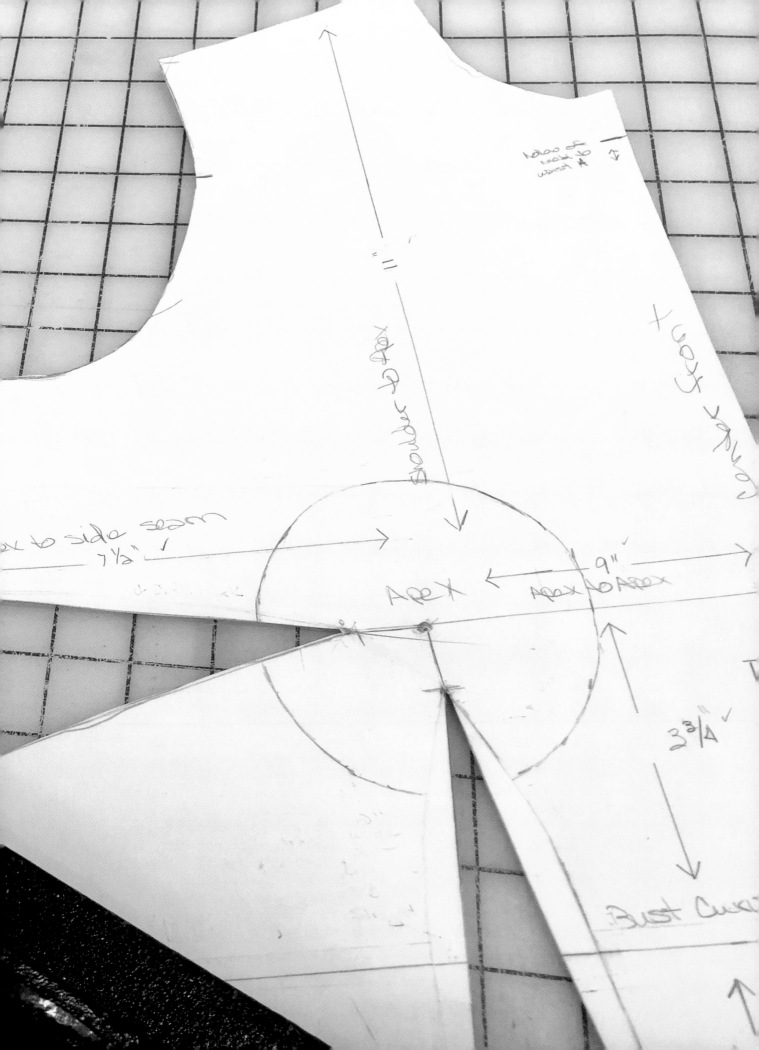

A trusty tape measure is
an essential tool in any
sewist's arsenal.

TAKING MEASUREMENTS

Fitting a dress from a commercial pattern begins with the basic process of measuring
your body. The only supplies you need are a tape measure and possibly some simple
marking dots, the kind available in an office supply store.

When measuring, wear the same style of undergarments that you will wear with
the finished garment. They should support your body, fit well, and create the desired
silhouette. Keep in mind that an ill-fitting silhouette can affect how a seam line
hangs on the body. It is important to wear the shoes you will wear with the garment
because they can affect your posture and body measurements. For example, a shoe
with a high heel will make you stand more upright and elongate your measurements,
whereas a flat, casual shoe may soften the spine, creating a squatter shape and
possibly wider measurements.

Have someone help take your measurements for the best accuracy; however,
many sewists fit themselves. To work around this challenge, use self-adhesive dots
to mark specific areas to measure. Stand in front of a mirror and place the dots on
your body.

It is much easier to take your body front and circumference measurements
by yourself; checking the tape in a full-length mirror will aid in finding back
measurements. Remember, for the absolute best fit, you should make a test garment
that will help fine-tune any discrepancy in measurements.

HOW TO MEASURE

Measure with the tape held closely to, but not tightly against, your body. Follow the instructions below and the guidelines on the figures. The red lines indicate measurements that generally appear on pattern envelopes. Blue lines are the optional measurements that are required to achieve the finer fit, which is a distinguishing characteristic of a perfect fit.

Note: Any area can be measured on the body. This is not a complete list, but only the most widely used, and not all measurements are necessary for every pattern.

1. **Height:** Stand erect, without shoes, flat against a wall. Place a 12" (30.5cm) ruler flat on your head and lightly mark the point where the ruler touches the wall. Measure from the mark to the floor.
- **Shoulder length:** Measure at the side from the base of your neck to the shoulder bone point.
2. **Full bust:** Measure around the fullest part of your bust with the tape horizontal in back.
- **Front bust:** Measure from side seam to side seam across the front.
- **Back bust:** Measure from side seam to side seam across the back.
- **Apex to apex:** Measure across the bust span from point to point.
- **Apex to side seam:** Measure from the apex to the side seam to determine the width of the side front area of the pattern.
3. **Full waist:** Tie a cord around the narrowest part of your waist and measure the circumference along the cord. Leave the cord at the waist as a guideline for other measurements.

- **Front waist:** Measure from side to side across the natural waist on the front.
- **Back waist:** Measure from side to side across the natural waist on the back.
- **Front-waist length:** Measure from the center of the base of your neck above the collarbone to the center of your waistline.
4. **Back-waist length:** Measure from the top of your spine to the center of the waistline cord.
- **Front shoulder apex length:** Measure from your shoulder to the bust point.
- **Apex to waist:** Measure from bust point to natural waist.
- **Shoulder to full upper back:** Measure from your shoulder to fullest width of the upper back.
- **Back shoulder waist length:** Measure from your shoulder to waistline.
- **Waist to hip length:** Measure at the side from the waistline to the fullest part of your hips.
5. **Full hip:** Measure around the fullest part of your hips with the tape horizontal in back.
- **Front hip:** Measure from side seam to side seam across the fullest part of the front.
- **Back hip:** Measure from the side seam to side seam across the fullest part of the back.
6. **Arm length:** Measure from your shoulder bone point to the elbow and down to the wrist bone.
- **Full bicep:** Measure around the fullest part of the upper arm. This area of the arm is often in line with the full bust line.
7. **Crotch length:** Sitting on a hard surface, measure from the waistline to the surface.
- **Full crotch length:** Measure from the waistline in back, under between the legs, then up to the waistline in front. Make sure it is not too tight.
- **Out seam length:** Measure from the waist down the side of the leg to the floor.

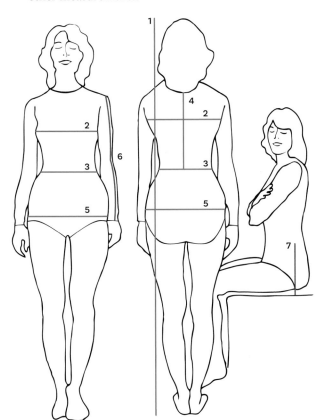

TIP

Wearing a fitted t-shirt or swimsuit while taking your measurements helps prevent skin irritation.

Pattern adjustment is the key to creating a garment that truly fits the wearer.

ADJUSTING THE PATTERN

Few figures are so perfectly proportioned that they match all the body measurements on which a pattern is based. The time to address the custom fit is in the pattern before cutting the fabric. Resist the temptation to hold the tissue pieces up and fit them to your body, adding a bit here and taking a snippet there. Tissue and paper patterns do not mimic fabric, nor do they conform to the body accurately. Professional clothiers know that creating a custom-fitted pattern and fit sample is the superior method to achieve the best results.

The steps used to alter a fashion pattern are the same from the most complex to the simplest garments. The basic processes can be adapted to any style, shape, and size. The final adjustments to achieve a superlative fit are made with the help of a muslin garment sewn from the adjusted pattern.

The traditional and most simplistic process to adjust your pattern is to compare your measurements to those on the pattern envelope and add or subtract the difference on the pattern piece at the side seam lines of the pattern pieces or on the printed adjustment lines. Numerically, this will result in a pattern that matches the overall body measurement in areas such as the full bust, full waist, and full hip. However, this approach is less custom and not much more accurate than tissue fitting. Beautiful fit happens within the body of a pattern and not on the edges.

For a true custom fit, simply compare your body measurements with the width (horizontal) and length (vertical) measurements of the pattern and make any necessary adjustments based on these differences. To avoid confusion, remove the seam allowance from the pattern before measuring. This will prevent you from adding the seam allowance back into the area of measure. First, work on the vertical adjustments, then the horizontal. Mark all measurement changes on the pattern piece and then blend the cutting and stitching lines to polish up the outer edges. By comparing your measurements to specific areas of fit on the pattern, the result is a more refined and pristine fit—one coveted by every sewist.

Additional fitting resource: For Joi's complete pattern fitting method, check out her book, *Create the Perfect Fit*.

THE PATTERN AS A TOOL

With a customized fit as the end goal, a few basic steps must be applied to each pattern piece to ensure you have the most successful results. But first, it is important to understand the differences between a sloper, a style block, and a stylized commercial pattern, so you have the right tool for the right purpose.

Sloper: This is a pattern with no seam allowance or ease. This basic pattern shape, or fitting shell, has no style lines other than a basic fitting dart and is meant to fit exact to the body measurements for scale and proportion. Pattern designers use the sloper as the starting point to create many kinds of fashion pattern designs using the slash and spread flat pattern method, including the bodice front, bodice back, sleeve, skirt front, and skirt back. The pant sloper is made from the skirt sloper. A perfectly fitted sloper is an ideal tool for any sewist. It can be used to design your own custom patterns, perfectly proportioned to your areas of measure. It can also be used to determine how a commercial pattern might fit your body.

Style block: This is a pattern that has been stylized using a sloper. It may or may not have ease and seam allowance. Variations on a block are based on how it is used and in what setting. In garment production, a style block is used like a sloper, but it refers to a specific garment style, such as a blouse or t-shirt. In custom sewing, a style block is a design you created from your custom-fit sloper. You use it to duplicate the garment or as a base for creative design as in flat pattern designing. Some patterns marketed as slopers are actually style blocks because they began as the basic fitting shell of a true sloper. A sloper or block purchased with seam allowance and sewing instructions is a commercial pattern that will need a custom fit like any other pattern.

Commercial pattern: These are patterns stylized from the basic sloper to create a specific fashion garment or silhouette. Patterns range from classic traditional styles to short-run, fad fashions. Pattern companies have their own unique sizing system and specific sets of body measurements that match specific sizes. Commercial patterns are not customized. Select your pattern size based off your full bust, waist, and hip measurements. This will be the launching point to create the style featured on the cover of the pattern; however, custom fitting is still required. Commercial patterns have seam allowance, comfort ease for movement, and design ease (anything extra for the silhouette) built into the design.

Sloper

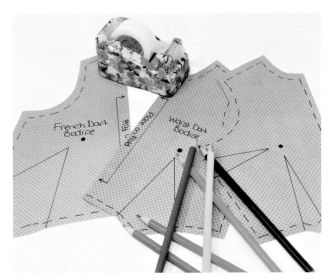
Style block

Commercial pattern

PATTERN ADJUSTING PROTOCOL

- **Remove seam allowance:** This is the first step if working with a block or commercial pattern.
- **Treat the front separate from the back:** Adjustments to the front may differ from the back.
- **The apex is the anchor point:** Avoid shifting the bodice pattern around. With the apex anchored, the pattern will self correct during the adjustment phase.
- **Adjust within the area of fit:** Measure between areas of fit such as shoulder to apex. When adjusting the pattern, cut approximately in the center, not on the shoulder or apex area. This will distribute the adjustments within the area of measure.
- **Adjustments are vertical and horizontal in the flat pattern:** Vertical adjustments will look horizontal and horizontal adjustments will look vertical. If this is confusing, focus on what the effect of the adjustment is on the pattern.
- **Some edges may be affected by an adjustment:** Areas like the arm opening and neckline will be polished after the adjustment is done.
- **Not all patterns need every adjustment:** If a pattern area matches your measurements exactly, no change is needed.
- **Not all areas of a pattern need ease:** Many vertical areas are baggy when too long and tight when too short. A literal match to measurements is most accurate.
- **Make a fitting muslin to refine the fit:** The fit pattern is the final step in fitting a design prior to sewing the fashion fabric.

The following examples (the rest of this section, through page 88) are the key areas to adjust on patterns, but remember that you can further customize by measuring any area of a pattern and adjusting it to fit your measurements, scale, and proportion.

ADJUSTING THE PATTERN VERTICALLY: BASIC STEPS FOR LENGTHENING

Most vertical areas of measure will match the body measurements exactly with little or no ease, unless there is a creative design reason to add or subtract. When vertical areas are too long, the garments are baggy, and when too short, they pull and are tight. When this happens in areas such as the apex, darts do not lay on the correct area of the body, resulting in a fit issue. This is true for all three types of patterns.

TIP

Measure your body in a specific area of fit and compare your unique measurement to the same area on the pattern. When the pattern is shorter than the body, the pattern needs to be lengthened or spread apart to match the body.

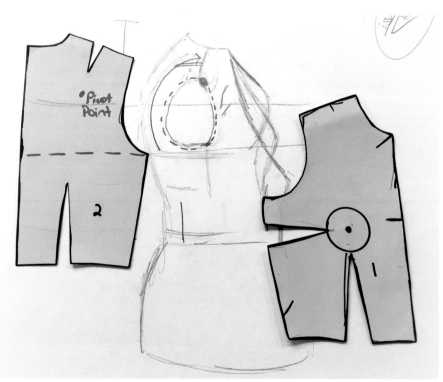

An unpolished work-in-progress pattern. You can see the paper pattern and the body sketch. The pattern should match the body.

ADJUSTING THE LENGTH VERTICALLY

1. To help visualize the area you are adjusting, draw a white vertical pencil line from the top to the bottom of the area of measure. In this example, the area to adjust is the shoulder to apex.
2. To lengthen, draw a blue horizontal adjustment line in the center of the area being adjusted.
3. Draw a vertical line down the center of a separate sheet of pattern paper slightly longer than the area you are adjusting. Normal printer paper or kraft paper works well and is inexpensive.
4. Cut the pattern along the adjustment line. Tape the cut-apart pattern so that the vertical lines are aligned and the pattern pieces are separated by the exact amount the section is to be lengthened. Connect the edges of the pattern and trim away excess paper. Your pattern should now match your body measurement of that area.

The following examples are vertical adjustments to the areas of measure as illustrated on the measurement chart featured on page 73.

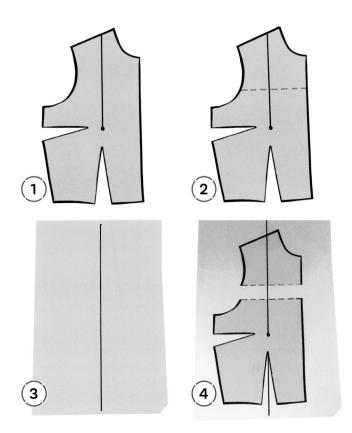

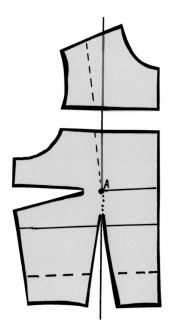

Front Shoulder to Apex

This is one of the simplest areas to measure, wearing a correct fitting bra with good support, lift, and natural shape. Compare your body measurement to the pattern. Lengthen if necessary. When adjusting this area of a pattern, the armscye (armhole) may temporarily be affected. Once you finish your adjustment, simply raise the underarm by the amount you lengthened and blend into the arm opening. This will be further refined in the muslin fit sample.

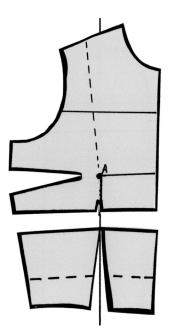

Apex to Waist

This area will give you the lower length of a torso pattern. Areas of fit affected by this measurement include the bust darts, the waist darts, and the transition from the full bust into the contour of the natural waist. If you are very busty, lengthen closer to the apex so the bust dart area is affected more. If you are smaller busted, adjust toward the center of the area of measure. Another area of fit that further refines the accuracy of bodice fitting is the bust curve.

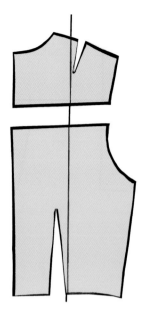

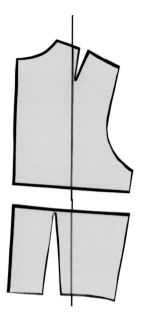

Shoulder to Full Upper Back

The fullest part of the back is the area approximately in the center of the arm opening on the pattern. It is usually the same on the body but may fall slightly above or below. This area of adjustment fits the contour and curve of the slope of the shoulder. Those with shoulders that tilt forward or slope to the front need to lengthen the upper portion of the pattern. Compare your body length to the pattern and lengthen as needed. This will prevent garments from pulling toward the back as a result of being too short in length. The arm opening will be temporarily affected. Simply raise the underarm by the amount lengthened and blend into the armscye.

Back Shoulder to Waist

Once the upper portion of the back is adjusted, measure from your shoulder down to the natural waist. Compare to the pattern and lengthen as needed. This adjustment should fall below the underarm approximately in the mid-back.

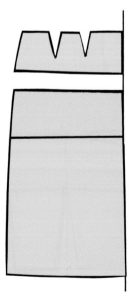

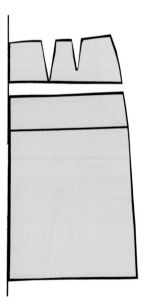

Waist to Full Hip Front

Hip lines are interesting. They are the fullest part of the body across the front. This can be an actual hip bone, a full tummy, or a fleshy contour at the side seam. However it presents itself, measure from the natural waist to the fullest part and compare to the pattern. Lengthen as needed to match. The garment needs to skim over the fullest part of the body. Once adjusted, you can additionally measure from the waist to knee or hem to determine any length adjustments.

Waist to Full Hip Back

The back natural waist to hip is adjusted the same as the front. Note that the front and back hips may not touch at the side seams. Treat them distinctively separate. The hip lines should fall parallel to the floor, but do not need to touch at the sides. In the muslin fit sample, you will blend the side seam for a natural look.

LENGTHENING THE LOWER PORTION OF A GARMENT

It is normal for the lower hem area of a garment to become too long or short during the process of custom fitting the upper part of a garment. Garments hang from the shoulder, waist, and hip area, so these should be modified first. After that, a simple correction at the hem will balance out the pattern.

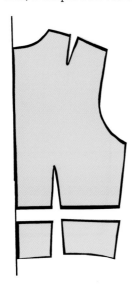

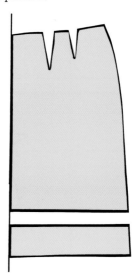

Dress Hem Length

Once the upper part of a top or dress is adjusted from the shoulder down to the apex, measure to the desired length of the garment. Lengthen or shorten near the bottom of the pattern as necessary to refine the length.

Skirt Length

Skirts fit at the waist and should skim over the full hip. Adjust this length in the pattern first. Then determine how long the skirt will be. Lengthen or shorten near the hem line and make sure the front and back have the same side seam length.

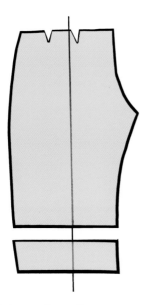

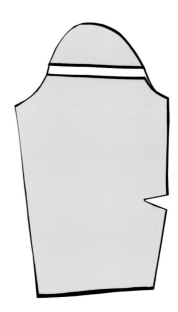

Pant and Leg Outseam Length

The upper part of the pant will be lengthened if any adjustments are needed in the crotch length or waist to hip area. Only after adjusting the upper part of the pant, measure from the natural waist to the floor to determine if you need to add additional hem length near the bottom. Make sure the side seams match on the front and back. Add additional length if you are unsure of the final hem finish.

Cap Height

The cap of the sleeve is the area from the full bicep to the top curve of the sleeve. This area fits differently than the arm of the sleeve. Find the fullest part of your bicep, which may be in line with the full bust or lay just below or above the horizontal bustline. Measure from the bicep to the shoulder point on your arm. Compare to the sleeve and add additional length if necessary. Connect the outer edge of the cap to polish the edge. You may not have adjusted the torso the same as the sleeve. These will be joined in the muslin fitting.

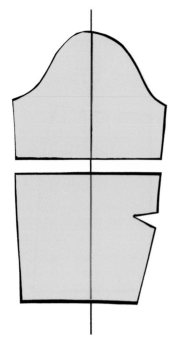

Arm Length/Sleeve

The arm of the sleeve has two areas of vertical fit: the bicep to the elbow and the elbow to the wrist. For patterns with an elbow dart or that are very fitted, use both areas of measure. For patterns without the elbow dart, you can measure from the bicep to the wrist and adjust in the middle of the area of measure.

Front Crotch Length

For pants, compare your crotch length measurement with the pattern's, measuring along the side of the pattern from the natural waist seam to a point opposite the bottom of the crotch seam (the fork of the seam). If your measurement is longer than the pattern's, you will have to lengthen the pattern at the crotch before you set the hem length.

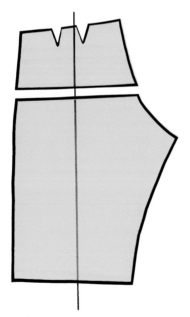

Back Crotch Length

Measure the adjusted front crotch length and subtract from your full crotch length measurement. The difference is how long your back crotch length should measure. Lengthen the back if needed.

ADJUSTING THE PATTERN VERTICALLY: BASIC STEPS FOR SHORTENING

Some vertical areas on a pattern will need shortening rather lengthening. It is also very normal to lengthen one area, yet need to shorten another. Although it may appear that they cancel each other out, you are actually customizing smaller areas of fit to match the smaller areas on your body. This attention to scale and proportion eliminates most fitting issues.

1. To help visualize the area you are adjusting, draw a white vertical pencil line from the top to the bottom of the area of measure. In this example, the area to adjust is the shoulder to apex.

2. To shorten, draw a blue horizontal adjustment line in the center of the area being adjusted.

3. Cut or fold the pattern along the adjustment line. Overlap the pattern pieces by the amount being shortened, dividing the amount between both sides. Use the white vertical pencil line to ensure they stay in the same placement line. When your pattern matches your body measurement, it is correct.

4. Place a separate sheet of pattern paper slightly wider than the area adjusting. Normal printer paper or craft paper works well and is inexpensive. Connect the edges of the pattern and trim away excess paper. Your pattern should now match your body measurement of that area.

TIP

Measure your body in a specific area of fit. Compare your unique measurement to the same area on the pattern. When the pattern is longer than the body, the pattern needs shortened or overlapped to match the body.

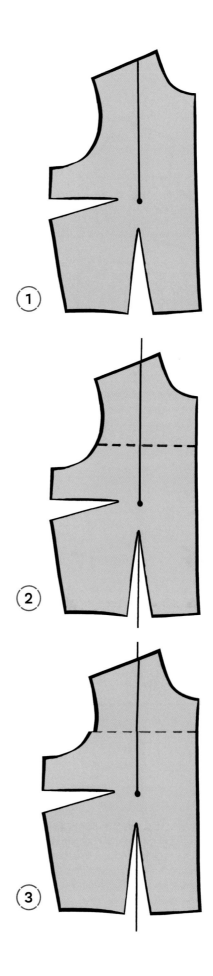

① ② ③

Examples: Shortening the Vertical Areas of a Pattern

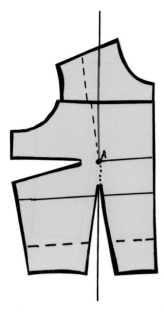

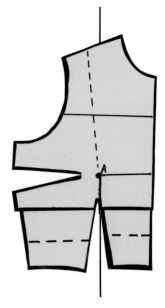

Compare your body measurement to the pattern. Shorten if necessary. When adjusting this area of a pattern, the armscye (armhole) may temporarily be affected. Once you finish your adjustment, simply lower the underarm by the amount you shortened in the upper torso and blend into the arm opening. This will be further refined in the muslin fit sample.

On the torso, the area from the apex to the waist may need shortened near the waist if you are shorter in that area, or the shortening of the pattern may occur closer to the actual apex if you are shorter in the curvature of the under bust area. Determine where you want to shorten the pattern so it will best match your body and cut across, overlapping by the amount being removed, and true up the outer edges of the pattern. This is an area of fit that can be further mastered by more study in how the front of the pattern fits the curve of the body.

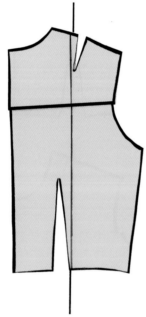

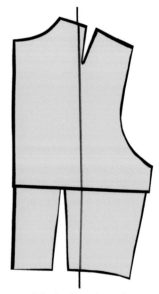

The fullest part of the back is the area approximately in the center of the arm opening on the pattern. It is usually the same on the body but may fall slightly above or below. This area of adjustment fits the contour and curve of the slope of the shoulder. Those with very square shoulders and no forward tilt or slope may need to shorten the upper portion of the pattern. Compare your body length to the pattern and shorten as needed. This will prevent garments from bunching in the back as a result of being too long in length. The arm opening will be temporarily affected. Simply lower the underarm by the amount shortened and blend into the armscye.

Once the upper portion of the back is adjusted, measure from your shoulder down to the natural waist. Compare to the pattern and take any remaining length out on the lower back as needed. This adjustment should fall below the underarm approximately in the mid-back.

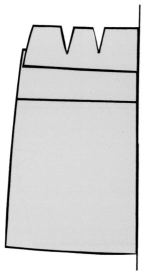 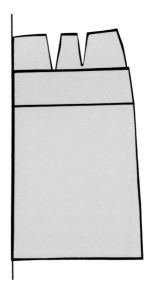

Measure from the natural waist to the fullest part of the hip and compare to the pattern. Shorten as needed to match. The garment needs to skim over the fullest part of the body. Once adjusted, you can additionally measure from the waist to knee or hem to determine any length adjustments.

The back natural waist to hip is adjusted the same as the front. Note that the front and back hips may not touch at the side seams. Treat them distinctively separate. The hip lines should fall parallel to the floor, but they do not need to touch at the sides. In the muslin fit sample, you will blend the side seam for a natural look.

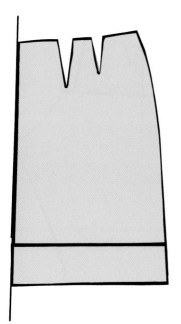 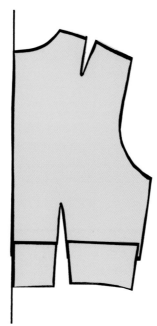 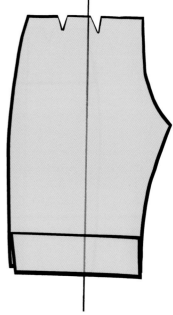

Skirts fit at the waist and should skim over the full hip. Adjust this length in the pattern first. Then determine how long the skirt will be. Shorten near the hemline and make sure the front and back have the same side seam length.

Many patterns for the upper body have a shorten line placed near the hem or lower edge of the garment. If that is the exact area where you need to remove length, such as if you are short-waisted, then this is the ideal area to shorten the pattern.

The upper part of the pant will be shortened if any adjustments are needed in the crotch curve or waist to hip area. Only after adjusting the upper part of the pant, measure from the natural waist to the floor to determine if you need to remove any additional hem length near the bottom. Make sure the side seams match on the front and back

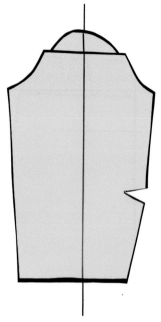

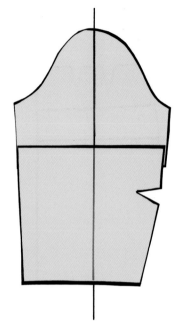

If you have a short distance from your shoulder point to the upper area of the arm, then most likely you will need to remove some height from the cap of the sleeve. A sleeve cap with too much height will bunch and have excess fabric.

The arm of the sleeve has two areas where the length can be shortened: the bicep to the elbow and the elbow to the wrist. For patterns with an elbow dart or that are very fitted, use both areas of measure. For patterns without the elbow dart, you can measure from the bicep to the wrist and adjust in the middle of the area of measure.

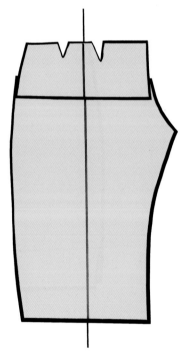

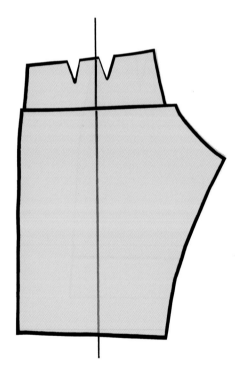

The front crotch length can be easily fitted on a pair of pants using the crotch curve template. This is the best way to shorten this area because it not only has a length, but it interacts with the back crotch curve. Reference Chapter 5 for exact instructions.

The back of the crotch curve is where the fit of pants is achieved. When the curve is too long, it interferes with how the pants move in conjunction with the body. The best way to shorten this area is to fit a template and then trace the crotch curve template onto the pattern for a more customized fit. Reference Chapter 5 for exact instructions.

ADJUSTING THE PATTERN HORIZONTALLY: BASIC STEPS FOR ENLARGING

Horizontal areas of a pattern match the circumference measurements that go around the body. At minimum, the horizontal area of a pattern should match the body measurements. Unlike vertical areas that have minimal to no ease, ease is added horizontally first for comfort and second for silhouette or design. Knit patterns are the exception due to their negative ease.

When a pattern is narrow horizontally, the garment pulls across the body and presents drag lines that may not close altogether. Excess width across the circumference makes a garment look sloppy, adds visual weight to the body, and inhibits movement in addition to preventing fitting elements such as darts, seams, and closures from matching the intended area of the body. Horizontally, the pattern should match the body in the center areas of the pattern and then toward the side front and side seam area. You need to find a balance between what looks aesthetically pleasing with what's comfortable for the fabric and pattern style. Ease will be added in once the key areas are fitted.

Adjusting Width Horizontally

1. To help visualize the area you are adjusting, draw a white horizontal pencil line from edge to edge of the area of measure. In this example, the area to adjust is the apex to side seam.
2. Draw a horizontal line across the center of a separate sheet of pattern paper slightly longer than the area you are adjusting. Overlap the edge of the pattern piece on the sheet of paper.
3. At the point where you need to enlarge your pattern piece, measure out from the edge of the pattern the amount to enlarge.
4. Draw a new outer edge of the pattern and transition into any area above or below the increase. Connect the edges of the pattern and trim away excess paper. Your pattern should now match your body measurement of that area.

The following examples are the horizontal areas of measure illustrated on the measurement chart featured on page 73.

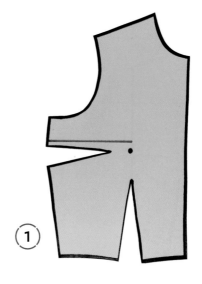

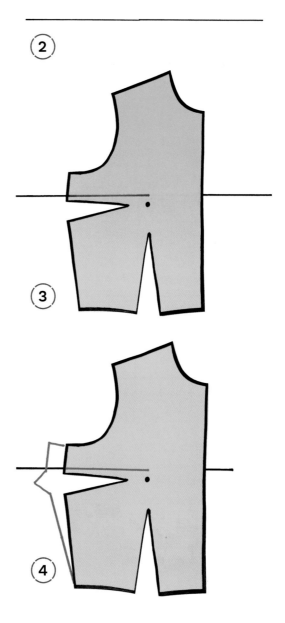

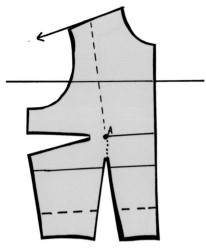

Shoulder Length

The shoulder length extends from the base of the neck to the shoulder point, where the sleeve joins the torso. Simply extend the shoulder outward to add additional length. A shoulder pad helps to shape the shoulder by adjusting the length and height for better support of your garment.

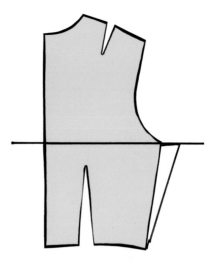

Full Bust Front and Back

The full bust measurement provides the overall circumference of the pattern. When you measure the front separate from the back, you further fine-tune your fit. Simply increase at the upper side seam. The increase may be different from the front to the back.

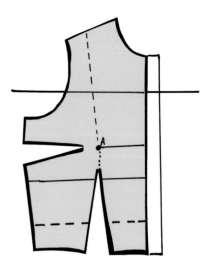

Apex to Apex

To increase the apex to apex measurement, increase the pattern width across the center front bust span. The center front is the main straight of grain on a woven garment, so the increase will vertically follow the entire center front. For apex to side seam: Subtract the apex to apex measurement from the full front bust. The remaining number will be placed on either side of the apex at the apex to side seam. Increase the side seam at the underarm.

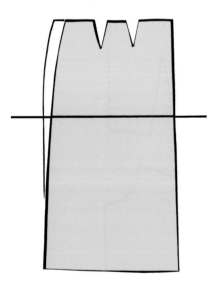

Front and Back Waist

The full waist measurement provides the overall circumference of the pattern. When you measure the front separate from the back, you further fine-tune your fit. Simply increase the side seam at the natural waistline.

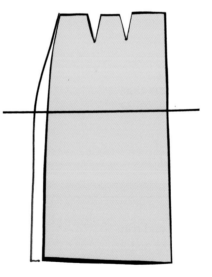

Front and Back Hip

The full hip measurement provides the overall circumference of the pattern at the hip. Increase the pattern side seam even with the fullest part of the hip. The amount added may be different from front to back.

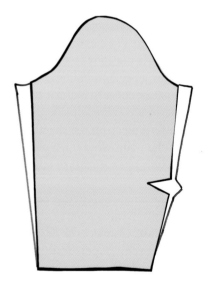

Full Bicep and Sleeve Width

The bicep is easily widened by extending the side seam outward. The cap of the sleeve may need reshaping due to the increase, which would be polished in the fit sample. Additionally, the elbow and wrist may need an increase. Measure the width of the wrist and increase to match. If the increase is equal the entire length of the sleeve, a slash and spread down the middle of the sleeve is an option.

ADJUSTING THE PATTERN HORIZONTALLY: BASIC STEPS FOR REDUCING

A custom-fitted commercial pattern may still have excess ease beyond what is necessary for your figure or what you prefer. If the pattern has been fitted first, it can be successfully contoured down the side seam to remove any excess ease.

A reduction in ease will slim down the silhouette and remove excess fabric that may be unflattering and bulky. For comfort reasons, the reduction should match the horizontal areas of the body at minimum unless the pattern is a knit—then the pattern may be smaller than the body due to negative ease. Any extra adjustment is up to you.

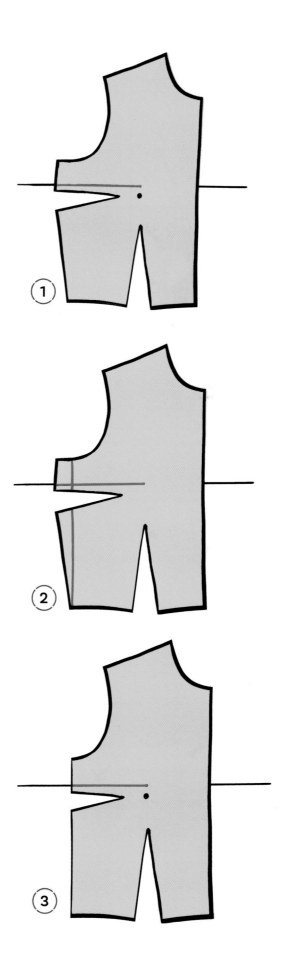

TIP
Measure your body in a specific area of fit. Compare your unique measurement to the same area on the pattern. When the pattern is wider than the body, the pattern needs to be reduced to match.

REDUCING WIDTH HORIZONTALLY

1. At the point where you need to reduce your pattern piece, measure in from the edge of the pattern and mark the amount to be reduced.
2. Draw a line and gradually transition into the pattern above and below the reduction.
3. Trim any excess and polish the pattern edge. Your pattern should now match your body measurement of that area with the desired amount of comfort and design ease.

TIP
It is not uncommon to reduce the front and back by different amounts.

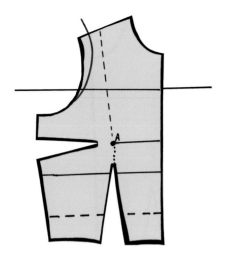

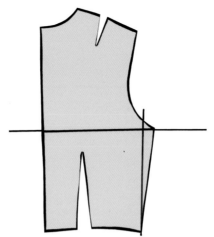

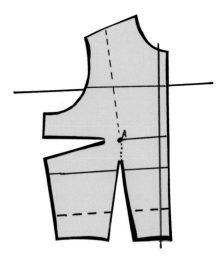

Shoulder Length Reduction

The shoulder length extends from the base of the neck to the shoulder point, where the sleeve joins the torso. If you have narrow shoulders, you will need to remove length from the edge of the shoulder until it matches your length. The garment measurement may be slightly longer than your body, so make sure you don't make it too short.

Full Bust Front and Back Reduction

The full bust measurement provides the overall circumference of the pattern. When you measure the front separate from the back, you further fine-tune your fit. Simply decrease at the upper side seam. The reduction may be different from the front to the back.

Apex to Apex Reduction

To decrease the apex to apex measurement, reduce the pattern width across the center front bust span. The center front is the main straight of grain on a woven garment, so the reduction will follow the entire center front vertically. For apex to side seam, subtract the apex to apex measurement from the full front bust. The remaining number will be placed on either side of the apex at the apex to side seam. Decrease the side seam at the underarm.

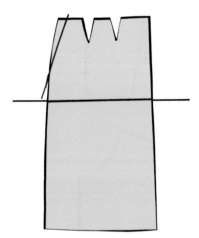

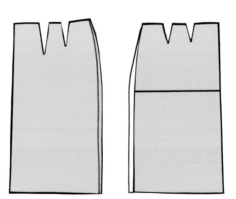

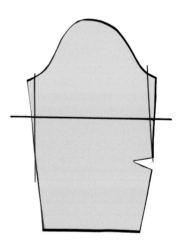

Front and Back Waist Reduction

The full waist measurement provides the overall circumference of the pattern. When you measure the front separate from the back, you further fine-tune your fit. Simply reduce the side seam at the natural waistline.

Front and Back Hip Reduction

The full hip measurement provides the overall circumference of the pattern at the hip. Decrease the pattern side seam even with the fullest part of the hip. The amount removed may be different from front to back.

Full Bicep and Sleeve Width Reduction

The bicep is easily narrowed by moving the side seam inward. The cap of the sleeve may need reshaping due to the decrease, which would be polished in the fit sample. Additionally, the elbow and wrist may need a decrease. Measure the width of the wrist and decrease to match. If the decrease is equal the entire length of the sleeve, a slash and spread down the middle of the sleeve with an overlap is an option.

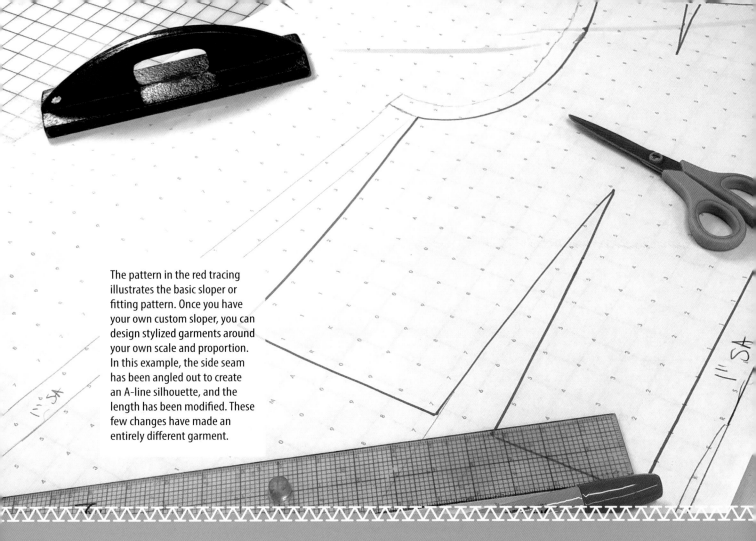

The pattern in the red tracing illustrates the basic sloper or fitting pattern. Once you have your own custom sloper, you can design stylized garments around your own scale and proportion. In this example, the side seam has been angled out to create an A-line silhouette, and the length has been modified. These few changes have made an entirely different garment.

ALL ABOUT EASE
WHERE TO ADD EASE

Ease is defined as any excess area in a pattern beyond body measurements. Comfort ease is the amount added to a pattern for movement and comfort. A common example is the ease added to sleeve and crotch curves for bending and sitting. Design ease is the extra added beyond comfort to create a fashion design or silhouette. In the sleeve, gathers added to the cap of the sleeve creates decorative fullness. In an A-line skirt, the triangular silhouette widens as it transitions from the waist to the hem, adding more space in the hip and hem area of the pattern; the silhouette of the skirt adds ease as part of the fullness in the design.

The ideal scenario is that the pattern is already custom-fitted to the scale of your body, leaving you to make the adjustments to the comfort ease and silhouette ease an easy modification. However, it is likely that most sewists will begin with an unaltered pattern out of the envelope with an incorrect amount of ease.

Here are some guidelines for adjusting ease:

- A sloper pattern has no ease. It is fitted to an accurate representation of the body.
- Most commercial patterns include ease based on the proportion of their standard and feature design ease necessary to the selected pattern.
- The ease on commercial patterns allows it to fit around many figures. Many times, that ease is far more than necessary to create a polished fit on most figures. Expect to contour the pattern to your body.
- Before addressing ease, make sure the pattern is fitted to your body both vertically and horizontally.
- Do not simply add ease to the edge of an unaltered pattern.
- Add ease to the side of a pattern only after the pattern has had a custom fitting.
- A fit sample is always necessary to test the fit and ease amount prior to sewing the fashion fabric.
- Not all areas of a pattern need ease (see vertical adjustments, page 76).
- The center front and back areas of patterns have minimal to no ease, because these areas fit exactly to body measurements. Ease is distributed at or near the side area of a fitted pattern.

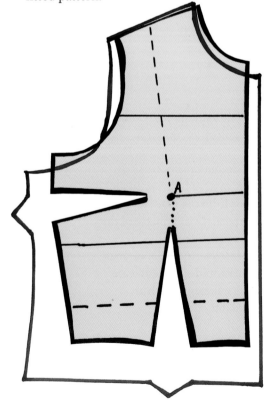

HOW MUCH EASE DO I ADD?

Ease is as unique to everyone as personal taste and style. What feels loose fitting on one person might feel snug on another. Commercial pattern envelopes often include an ease chart with terms such as "fitted," "semi-fitted," "tailored," and "loose fitting." These are simply a guide, because your own personal amount of ease will be determined by fitting your muslin fit sample. Of course, different fabrics will require more or less ease based on the fabric characteristics.

To understand the ease in your pattern, apply the following steps:

- Fit the pattern to your body by first matching all key areas of the pattern to your body proportions. Make sure you have removed the seam allowance from your pattern.
- The design details on a stylized block or commercial pattern should match the corresponding areas on the body, which is the reason we adjust the pattern first. By fitting the pattern, you will naturally reduce or enlarge areas that need customization. For patterns that have a lot of ease in them already, determine which areas are key fitting areas that should match the body exactly and adjust those.
- Next, add ease using the 1" to 2" (2.5 to 5cm) formula to each side seam: front left, front right, back left, and back right. If your pattern already has ease, you can omit or blend into the fitted area. For example, an A-line skirt has a full silhouette around the hip and hem and already includes ease; you would fit the waistband to your body and blend the side seam into the skirt with a ruler.
- While the final garment may not include all the added ease, you will now have a generous amount down the side seams to work with for contouring, comfort, and design. This will be refined in the muslin fitting.
- Add seam allowance around the edges of the pattern.
- Create a fit sample. Baste it together and pin fit for final shaping (page 92).
- By doing the pattern fitting first, you can see that the ease is easily adjusted in the side without interfering with the fit of the garment. This only works with a fitted pattern.

In this example, the fit pattern is transposed over a tracing of a stylized pattern. Using your custom fitted sloper, you can more easily utilize your commercial patterns. If you compare the shoulder, side seam, and arm area, you would know right away if the commercial pattern will fit. Any area that is smaller than your custom fitted pattern will automatically be too tight, and any areas much larger also indicate fit issues. This quick pattern evaluation will tell you where you need to modify any pattern.

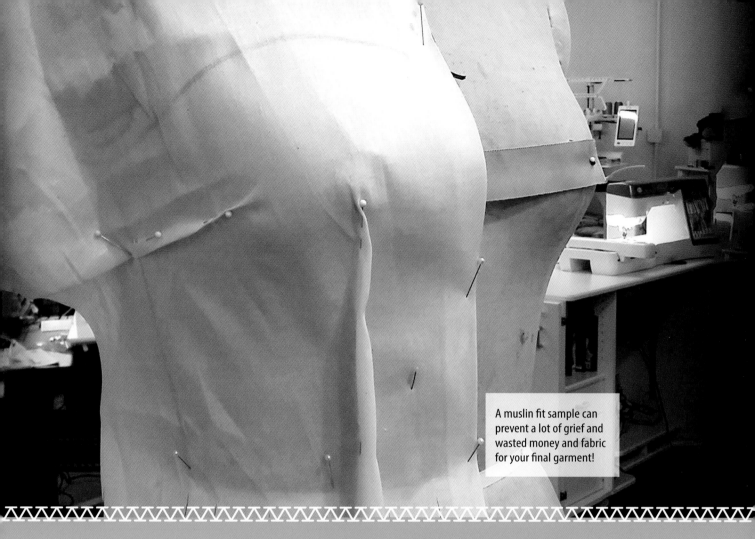

A muslin fit sample can prevent a lot of grief and wasted money and fabric for your final garment!

MAKING A MUSLIN FIT SAMPLE

Professional dressmakers and tailors know the muslin fit sample is the true key to a perfect fit. Avoid thinking that fitting samples are a waste of time. Instead, they are the best tool to refine the details of the pattern and polish the fit prior to sewing your fashion fabric. Once fitted, you can sew the final garment from start to finish knowing the end results will be a success. That is a huge time saver! The muslin will also spare the garment fabric from repeated basting and stitch removal during the fitting. Equally, tissue fitting simply cannot mimic the fashion fabric. The muslin clearly illustrates how the final design will look, fit, and hang on the specific body.

To make a muslin for fitting, cut out the adjusted pattern in a quality muslin or fabric similar in weight and drape to the fashion fabric to be used in the final design. Make sure seam allowance is added along with desired ease. Next, cut out, mark, and assemble the muslin on the main seam areas like the shoulder, side seam, princess seams, and waistline. There is no need to add decorative pockets, main collar pieces, or hand stitching. Use the muslin to refine the body of the garment.

Now the actual garment can be cut out and sewn. Regardless of how skillful a job you do on the muslin, you may still have to adjust on the actual garment because the real fabric drapes differently. Such changes, however, will be minor. Once the muslin is fitted, it can be carefully removed from the body and the changes marked—it will be your new pattern with a custom fit.

FITTING THE MUSLIN

Most fitting issues are eliminated with the vertical and horizontal adjustments made to the custom pattern. The next step is to construct the garment in muslin using machine basting stitches, which are easy to adjust, so that you can try on the muslin and see how well it follows the contours of your body. Once a muslin is made, contouring of the edges of the pattern and other subtle refinements that are not visible in the paper and tissue pattern are easily polished in the muslin.

When approaching fit with a muslin created from an unaltered tissue or a sewn garment with minimal to no adjustments prior to sewing, additional adjustments are necessary. Eliminating imperfections with the techniques shown on the following pages will ensure you also have a perfectly fitted garment.

Because garments for the upper body hang from its shoulder seams, start the fitting there and work down, adjusting one seam at a time with pins; re-baste, then try on again if necessary. For the lower body, fit the waist and then work down. Your fitted muslin will be your new pattern. Transferring the markings to the paper pattern is also a common technique.

After completing each alteration in a seam of the muslin, transfer the revision to the paper pattern with pins and a pencil. When the muslin fits impeccably and the grain lines fall straight, you can safely ink in and tape down the revisions on the paper pattern.

The dress fabric may drape differently from the muslin and require further changes at the basting stage; however, making the major fitting adjustments on the muslin ensures that these final corrections will only be minor.

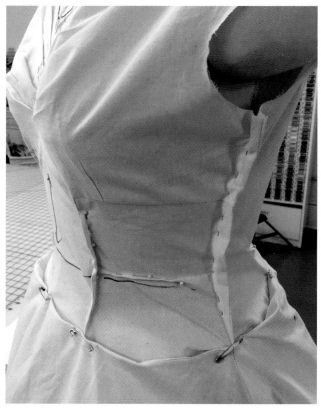

This working fit sample is a real example of a design in development. The skirt is pinned up for a better placement, a reduction has been pinned out vertically and horizontally in the front torso, and the side seams have been easily contoured for a custom fit. These types of adjustments are part of refining a flat paper pattern that has been sewn into a three-dimensional garment. The muslin allows for preliminary fitting as well as removal of any unsightly issues that you won't want in a final garment. While the side seams can always be contoured, the other adjustments may not be possible on a garment already sewn in the fashion fabric.

MARKING AND MEASURING MUSLIN ADJUSTMENTS

If the muslin has been tucked:
1. Baste the tuck along its base and remove the pins. Then baste the tuck flat.
2. If transferring markings to the paper pattern, measure the depth of the tuck at its widest point. Transfer the marking to the pattern.
3. If using the muslin as your new pattern, press the tuck flat. Do not make a tuck in your final garment.

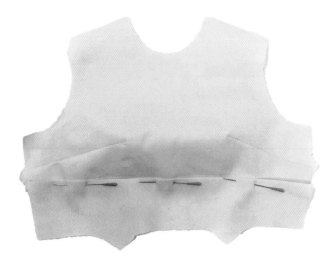

If the muslin has been tucked

If the muslin has been slashed:

1. Pin a muslin scrap underneath the opening. Baste the muslin insert to the garment fabric along the cut edges of the slash.
2. If transferring markings to the paper pattern, measure the depth of the slashed adjustment at the widest point. Transfer the markings to the pattern.

If the muslin has been tucked at a seam:

1. Turn the muslin wrong side out and fold the garment along the tucked seam.
2. Locate the pins along the folded edge of the muslin. Mark each pin position with chalk.
3. Mark the beginning and end of the tuck with a small chalk mark at a right angle to the seam.
4. Unpin the tuck to make the new seam line. Connect the chalk marks.
5. Some tucks transition into the seam or edge of the fabric at long angles and others with a short distance. Make sure you mark precisely so the adjustment will look exactly how the muslin was pinned.
6. Transfer the adjustment measurements to the paper pattern or mark a corrected seam allowance and trim off the excess removed in the adjustment.

If the muslin has been slashed (photo shows garment right side)

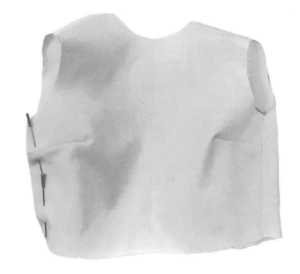

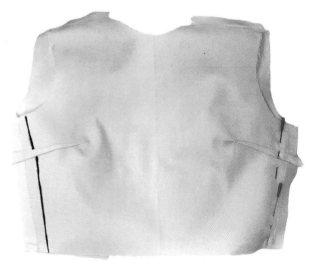

If the muslin has been tucked at a seam (photos show garment wrong side)

If the muslin seam needs to be let out:

1. Carefully seam rip or remove the stitches on the seam, letting it open. Once the seam relaxes and fits the body, place a mark on the seam at the end of the opening.

2. Measure the width of the seam opening at its widest point. This will be the amount that is needed to add to the edge of the pattern. This amount may be divided equally on either side of the seam or when a seam needs to be balanced. You may add more to one edge than the other.

3. Measure the length of the adjustment from end-to-end and transfer the marking to your pattern.

TIP

Measure additional areas on the length of the adjustment and transfer those markings to the pattern..

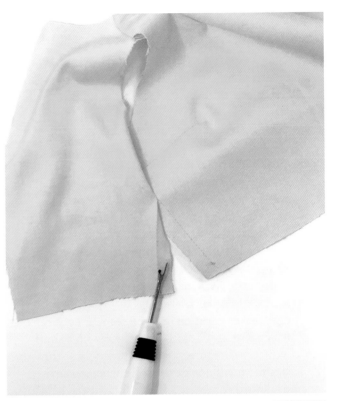

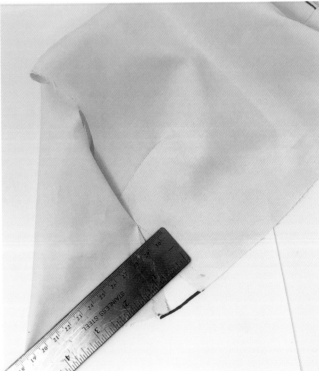

If the muslin needs to be let out

TROUBLESHOOT: A TIGHT INSET SLEEVE SHOULDER

Symptoms (A):
- The shoulder seam feels too tight.
- Creases appear just below the shoulder near the armhole.

Refitting the shoulder seam (B):
1. Open the armhole stitching and remove the sleeve. Open the shoulder seam from neck to armhole. Pull the shoulder seam allowances outside the muslin.
2. Starting at the neck, let out the seam allowance by taking more fabric from one side than the other, if necessary, until they lie smooth and comfortable. Pin the new shoulder seam, tapering it evenly from neck to armhole. Take off the muslin.
3. Measure from the new shoulder seam line to the original one at the armhole seam line on the bodice front. Mark the change on your tissue pattern.

Adjusting the pattern (C):
1. Slash the bodice front pattern diagonally from about 1" (2.5cm) below the shoulder seam line on the armhole to the intersection of the shoulder and neck seam lines.
2. Spread the slash at the armhole the distance measured in step 3 above. Slide pattern paper under the slash and pin it to the pattern. Draw the armhole seam line on the paper insert. Draw a new cutting line ⅝" (1.5cm) outside the new seam line and parallel to it. Trim the excess paper away.
3. Raise the base of the armhole on the bodice front pattern by the amount added in the shoulder.
4. Repeat steps 1–3 on the bodice back pattern.
5. Using the revised armhole seam and cutting lines, re-cut the armhole of the dress muslin and baste the sleeve into the revised armhole.

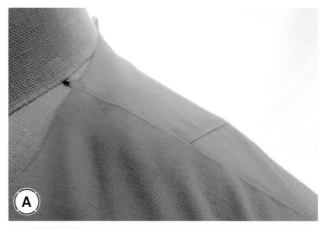

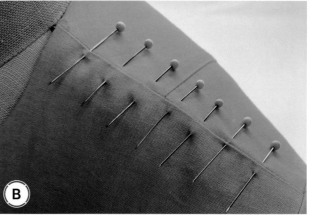

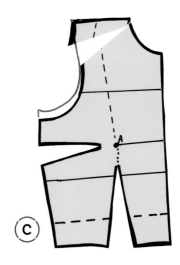

TROUBLESHOOT: A LOOSE INSET SLEEVE SHOULDER

Symptoms (A):

- The shoulder seam of the dress muslin stands up above natural shoulder line.
- Crossways creases appear on the bodice along the armhole.

Refitting the shoulder seam (B):

1. Remove the stitching around the armhole and take out the sleeve.
2. Starting at the armhole and working toward the neck, pull the shoulder seam straight up and pin the front and back shoulder, taking more fabric from one than the other if necessary, until they lie smooth and meet along the center of your shoulder.
3. Pin the new shoulder seam, tapering it evenly from the armhole to the neck. Take off the muslin.
4. Measure along the new shoulder edge and make the changes on the paper pattern.

Adjusting the pattern (C):

1. Trace the original armhole and shoulder seam lines and other markings of the front bodice pattern on a sheet of tracing paper.
2. Draw the new seam line on the pattern making the reduction. Draw a new cutting line ⅝" (1.5cm) outside the new seam line and parallel to it.
3. Slide the tracing of the armhole under the pattern and align the shoulder seam line of the tracing with the new shoulder seam line on the pattern, matching the side seam edge of the tracing to the side seam of the pattern.
4. Following the line on the tracing paper, draw a new armhole seam line, complete with pattern markings, lower than the original one, on the bodice front pattern. Then draw a new cutting line ⅝" (1.5cm) outside the new seam line and parallel to it.
5. Repeat steps 1–4 on the bodice back pattern.
6. Using the revised armhole seam and cutting lines, re-cut the armhole of the dress muslin and baste the sleeve into the revised armhole.

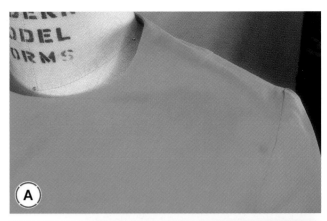

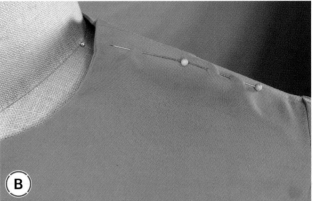

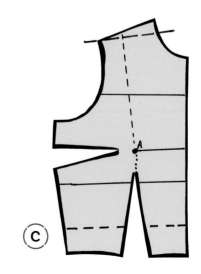

TROUBLESHOOT: A TIGHT INSET SLEEVE TOP

Symptoms (A):
- The sleeve top feels too tight around the upper arm.
- Creases radiate from the armhole on both the sleeve top and the shoulder.

Refitting the sleeve top (B):
1. Open the armhole seam around the sleeve top, releasing at least 4" (10cm) on either side of the shoulder seam.
2. Let out enough seam allowance at the cap until the sleeve can be comfortably re-pinned to the shoulder.
3. Pin the folded edge to the armhole seam line of the bodice at the shoulder seam line. Continue folding under the seam allowance from the shoulder seam line around the sleeve, tapering the fold into the original seam line of the sleeve top. Take off the muslin.
4. At the shoulder seam line, measure from the edge of the fold to the original armhole seam line on the sleeve top.

Adjusting the pattern (C):
1. Measure down on the sleeve pattern halfway between the shoulder point to the bicep and draw a horizontal line across the pattern.
2. Cut the sleeve top along the line.
3. Slide a piece of pattern paper under the cut pattern and spread until the distance between the edges of the pattern pieces is equal to the measurement of the amount let out of the cap. Make sure the edges of the pattern pieces are parallel, then pin them to the paper.
4. On both sides of the sleeve, draw new seam lines on the shelf paper joining the original seam lines. Draw new cutting lines ⅝" (1.5cm) outside the new seam lines and parallel to them. Trim excess shelf paper.

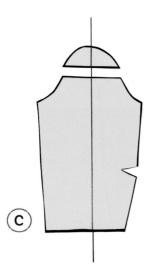

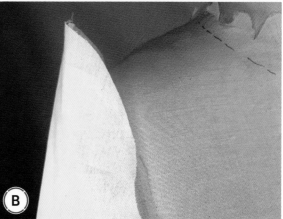

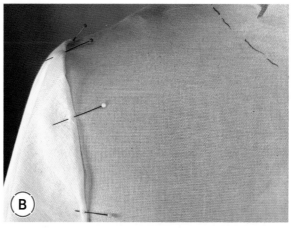

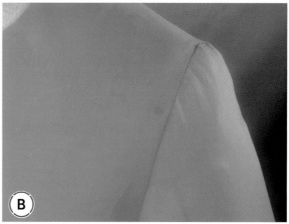

TROUBLESHOOT: A LOOSE INSET SLEEVE TOP

Symptoms (A):
- The top rolls up above the shoulder seam of the muslin to create a puffed effect.
- Fullness appears across the top along armhole seam.

Refitting the sleeve top (B):
1. Open the armhole seam around the sleeve top, releasing at least 4" (10cm) of the sleeve top on either side of the shoulder seam.
2. Re-pin the sleeve top over the upper arm to the armhole at the shoulder seam, then fold under the fabric at the center edge of the sleeve top. Pin the fold at the point where the shoulder seam line intersects the armhole seam line.
3. Fold under the seam allowance of the sleeve top in front and back and pin it to the armhole seam line, tapering into the original seam line midway down the armhole. Take off the muslin.
4. Measure the distance at the shoulder seam line from the new sleeve top seam line to the original one.

Adjusting the pattern (C):
1. Measure down on the sleeve pattern halfway between the shoulder point to the bicep and draw a horizontal line across the pattern.
2. Fold the pattern on the line and create a tuck removing the amount removed from the sleeve cap.
3. Pin a piece of pattern paper under the tuck.
4. Draw new seam lines on each side of the sleeve from the bottom of the tuck to taper into the original seam line along the top of the sleeve 1" (2.5cm) or so above the tuck. Draw new cutting lines on the paper ⅝" (1.5cm) outside the new seam lines and parallel to them. Trim away excess paper.

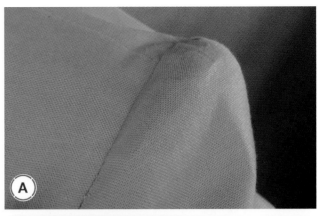

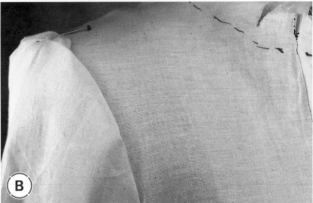

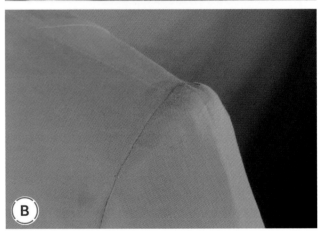

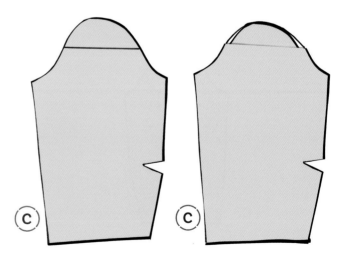

TROUBLESHOOT: A POORLY PLACED INSET SLEEVE TOP

Symptoms (A):
- The muslin feels lose in back at the armhole but tight in front, or vice versa.
- Creases appear close to the armhole seam line on the loose side of the sleeve top.

Refitting the sleeve top (B):
1. Open the armhole seam at the top of the sleeve between the notches on either side of the sleeve top or 1"–2" (2.5–5cm) beyond where the sleeve is tight.
2. If the looseness is in the front of the sleeve top, move the center of the sleeve top back from the shoulder seam until the fullness of the sleeve top is evenly distributed. If the looseness is in the back of the sleeve top, move the center of the sleeve top forward.
3. Pin the seam line of the sleeve cap to the armhole seam line of the bodice at the shoulder seam. Take off the muslin.
4. Measure along the sleeve top seam line from the pin at the shoulder seam to the original pattern mark indicating the shoulder seam attachment point.

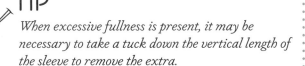

TIP

When excessive fullness is present, it may be necessary to take a tuck down the vertical length of the sleeve to remove the extra.

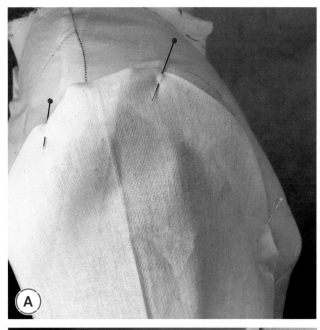

(A)

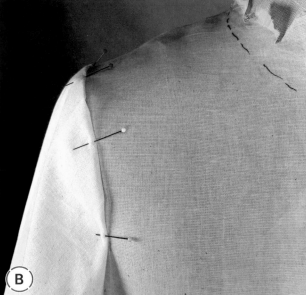

(B)

Adjusting the pattern (C):
1. Measure along the sleeve cap seam line of the pattern from the original top center, marking the distance measured, and mark with a new dot. Check the notches identifying front and back to be sure that the measurement corresponds in direction to the one previously made.
2. With the ruler parallel to the original grainline, rotate the top of the ruler toward the new dot created for the shoulder placement.
3. Draw a new grain line from this dot to the bottom end of the original grain line.

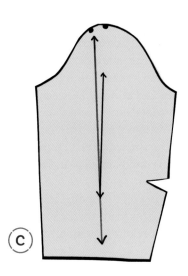

(C)

TROUBLESHOOT: A LOOSE, ROUND HIGH NECKLINE

Symptoms (A):

- The neck seam line stands away from the base of the neck. Check for this symptom before attaching collar or facing, but after the neck seam line has been stay-stitched and the seam line clipped.

Refitting the neckline (B):

1. Measure the circumference of the neck seam line with a measuring tape, then cut a bias strip of muslin ¾" (1.9cm) wide and 2" (5cm) longer than the neck circumference.
2. Using a pressing cloth, shape and press the bias strip into a curve like that of the neckline.
3. Fit the bias strip around the base of your neck so that the inner curved edge lies comfortably along the base of your neck. It is not attached to the fit sample yet. The inner edge will represent the new neck seam line.
4. Pin the strip to the muslin and take off the muslin.
5. Measure from the inner curved edge of the bias strip to the original neck seam line at the center front, center back, shoulder seams, and midway between each of these points.

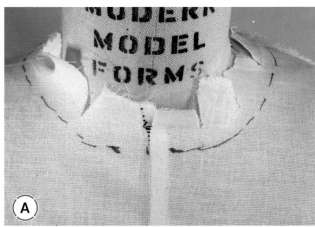

TIP

You can use a fabric glue stick to also adhere the bias strip to the muslin.

Adjusting the pattern (C):

1. Pin a piece of pattern paper under the neckline of the bodice front pattern.
2. Using the distances measured in step 5 of the previous sequence, mark dots outside the original bodice front neck seam line at the center front, at the shoulder, and midway between these points.
3. Connect the dots with a smooth curve similar in shape to the original neck seam line. Draw a new cutting line on the paper ⅝" (1.5cm) outside the new seam line and parallel to it. Trim away the excess paper.
4. Repeat steps 1–3 on the bodice back pattern using the measurements made on the muslin bodice in step 5 of the previous sequence.

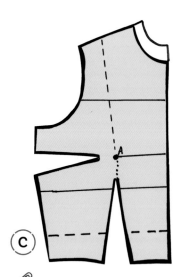

TIP

A properly fitted neckline is important for achieving the correct fit of a collar so that the collar hugs the neck well..

TROUBLESHOOT: A TIGHT, ROUND HIGH NECKLINE

Symptoms (A):

- The neck is tight in the front, back, or both places. Check for this symptom before attaching the collar or facing, but after the neck seam line has been stay-stitched and the seam allowance clipped.
- The fabric bunches and small crossways creases appear below the neck seam line.

Refitting the neckline (B):

1. Starting at the center front and working around the neckline, clip through the machine stitching on the neck seam line at ½" (1.5cm) intervals.
2. Taking tiny cuts each time, gradually extend the depth of the clips around the neckline until the muslin lies comfortably along the base of your neck and the creases disappear.
3. Draw a new neck seam line directly on the muslin around the bottom ends of the clips. Take off the muslin.
4. Measure from the new neck seam line to the original one at the center front, center back, shoulder seams, and midway between each of these points.

Adjusting the pattern (C):

1. Using the distances measured previously, mark dots inside the original bodice front neck seam line at the center front, at each shoulder, and midway between these points.
2. Connect the dots with a smooth curve similar in shape to the original neck seam line but custom to your shape. Draw a new cutting line ⅝" (1.5cm) outside the new seam line and parallel to it.
3. Repeat steps 1 and 2 on the bodice back pattern using the adjustments made on the muslin bodice back.

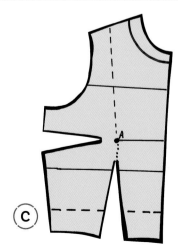

TROUBLESHOOT: A TIGHT UPPER BACK

Symptoms (A):
- The back of the bodice feels too tight over the shoulders.
- The neckline stands away from the back of neck.
- Creases radiate from the upper back toward the armholes.

Refitting the upper back (B):
1. Take off the muslin. Cut horizontally from the point of one shoulder dart across the back to the point of the other, then extend the slash from the darts horizontally to each armhole seam line. Put the muslin on again.
2. Slip an insert of muslin under the slash and spread the slashed edges of the bodice back apart until the muslin feels comfortable.
3. Pin the cut edges of the slash to the muslin insert. Take off the muslin.
4. Measure along the center back seam from one edge of the slash to the other to determine the amount of space being added to the pattern.

TIP
Can you see why scaling your pattern vertically and horizontally is beneficial for avoiding these additional steps?

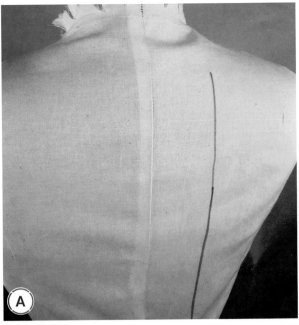

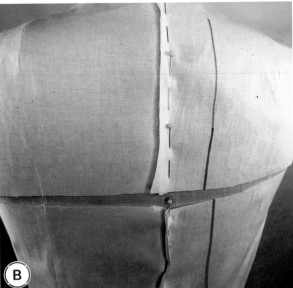

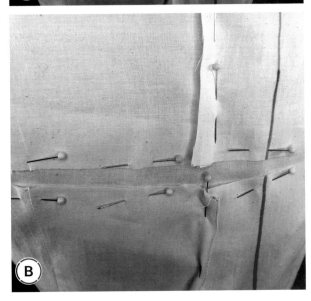

Adjusting the pattern (C):

1. With the ruler at the point of the back shoulder dart and at a right angle to the center back line, draw a line from the center back through the point of the dart to the armhole seam line. Cut along this line.
2. Cut the back shoulder dart down the center from the shoulder cutting line to within ⅛" (3mm) of the point.
3. Cut a square insert of pattern paper, center it under the top of the bodice back pattern, and pin the pattern to the paper below the horizontal slash.
4. Lift up the upper section of the pattern. Extend the center back line of the bottom section on to the shelf paper 6" (15.2cm) above the horizontal slash.
5. Mark the opening on the insert along the center back line up from the horizontal slash the amount being added to the pattern. Mark with a dot.

If the upper back is tight (D):

1. Place the upper pattern section over the insert, aligning the center back line with the line on the insert and the slashed edge of the pattern section with the dot made in the previous step.
2. Pin the top of the pattern flat against the insert, first along the center back line, then along the edges of the back shoulder dart, which will have spread to form a dart wider than the original one. Finally, pin along the upper edge of the horizontal slash.
3. Draw a new shoulder cutting line by extending the original cutting lines until they intersect in an inverted V above the center of the widened dart. Trim away excess shelf paper.

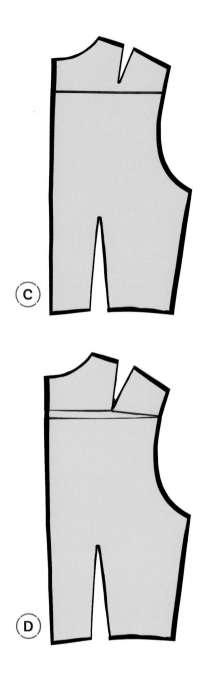

TROUBLESHOOT: A LOW, WIDE BUST LINE

Symptoms: (A)

- The under-bust dart of the muslin angles inwards and ends less than 1" (2.5cm) below the apex or forward point of the bust.
- The side-bust dart angles upwards and ends less than 1½" (4.5cm) from the apex or forward point of the bust.

Refitting the bust line (B):

1. Mark the muslin at the forward point of the bust.
2. Measure 1" (2.5cm) down toward the waist from the point marked in step 1 and mark with a dot. Chalk mark or insert pins end to end from this dot to the waist seam line to mark the new under-bust dart.
3. To mark the new side-bust dart, measure 1½" (4cm) toward the side seam from the forward point of the bust and mark with a dot. Insert pins end to end from this dot to the base of the original side-bust dart. Take off the muslin.
4. Measure along the new under-bust dart seam line from the dot to the waist seam line.
5. Insert a pin on the original under-bust seam line at the distance from the waist seam line measured in step 1.
6. Measure from the pin inserted in step 2 to the dot at the top of the new under-bust dart seam line.
7. Repeat steps 1–3 on the side-bust dart, using corresponding dots and measurements from the base of the original dart at the side seam line.

Adjusting the pattern (C):

1. On the bodice front pattern, measure from the waist seam line along the under-bust dart seam line that is nearer the side seam, using the distance measured in step 4 of the previous sequence. Mark with a dot.
2. With a ruler at the dot and at a right angle to the center line of the under-bust dart, measure toward the side seam the distance measured in step 2 of the previous sequence. Mark with a dot.
3. Measuring from each base point of the original dart seam lines along the waist seam line toward the side seam, mark the distance measured at the top of the new under-bust dart seam line with dots.
4. Draw lines from the dot made above.
5. Repeat steps 1–4 to lower the point of the side-bust dart using corresponding measurements and dots, but omit step 3 and use the base points of the original dart instead of marking new ones.

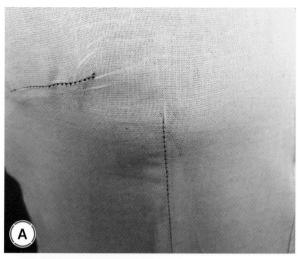

A

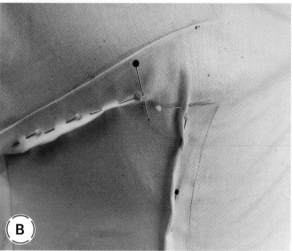

B

TIP

In custom fitting, your dart may stop slightly closer or a little further back from the apex based on how you fit and the fabric. Where the fitting darts angle is most important.

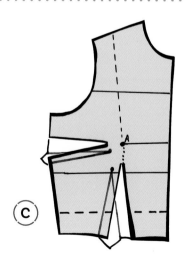

C

TROUBLESHOOT: A HIGH, NARROW BUST LINE

Symptoms (A):
- The under-bust dart of the muslin angles outward and ends more than 1" (2.5cm) below the apex or forward point of the bust.
- The side-bust dart angles downward and ends more than 1½" (4cm) from the forward part of the bust.

Refitting the bust line: (B)
1. Mark the muslin at the forward point of the breast.
2. Measure 1" (2.5cm) down from the point marked in step 1 and mark with a dot. Chalk mark or insert pins from this dot to the waist seam line to mark the new under-bust dart.
3. To mark the new side-bust dart, measure 1½" (4cm) toward the side seam from the forward point of the bust and mark with a dot. Chalk mark or insert pins end to end from this dot to the base of the original side-bust dart. Take off the muslin.
4. Measure along the new under-bust dart seam line from the dot to the waist seam line.
5. Measure along and beyond the original under-bust dart seam line from the waist seam line the distance measured in step 4. Mark with a pin.
6. Measure from the pin inserted in step 5 to the dot at the top of the new under-bust dart seam line.
7. Repeat steps 3–6 on the side-bust dart using corresponding dots and measurement from the base of the original dart at the side seam line.

Adjusting the pattern (C):
1. On the bodice front pattern measure along and beyond the center of the under-bust dart, using the distance from the waist seam line measured in step 1 of the previous sequence. Mark with a dot.
2. With the ruler at the dot and at a right angle to the center line of the under-bust dart, measure toward the bodice center front the distance figured in step 2 of the previous sequence. Mark with a dot.
3. Measuring from each base point of the original under-bust dart along the waist seam line toward the bodice center front, mark the distance measured in step 6 of the previous sequence with dots.
4. Draw lines from the dots made above.
5. Repeat steps 1–3 to raise the point of the side-bust dart, using corresponding measurements and dots, but omit step 4 and use the base points of the original dart instead of marking new ones.

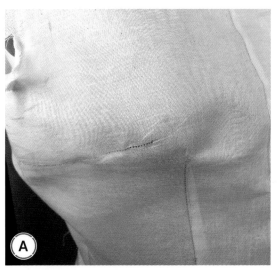

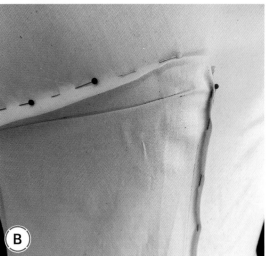

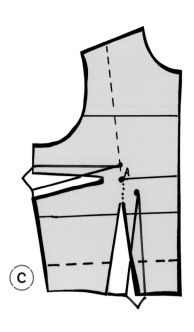

TROUBLESHOOT: A ROUND BUST LINE

Symptoms (A):
- Diagonal creases form in the muslin below the side-bust dart and radiate down from the armhole toward the center front of the bodice.

Refitting the bust line (B):
1. Open the side seam of the muslin from the armhole to 1" (2.5cm) or so below the side-bust dart. Then open the side-bust dart and pull the folded fabric of the dart outside the muslin.
2. Working from the side seam line to the point along the center of the original dart, pinch the fabric between thumb and index finger into a horizontal fold smaller than original dart.
3. Insert pins end to end along the base of the fold to mark the new dart seam line. Taper the fold evenly from the side seam toward the point. Take off the muslin.
4. At the side seam line, measure from the pin markings to one of the original seams of the dart.

Adjusting the pattern (C):
1. On the bodice front pattern, measure along the side seam line, from its intersection with each original dart seam line, the distance measured above. Measure toward the center of the dart in each case. Mark with dots.
2. Draw lines from the dots to the point of the original dart.
3. To correct the side seam line of the bodice front, which is lengthened by the smaller dart, lower the armhole a distance equal to twice the measurement made in step 1, measuring down the side seam line from its intersection with the armhole seam line. Mark with a dot.
4. Draw the new armhole seam line below the original seam line, curving it smoothly between the side seam dot and the armhole notch. Redraw the cutting line ⅝" (1.5cm) outside the new seam line and parallel to it.

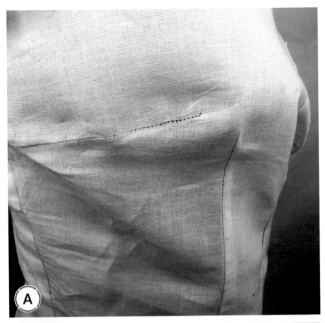

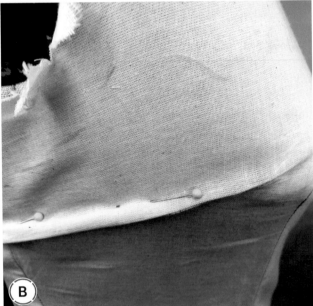

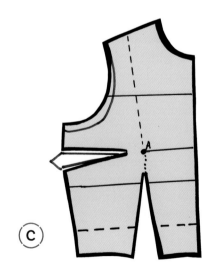

TROUBLESHOOT: A FLAT BUST LINE

Symptoms (A):
- Diagonal creases form in the muslin below the forward point of the bust and radiate down toward the side seams.

Refitting the bust line (B):
1. Open the side seam from the armhole to 1" (2.5cm) or so below the side-bust dart. Then open the side-bust dart and pull the folded-fabric of the dart outside the muslin.
2. Working from the side seam line toward the point along the center of the original dart, pinch the fabric between thumb and index finger into a horizontal fold larger than original dart.
3. Insert pins end to end along the base of the fold to mark the new dart seam line. Taper the fold evenly from the side seam to the point. Take off the muslin.
4. At the side seam line, measure from the pin markings to one of the original seams of the dart.

Adjusting the pattern (C):
1. On the bodice front pattern, measure along the side seam line, from its intersection with each original dart seam line to a point outside the dart. Mark with dots.
2. Draw lines from the dots to the point of the original dart.
3. To correct the side seam line of the bodice front, which is shortened by the larger dart, pin shelf paper under the armhole and raise the lower part of the armhole a distance equal to twice the measurement made in step 4 of the previous sequence, measuring from the intersection with the armhole seam line. Mark with a dot.
4. Draw the new armhole seam line above the original seam line—on the shelf paper if necessary—curving the new line smoothly between the side seam dot and the armhole notch. Redraw the cutting line ⅝" (1.5cm) outside the new seam line and parallel to it. Trim away excess shelf paper.

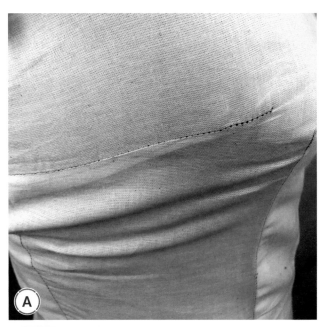

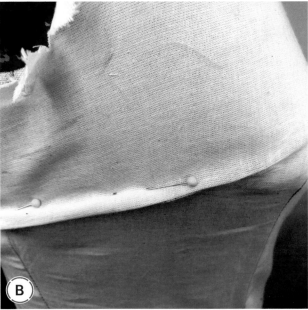

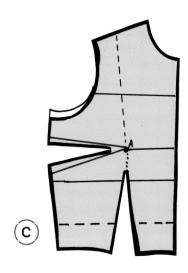

TROUBLESHOOT: A LONG LOWER SKIRT BACK

Symptoms (A):
- Crossways creases appear just below the waist in the back of the skirt.

Refitting the skirt back (B):
1. Starting in the center back of the skirt just below the waistline, pinch the excess fabric between thumb and index finger into a horizontal tuck and insert a pin at the base of the tuck.
2. Extend the tuck to both side seams, tapering it to a point on each side and inserting pins as you do so. Take off the muslin.
3. Measure along the center back seam line of the skirt from the pin inserted above to the top edge of the tuck. Double the measurement taken.

Adjusting the pattern (C):
1. With the ruler at a right angle to the center back seam line on the skirt back pattern, draw a line from the intersection of the waist seam line and the center back seam line to the side seam line.
2. Measure down the center back seam line from the waist seam line the distance calculated above and mark with a dot. Draw a line from the dot to the intersection of this line and the side seam line.
3. Fold the pattern piece along the line made in step 2, then turn the folded edge up to coincide with the line made in step 1, forming a tuck that is wide at the center back and tapers to a point at the side. Pin the tuck flat. Re-draw the dart seam lines over the tuck.

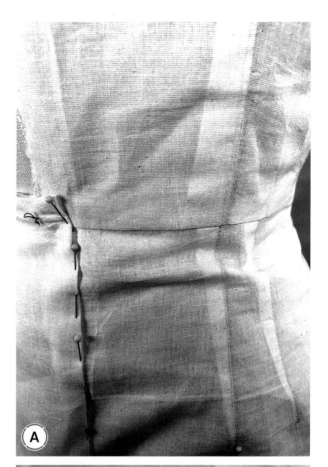

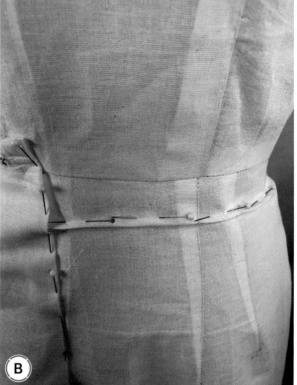

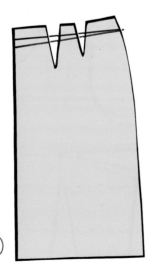

TROUBLESHOOT: A TIGHT SKIRT FRONT

Symptoms (A):
- The skirt feels too tight across your abdomen.
- Creases radiate from your abdomen toward the side seams.

Refitting the skirt front (B):
1. Open the front waist seam from one side seam to the other.
2. Slide the skirt front down away from the bodice until the creases below the darts disappear.
3. Starting from the center front and tapering evenly into the original waist seam line toward the sides, pin the seam allowance of the skirt waist to the bodice waist seam line.
4. Open the skirt front darts and shorten the darts until all creases disappear. Insert pins end to end along the base of each dart. Take off the muslin.
5. At the center front of the skirt, measure from the new waist seam line to the original one.
6. Measure the length of each shortened dart.

Adjusting the pattern (C):
1. On the skirt front pattern, draw a line at a right angle to the center front line from the intersection of the center line and the waist seam line to the side seam line. Cut along the pencil line to the side seam line but do not cut the pattern apart.
2. Slide an insert of shelf paper under the slash and spread the sections of the pattern apart at the center line to the distance measured above and pin them to the shelf paper.
3. Draw a line to connect the original center front line of the two edges. Trim away excess shelf paper.
4. On both original darts, measure down the center from the waist seam line a distance equal to the measured length of the shortened darts and mark with dots.
5. Draw new seam lines from the dots to the base of the original darts at the waist seam line.

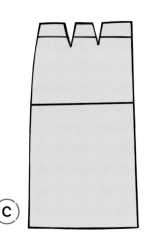

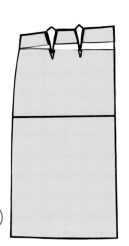

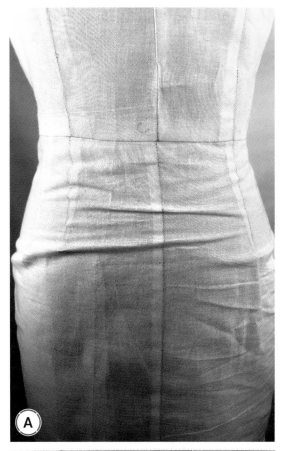

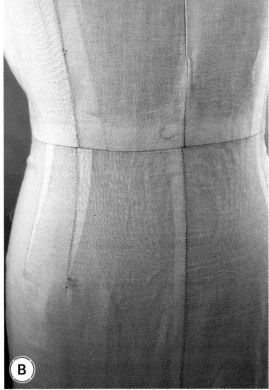

TROUBLESHOOT: A CROOKED SIDE SEAM

Symptoms (A):

- The side seam of the muslin fails to run vertically from armhole to hem. It may be curved in one or more places, or it may veer diagonally forward or backward.

Refitting the side seam (B):

1. Starting where the side seam departs from the vertical, insert pins in a vertical line along the crooked section.
2. Open the crooked section of the side seam so that the fabric sections separate.
3. With your fingertips, roll fabric out from the seam allowance of the garment section that has no pins until the fold is aligned with the pinned line. Insert pins horizontally to hold it in place. Take off the muslin.
4. Measure along the side seam line from the point where the adjustment begins to the nearest horizontal seam. Then measure the length of the pinned section.
5. At the widest point of the adjustment, measure the distance from the folded edge to the original stitching line.

Adjusting the pattern (C):

1. On the pattern corresponding to the unfolded edge of the seam, measure along the side seam line from the horizontal seam line that corresponds to the one used above, using the same measurements, and mark with dots to indicate where the adjustment begins and ends.
2. Repeat step 1 on the pattern corresponding to the folded edge of the seam.
3. On the pattern piece corresponding to the unfolded edge of the seam (left in drawing), measure in from the original seam line the distance figured above and mark with a dot.
4. Repeat at 2" (5cm) intervals along the middle of the adjustment. Draw a new side seam line that connects the dots and tapers into the original seam line at both ends of the adjustment. Draw a new cutting line ⅝" (1.5cm) outside and parallel to the new seam line.
5. With the pattern piece corresponding to the folded edge of the seam (right in drawing), slip shelf paper under the seam line and measure the distance figured above from the original side seam line and mark with a dot.
6. Repeat at 2" (5cm) intervals along the middle of the adjustment. Draw a new side seam line that connects the dots and tapers into the original seam line at both ends of the adjustment. Draw a new cutting line ⅝" (1.5cm) outside the new seam line and parallel to it.

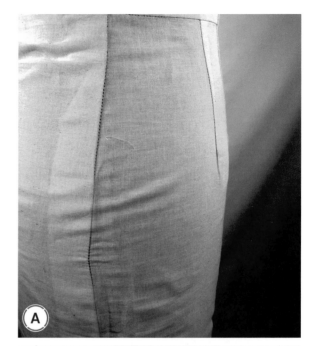

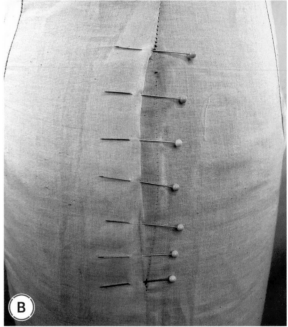

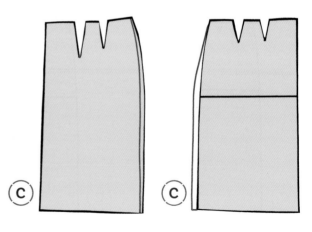

STYLIZED SLEEVE ADJUSTMENTS: THE RAGLAN AND DOLMAN SHOULDER

A raglan sleeve has a seam angling from the underarm to the neckline with a dart contouring over the shoulder. The dolman sleeve has a seam that extends from the neckline down the center of the arm the length of the sleeve.

Symptoms of a loose shoulder (A):
- The shoulder seam or dart of the muslin stands up above natural shoulder line.
- Crossways creases appear on the bodice along the armhole.

Refitting the shoulder seam (B):
1. Remove the stitching around the armhole and take out the sleeve.
2. Starting at the armhole and working toward the neck, pull the shoulder seam straight up between thumb and index finger. Pinch the front and back pieces of the bodice, taking more fabric from one than the other if necessary, until they lie smooth and meet along the center of your shoulder.
3. Measure the change on the dart or seam from the original to the new dart or seam location.

Adjusting the pattern (C):
1. On the paper pattern, mark the new dart position at the distance from the old one measured in previously.
2. Repeat on the sleeve back dart or seam line.

A

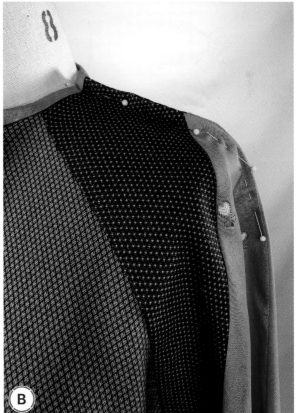

B

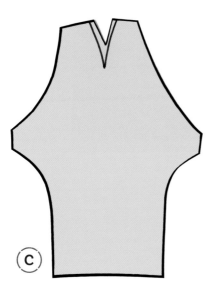

C

Symptoms of a tight shoulder (A):

- The shoulder dart feels very taut.
- Vertical creases appear below the shoulder dart near the arm.

Refitting the shoulder dart (B):

1. Open the shoulder dart and pull the seam allowances outside the muslin.
2. Starting at the neck and working toward the arm, smooth the front and back of the sleeve upwards against your shoulder and pinch them together, releasing fabric to relax the dart or seam, taking more fabric from one side than the other if necessary, until both lie smooth and meet along the center of your shoulder.
3. Measure the change on the dart or seam from the original to the new dart or seam location.

Adjusting the pattern (C):

1. On the paper pattern mark the new dart position at the distance from the old one measured previously.
2. Repeat on the sleeve back dart or seam line.

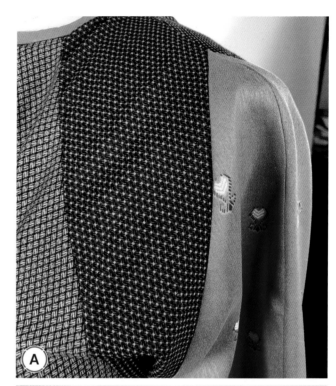

A

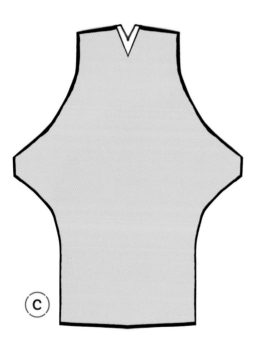

C

B

Symptoms of a tight sleeve cap (A):

- The muslin pulls over the shoulder and down the top of the arm.
- Creases radiate from the shoulder point.

Refitting the sleeve top (B):

1. Mark the natural shoulder point on the shoulder dart or seam of the muslin.
2. Take off the muslin. On a raglan sleeve, cut around the shoulder from the shoulder point down the front of the shoulder to the front sleeve seam, then down the back to the back sleeve seam, leaving the seams intact. On a dolman sleeve, cut from the shoulder point down the front of the dress to the middle of the underarm curve, leaving the underarm seam line intact. Do the same down the back.
3. Put the muslin back on and slip an insert of muslin under the slash opening.
4. Slide the arm section of the sleeve down your arm until it lies smooth and all creases disappear. Pin the cut edges of the sleeve to the muslin insert. Take off the muslin.
5. Measure along the shoulder dart or seam line from the neck seam line to the upper edge of the slash.
6. Measure the distance between the cut edges of the slash in the sleeve at the shoulder dart seam line.

Adjusting the raglan sleeve pattern (C):

1. On the raglan sleeve pattern, measure along both dart seam lines from the neck seam line the distance measured previously and make dots to mark the shoulder point.
2. With the ruler at the dot made above on one side of the dart at a right angle to the dart seam line, draw a line to the bodice-to-sleeve seam line. Repeat on the other side of the dart. Cut the pattern along these lines to the bodice-to-sleeve seam lines, but do not cut the pattern apart.
3. Slide an insert of pattern paper under both slashes and spread the cut edges apart until the distances between the edges of each slash match the measurement of the distance in the slash made on the sleeve.
4. Pin the insert in place. Draw dart seam lines on both sides of the dart on the pattern paper, connecting the original dart seam lines on the pattern. Draw new cutting lines ⅝" (1.5cm) outside and parallel to the new seam lines. Trim away excess paper. Repeat on back pattern.

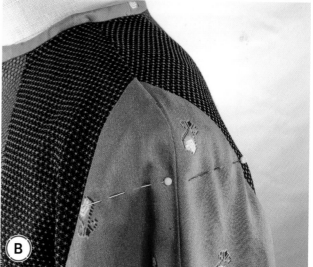

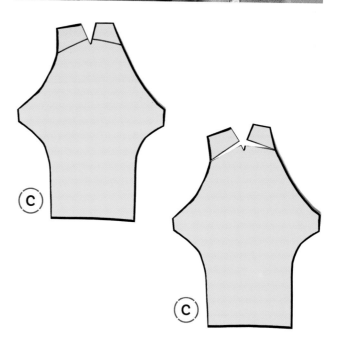

Adjusting the dolman sleeve pattern (D):

1. On the bodice front pattern, measure along the shoulder seam line from the neck seam line the distance measured previously and mark with a dot.

2. Draw a line from the dot made in step 1 to the middle of the curve in the underarm seam line. Cut along this pencil line, but do not cut the pattern apart.

3. Slide pattern paper under the slash and spread the cut edges apart until the distance between the edges of the slash at the shoulder seam line is equal to the measurement. Pin the insert in place.

4. Draw a seam line on the shelf paper to connect the original seam lines on the pattern. Draw a new cutting line ⅝" (1.5cm) outside the new seam line and parallel to it. Trim away excess pattern paper. Repeat on the bodice back pattern.

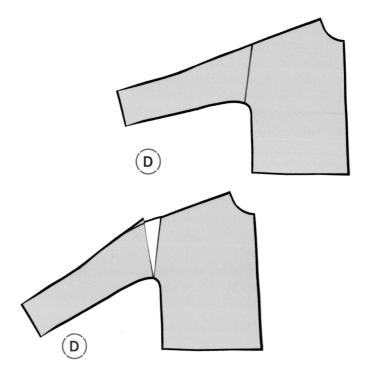

Symptoms of a loose sleeve cap (A):

- The sleeve droops from the shoulder over the arm.
- Folds appear at the top of the arm.

Refitting the sleeve top (B):

1. At the natural shoulder point, pinch the fabric from the shoulder and arm area of the sleeve together until the sleeve lies smooth over the top of your arm.

2. Insert a pin across the dart or seam at the natural shoulder point to form a small tuck. On the raglan, continue pinning across the sleeve tapering out to the sleeve seam front and back. On the dolman, continue pinning the tuck across the sleeve tapering to the underarm seam line. Take off the muslin.

3. Measure the distance from the neckline to the natural shoulder point.

4. Measure from the pin inserted in step 2 to the top edge of the tuck. Multiply this measurement by two.

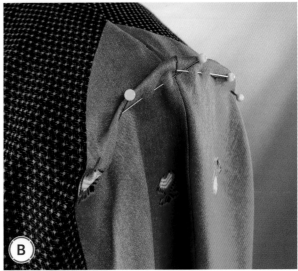

Adjusting the raglan sleeve pattern (C):

1. On the sleeve pattern, measure along both dart seam lines from the neck seam line and the distance measured previously, then make dots to mark the shoulder points.

2. Measure along each dart seam line from the shoulder point the distance calculated in step 1 and make a dot.

3. With the ruler at the shoulder point on one side of the dart and at a right angle to the dart seam line, draw a line to the bodice-to-sleeve seam line. Then draw a line from the dot above to the point where the pencil line on that side intersects the bodice-to-sleeve seam line. Repeat on the other side of the dart.

4. On each side of the dart, fold the pattern along the upper pencil line. Turn the folded edge over so that it coincides with the second pencil line, forming a tuck that tapers to a point at the bodice-to-sleeve line. Pin the tuck flat.

5. Pin a piece of pattern paper under both tucks and re-draw the dart seam lines from the folded edge of the tuck toward the dart point, tapering into the original dart seam line about 1"–2" (2.5–5cm) above the fold.

6. Re-draw the cutting line on to the pattern paper ⅝" (1.5cm) outside the new seam line and parallel to it. Trim away the excess paper. Repeat on the back.

Adjusting the dolman sleeve pattern (D):

1. On the bodice front pattern, measure along the shoulder seam line from the neck the distance measured previously. Draw a line from the shoulder point to the underarm seam in the middle of the underarm curve.

2. Fold along the line the amount needed to make the reduction.

3. Polish the edge with pattern paper. Redraw the cutting line and repeat on the back pattern.

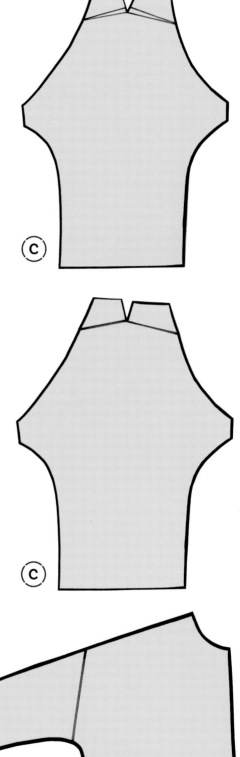

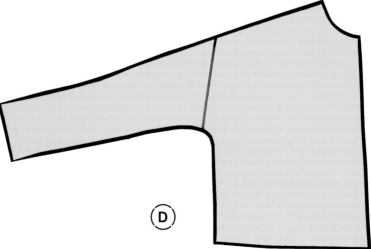

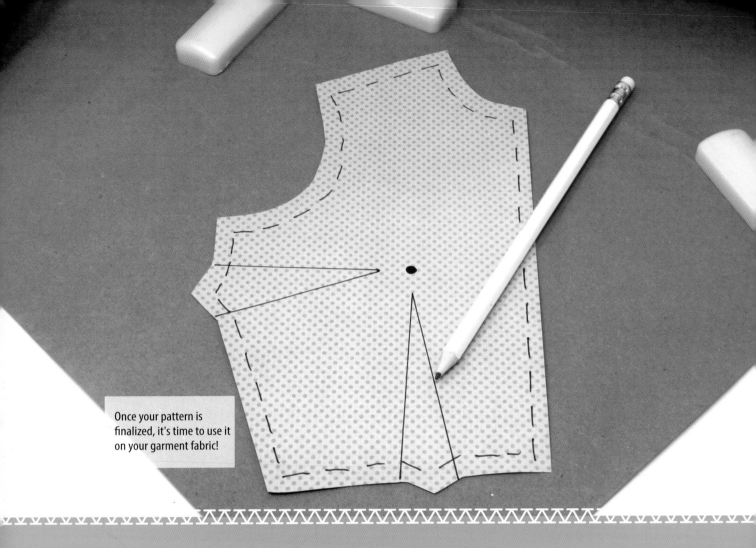

Once your pattern is finalized, it's time to use it on your garment fabric!

PATTERN LAYOUT AND CUTTING

When the right fabric for the right pattern is selected and the fitting adjustments have been made, you are ready to construct your actual garment. Find a flat, firm cutting surface large enough to hold the entire length of your fabric—a table or even the floor, if necessary. To protect your cutting surface, use table pads, a dressmaker's cutting board, or a self-healing cutting mat. Check the grain alignment of the fabric (see Chapter 2: Understanding Grain and Bias, page 58). Fold the fabric lengthwise. If the raw edges do not match each other and the corners do not form right angles, the grain is off. Straighten using the steps on page 64.

Arrange the pattern pieces on the straightened fabric following the guide sheet that comes with your pattern. It will provide cutting guides, or diagrams, showing how to arrange the pattern on the material according to the size and the width of the material. For both straight and bias cuts, the grain line arrows on the pattern pieces must be parallel to the selvages. Pin and cut out the entire pattern without moving the fabric. For pattern pieces that are awkward to reach, cut loosely around the entire section, remove it and trim the pieces separately at the cutting line.

After cutting out your garment, transfer all pattern markings to the wrong side of the fabric before you remove the pattern. This may be done with a tailor's hand tack, chalk, or by using a tracing wheel and dressmaker's carbon paper to do the job quickly and accurately.

PREPARING TO SEW

Because fabric is flat and the human body is not, the paper patterns that are used as a guide for cutting and sewing garments include numerous instructions, some in the form of symbols, to help you convert a two-dimensional fabric into three-dimensional clothing.

For example, the grain line and fold line tell how to align the pattern piece with the weave so that the fabric curves properly. Other symbols guide steps, such as the joining of two pieces to conform to general body contours with numbered notches, and the seaming of individual pieces to fit around pronounced curves such as the bust or buttocks with broken lines.

PATTERN MARKINGS AND SYMBOLS

Grain line: This arrow indicates how to align the pattern piece with the threads of the fabric. Place the line between the arrows, as specified on the pattern piece, on either the lengthwise or the crosswise grain of the fabric—the thread that runs parallel to or at right angles to the finished edge (the selvage) of the fabric.

Fold line: Either of these two symbols indicates how the edge of the pattern piece aligns with the fabric fold: the bold line of the arrow should line up with the fold.

Seam allowance: Either of these two symbols indicates the distance between the cutting line, where the pattern piece is cut, and the stitching line (sometimes called the seam line), where it must be sewn. This distance, usually ⅝" (1.6cm), is marked in numerals in at least one place on the pattern piece.

Cutting line: A heavy solid line, frequently accompanied by a drawing of scissors, marks the exact line along which the pattern piece must be cut.

Stitching line: A thin broken line, frequently accompanied by a drawing of a sewing machine presser foot, marks the exact line along which seams, darts, and other construction areas must be stitched. An arrow along the stitching line, or seam line, shows the direction in which the seam must be sewn.

Adjustment line: A heavy double line indicates the points on the pattern piece at which it may be shortened or lengthened. To lengthen the piece, cut the pattern between the printed lines and add paper. To shorten, pin the pattern up between the double lines.

Notches: These symbols, which are used alone, in pairs, or in threes, are always numbered. They mark the exact points along the outer seam lines where sections are joined together; the single notches are joined to single notches, No. 8 notches to No. 8 notches, etc.

Construction symbols: Large dots, squares, and triangles guide construction of a garment—indicating the center front of a sleeve, for example, or marking the point where pieces such as collars and neckline facings must be attached to the garment body. Small dots guide alignment of seams.

Fabric layout symbols: A black star indicates that the fabric must be laid out in one thickness, wrong side down, and a single piece of fabric cut. The shaded bar indicates that the pattern piece shaded in the pattern cutting layout is to be placed on the fabric with its printed side down. The other three construction symbols—the large asterisk, dagger, and double dagger—are keys to special cutting directions in the pattern instruction sheet.

Button marking: The horizontal line on this symbol shows exactly where the buttonhole is to be placed, and its length is the buttonhole length. The button drawing is the size of the button to be used (the pattern envelope also specifies button sizes).

Zipper marking: This symbol on the pattern marks the position of the zipper on the garment, and the symbol length is the exact opening length. The top of the slider tab indicates the top of the zipper opening, and the bottom stop indicates the bottom of the opening.

Using Tailor Tacks to Transfer Pattern Markings

1. Mark all notches by making ⅛" (3mm) clips into the seam allowances at the center of each pattern notch. Be sure to clip through both layers of fabric.

2. By making rows of tailor tacks (page 21), transfer all seam lines except for dart seam lines, which will be drawn in chalk at the time of construction. Space the stitches at ½" (12mm) intervals around curves and on long straight seam lines that can be farther apart.

3. Transfer all pattern dots or circles, including those along the dart seam lines, by making a single tailor tack on each one. If the marking is along a seam line, make the tack at right angles to the row of tacks or use thread of another color.

4. Mark the position of each buttonhole by making a single tailor tack at the intersection of the center and the outer placement lines. If you are making pants, skip to step 8.

5. If you are making a jacket, transfer the collar and lapel roll lines, the vent fold line, and the placement lines for patch pockets, if any, by making a row of tailor tacks along each. Transfer the center-front line from the bottom edge to a point just below the lapel roll line.

6. Mark the position of a welt pocket by making a single tailor tack at each end of the long bottom line.

7. Mark the position of double-piped pockets by making a single tailor tack at each end of the long middle line.

8. Cut the loops of the tailor tacks and carefully remove the paper pattern.

9. Mark an "X" with chalk on the wrong side of each layer of fabric.

10. Separate the layers of fabric, clipping the tailor tacks between the layers as you do.

IF YOU ARE LEFT-HANDED

Follow the directions in steps 1–5, starting at the left edge of the line to be marked and stitching from left to right as shown.

Transferring Pattern Markings with a Tracing Wheel and Dressmaker's Carbon Paper

1. If you are marking two layers of fabric, remove just enough pins from one area at a time so you can slip dressmaker's carbon paper, carbon side up, under the bottom layer of fabric. Then place another piece of carbon paper, carbon side down, over the top layer of fabric.

2. With the pattern on top, run a tracing wheel along all stitching, placement, and fold lines. Use a straight-edged ruler as a guide for straight lines; trace curves freehand. Use a plain (not sawtooth) wheel for knits.

3. Using a dull pencil, trace the notches and draw an "X" through the center of all dots and circles.

4. Remove the pattern from the fabric and make a line of basting stitches or tailor tacks along any markings that must show on both sides of the fabric, such as the placement lines for pockets.

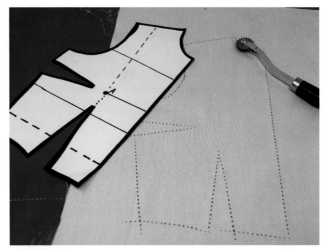

Tracing paper comes in many varieties. Test the paper on a sample fabric prior to your fabric yardage. The tracing wheel may feature a solid wheel for delicate fabrics or a needlepoint wheel for fabrics such as cottons, wool suitings, and others that will not be affected by the sharp points.

PINNING THE PATTERN TO A SOLID FABRIC

1. Separate all pattern pieces having a line marked "place on fold" and place them on the fabric so that the mark aligns with the fold of the fabric. Pin these pieces to the fabric along the fold.

2. Loosely arrange the other pieces according to the pattern cutting guide with the printed grain line arrows parallel to the fold and selvage edges. Fabric length and width may vary, so you may need to modify how you place the pattern on the fabric as long as the grain is still following the correct direction.

3. Measure from the fabric edge to both ends of the grain line arrow on each pattern piece; make sure that the arrow is uniformly distant from the edge and parallel to it.

4. Smooth each pattern piece to make sure it lies flat. Then pin each piece to the fabric, placing the pins diagonally at the corners and parallel to, and just inside, the cutting line.

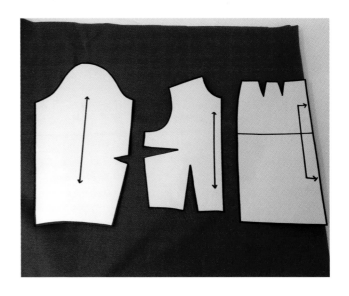

PINNING THE PATTERN TO A STRIPED OR CHECKED FABRIC

1. Loosely arrange the pattern pieces on the fabric according to the directions in the pattern layout guide. To make the fabric design match where the pattern must be seamed together, make sure that corresponding notches or pattern details lie in the exact same position relative to the checks or stripes. Use a tracing to help line them up precisely.

2. To match a fabric design along the most important seam lines of a dress, blouse, or shirt, line up notches in the following order: side seams (notches marked 1), armhole and sleeve seams (notches 2 and 3), then underarm sleeve seams (notches 4).

3. To match seam lines of a skirt, line up the side seams (notches marked 1). The center front seam will match because both halves are cut out at once. If the waistband is cut parallel to the grain of the fabric, as in this example, line up the waistband with the waistline edge at the front (notch 2) and then the back (notch 3).

4. To match seam lines of pants, line up the side seams (notches marked 1) and the inner leg seams (notch 2). If the waistband is cut on the bias, as in this example, the waistband is not matched to the waistline edge.

5. Pin at the notches.

6. Check to be sure that the grain line is parallel to the selvage, or lengthwise edge of the fabric, as in step 3, and adjust where necessary.

7. Pin the entire pattern to the fabric.

 TIP

Notches can have numbers or simply match the same notch on a corresponding pattern piece. These are used to help line up pieces as well as fabric designs. For higher end results, trace the design of the fabric onto tracing paper. Overlay the tracing on the main pattern piece. Determine where the pattern, such as a stripe, will fall on the pattern. Trace the pattern shape onto the tracing paper and use it as a tool for placing the corresponding pattern piece on the fabric with the design matching exactly. Avoid cutting through two layers of a plaid to get a right and left pattern piece.

Dress, blouse, or shirt

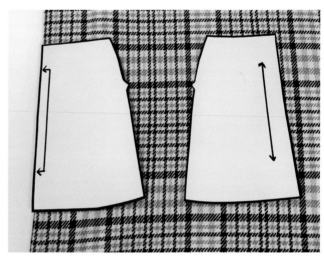

Skirt

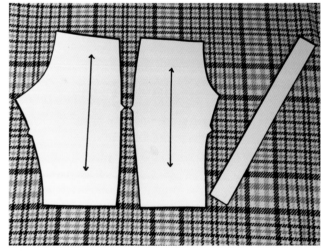

Pants

LAYING OUT BIAS CUT PATTERNS

"True bias" refers to a diagonal line that is at a 45-degree angle from both selvage edges. Characteristics of bias include:

- Does not ravel
- Softness and drapability
- Garments grow as they hang
- Inherent stretchability of the fabric
- Stretchability can be positive or negative

1. Make a duplicate pattern for each pattern piece from which multiple garment sections will be cut, such as a left skirt back that must be reversed to cut a right skirt back. Trace the grain line arrow on each duplicate piece.
2. Spread open the straightened fabric and loosely arrange the pattern pieces according to the accompanying pattern cutting guide, making certain the grain line arrows are parallel to the selvages.
3. Pin each pattern piece diagonally at the corners; then pin parallel to, and just inside, the cutting line. Arrange and pin all pattern pieces before cutting any. Note: Layout is suitable for fabrics with nap.

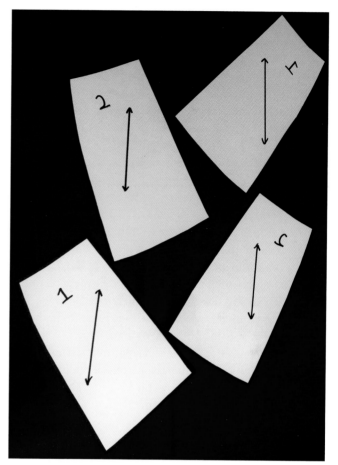

The layout for a bias pattern on solid fabric requires a mirror image tracing of the pattern, which is then placed on the fabric and matches the grain lines. Notice how the patterns look like they are going different directions, but if you evaluate the grain lines, they are using the same grain. Additional markings on your pattern will help with clarity on where the patterns should be placed.

Understanding Bias Cut Garments

Bias sewing tips:

- Press all bias fabric pieces before you sew.
- Mark seams with thread basting on the seam allowance.
- Stretch slightly as you sew (except shoulder seams).
- Start at the center seam and do final fitting at the side seams.
- Let garments hang and grow before final fitting and finishing.
- Garments may grow often, so repeat hanging as necessary.
- Any zipper sewn on the bias should use stay tape and extend pass the zipper opening to weight down the seam allowance.
- Use weights such as small washers, garment chains, or charms in a cowl design to hold the shape.
- Use directional sewing on the bias. Start in the middle of a seam and work your way out.
- If a bias angle in a garment has too much stretch, experiment with cutting the pattern more on grain.
- Do not hang bias garments on a hanger. Lay them flat to store to prevent continual stretching.

Bias layout tips:

- Fabric has two lines of bias. Cut pieces on the same bias line.
- Opposite bias lines can vary in the same fabric for characteristics.
- Create a pattern piece for left and right such as front, back, and sleeve.
- Do not cut patterns mirror image. The grain would be opposite, and the pieces will behave differently.
- Avoid cutting on the fold.
- Bias patterns are cut in a single layer.
- Bias takes more yardage, so plan generously. One yard for each major piece is a good formula.
- Add extra seam allowance ½" to 1" (1.5 to 2.5cm more) to allow for growth.
- Mark pieces before you remove the pattern.

This classic tank top sewn in several different draping rayon fabrics is further accentuated by utilizing the bias of the fabric. The front of this design is cut on the true bias, which creates a beautiful drapy effect in the hem and folds of the fabric.

Using bias in a garment can also be a special feature and may only be applied in a few specific areas. The bias-cut ruffle adds a lovely drape while the garment is cut on the straight of grain.

PRINTS, STRIPES, AND PATTERNS: WORKING WITH BOLD DESIGNS

The pattern of the fabric itself is often the garment's most eye-catching element. Although small prints can often be treated almost like solids, bold patterns restrict the choice of style, calling for a simple design with a minimum of darts and seams. Even so, prints demand special care in cutting and stitching and require special techniques of the sewist when the material is boldly patterned.

Bold repeat prints go well on pleated or gathered skirts and long unfitted garments. They are unsuited for trousers or close-fitting blouses or jackets.

Both the design elements themselves and the repeats affect sewing. The way a bold plaid is cut, and even the kind of garment that can be made from it, depends on whether it is regular with its lengthways and crossways lines equally spaced in each direction from the most dominant lines.

A special problem is raised by the border print, which is fabric bearing a pattern only along one selvage. The design is meant to appear at the hemline, jacket edge, or cuff. This arrangement is possible only if there is a separate bodice or a seamed waistline. A border print will not work with a floor-length A-line or shift dress unless careful attention is taken to shape the border to work with the curve of the hem.

To match irregular plaids and to position bold patterned fabrics whose designs run in one direction, it is necessary to use a nap layout—that is, all the pattern pieces must face in one direction. All nap layouts require some extra fabric. If the pattern envelope does not advise otherwise, allow ½ yard more fabric than normally required.

Placement of design details demands more than mechanical alignment. The motif of a large floral or repeat print must be placed over the body in a balanced and attractive arrangement so that the eye sees the fabric as a whole and is not distracted by one large, dominating point.

Always match the sections of the garment at important seams—sides, center front, back, and on the seam lines, not on the cutting lines. On plaids and bold repeat prints, always match horizontal lines and make sure the design runs continuously from the bodice front into the sleeve.

The techniques of cutting and positioning fabrics with bold designs may seem more formidable than they really are. Some care and attention to detail will enable you to handle patterns that at first glance raise difficulties. If you choose a plaid or print that is in scale with your figure, you can have a striking garment—one that is eye-catching and uniquely your own.

A stripe fabric can add interest to a design when cut on the bias or placed at other angles besides straight up and down or horizontal to the floor. Interesting placement of the stripe can soften the line and garment details and also manipulate the line of the fabric.

A plaid fabric is an ideal fabric for adding interest to any garment. Similar to stripes, simply using vertical or horizontal placement may not add as much interest or many not be as flattering as utilizing different angles or even different placement on the pattern. In this example, the plaid is effective because it adds interest, is not overwhelming the body shape, and is not right next to the face. Instead, it adds contrast, but it does not make the figure look too big.

SLIP STITCH BASTING: MATCHING DESIGNS

1. Unless you have already done so, run a line of basting stitches (page 20) along the seam lines where the design is to be matched.

2. Press under the seam allowance of one section. Place the folded edge on top of the seam line of the other section's right side, carefully matching the design. Pin through all fabric thicknesses at ½" to 1" (1.5 to 2.5cm) intervals.

3. Using a knotted thread, draw the needle up from the back of the single thickness of fabric just below the fold and pull it through.

4. Insert the needle into the folded seam allowance just above the fold and directly above the stitch made above. Bring the needle out just below the fold and ¼" to 1" (0.5 to 2.5cm) to the left of the first stitch, depending on the size of the design to be matched.

5. Continue the process, removing the pins as you go. End with a loose fastening stitch (page 26) through all layers of fabric.

6. When you are finished and the folded seam allowance is opened out, long slanted stitches will appear on one side and a row of small stitches will appear on the other side. The machine stitching for the seam will run directly over the small stitches.

TIP

When matching prints, give priority where possible to front seams over back ones and to horizontal seams over vertical ones.

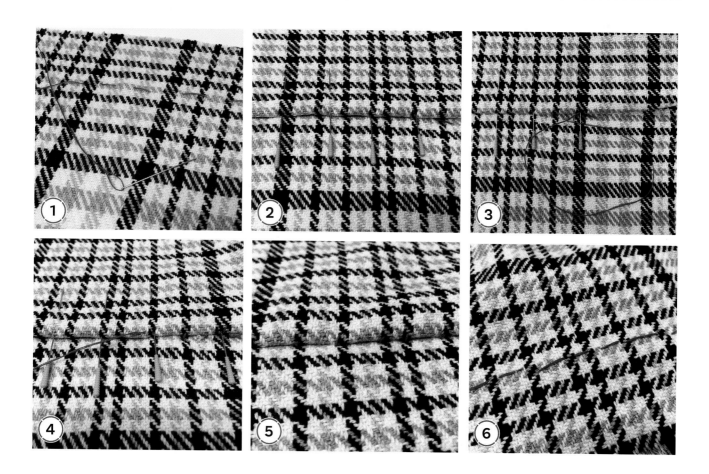

PATTERN LAYOUT: FABRIC WITH NAP

Fabric with nap has a distinctive direction, which is illustrated dramatically by the characteristics of fur fabric. If you brush fur one direction, it will lay flat and smooth. However, when brushing against the direction of the hair, it looks messy, does not lay flat, and is difficult to place a pattern on. Pattern pieces cut in all sorts of directions will not look the same on a garment. Velvet, corduroy, suede, and terry cloth are common fabrics with a nap.

The first rule for laying out the pattern on a fabric with nap is to arrange all pieces in one direction from top to bottom. Standard cutting guides will call this a nap layout because it follows the direction of the fabric nap. Such layouts should be used not only for fabrics having an obvious nap, but also for those with a smooth surface. This is because some tailoring fabrics, even those that look smooth, have a subtle nap, and others have a visible directional weave. In the finished garment, light will be reflected from each section at a different angle, emphasizing color variations that would arise if the nap directions varied.

In laying out the pattern on striped or plaid fabrics, pay attention also to the way the design will meet when the garment is assembled.

PATTERN LAYOUT: LARGE FLORAL PRINTS

Bold prints are striking fabrics that delight designers. The few special problems they pose are easily handled. Besides requiring careful matching and cutting, large-scale prints must be positioned on the body so that no focal point jars the eye, such as a big rose right on the hips or buttocks! The key to handling boldly patterned fabrics is to make duplicates of all pattern pieces in which matching or positioning is crucial. Then, lay out all the pattern pieces on the spread out fabric and cut nothing until everything is matched and attractively positioned. Flowers in large-scale floral prints should be matched whenever they fall on seams.

Floral print layout tips:

1. Lay the fabric right side facing up and pin the original dress front pattern piece to the fabric with markings up. Align it so that the designs fall off-center vertically, above or below the bust line, and are balanced by designs near the bottom.

2. Pin the duplicate dress front piece to the fabric, markings down (creating the mirror image), aligning its center fold line with that of the original piece and following the other instructions in step 1. Adjust both pieces to make the designs symmetrical.

3. Pin the original pattern piece for the dress back to the fabric with pattern markings facing up, making sure that any large designs are placed off-center vertically and are above or below hip level.

4. Pin the duplicate pattern piece for the dress back to the fabric with pattern markings facing down, following the placement instructions in step 3.

5. Cut out first those pieces for which the original pattern piece was marked with a fold line. The original and duplicates of such pieces must be cut together so that the fabric for both parts of each section form a single unit.

6. Cut out the other pinned pieces separately.

7. Pin and cut out any remaining pattern pieces that are not part of the basic body section, such as collars and facings, without any further attempt at positioning the design.

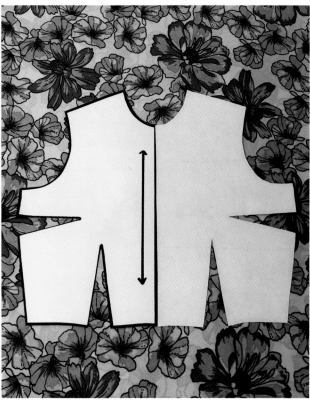

PATTERN LAYOUT: DIAGONAL STRIPES

Diagonal stripes are best matched at the back of a garment, although a seam down the center front or at the side seam creates a chevron effect that can be slimming and fashionable.

Diagonal stripe layout tips:

1. Lay out the fabric right side facing up and pin the original pattern piece for the tunic front to the fabric with pattern markings facing up.

2. Pin the duplicate pattern piece for the tunic front to the fabric with pattern markings facing down, aligning the center front fold line with that of the original pattern piece.

3. Pin the original pattern piece for the tunic back to the fabric with pattern markings facing up, aligning the hemline with that of the front and making sure that the notches on the side seam fall in the same position on the stripe as their numbered counterparts on the tunic front.

4. Pin the duplicate pattern piece for the tunic back to the fabric with pattern markings facing down, following the placement instructions in step 3 and making sure that the notch on the back seam falls in the same position on the stripe as its numbered counterpart on the original pattern piece.

5. Pin the original pattern piece for the sleeve to the fabric with pattern markings facing up, aligning the pattern piece in the same lengthways direction as the pattern pieces for the tunic front and back. However, make no attempt to match the stripes to the armholes of the body sections. Pin the duplicate pattern piece for the sleeve to the fabric with pattern markings facing down.

6. Pin the original pattern piece for the cuff to the fabric with pattern markings facing up, aligning it so that the diagonal lines run in the same direction as those on the sleeve. Then pin the duplicate pattern piece for the cuff to the fabric with pattern markings facing down and aligned with the original.

7. Cut out, following the instructions for laying out a large floral print, steps 5 and 6 (page 127).

8. Pin and cut out any remaining pattern pieces according to the instructions for laying out a large floral print, step 7 (page 127).

PATTERN LAYOUT: BORDER PRINTS

The border of a border print may be used at a straight-edged hem. Some border fabrics, such as laces, can be clipped and molded to a contoured edge. The pattern pieces must be placed vertically on the crossways grain of the fabric. Bold repeat prints also need straight-hem patterns to use effectively.

Border print layout tips:

1. Lay the fabric with right side facing up and pin the original pattern piece for the skirt front to the fabric with pattern markings facing up. Align the pattern so that the hemline marking is ½" (1.5cm) above the selvage of the fabric and the center fold line falls in the middle of one main element in the design (the center of a flower in this example).

2. Pin the duplicate pattern piece for the skirt front to the fabric with pattern markings facing down, aligning its center fold line with that of the original pattern piece and following the other placement instructions in step 1.

3. Pin the original piece for the skirt back to the fabric with pattern markings up, the hemline marking ½" (1.5cm) above the selvage and the center seam line—not the cutting edge—in the middle of a main element in the design.

4. Pin the duplicate pattern piece for the skirt back to the fabric with pattern markings facing down, following the placement instructions in step 3.

5. Cut out the pattern pieces following the instructions for laying out a large floral print, steps 5 and 6 (page 127).

6. Pin and cut out remaining pattern pieces.

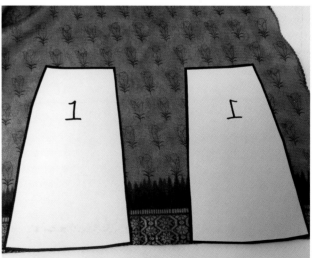

PATTERN LAYOUT: BOLD REPEAT PRINTS

Print layout tips:

1. Lay out the fabric right side facing up. Pin the original pattern piece for the skirt front to the fabric with pattern markings facing up, aligning it so that the hemline marking of the pattern falls on a heavier line of the print and the waistline falls on a lighter section.

2. Pin the duplicate pattern piece for the skirt front to the fabric with the pattern markings facing down, aligning its center fold line with that of the original pattern piece and following the other placement instructions in step 1.

3. Repeat with original and duplicate pattern pieces for skirt back, aligning them so that the hemline marking falls along the same heavy line as the two front pieces and the notch on the side seam falls in the same position on the design as its numbered counterpart on the skirt front.

4. Pin the original and duplicate pattern pieces for the bodice front to the fabric with pattern markings facing up, aligning them so that the heavier lines of the design fall above and below the bustline, which is at the apex of the dart.

5. Pin the original and duplicate pattern pieces for the bodice back to the fabric with pattern markings facing up, aligning them so that the numbered notch on the side seam falls in the same position on the design as its numbered counterpart on the bodice front.

6. Pin the original and duplicate pattern pieces for the sleeve to the fabric with pattern markings facing up.

7. Cut out the pattern following the instructions for laying out a large floral print, steps 5 and 6 (page 127).

8. Pin and cut out the remaining pattern pieces following the instructions for laying out a large floral print, step 7 (page 127).

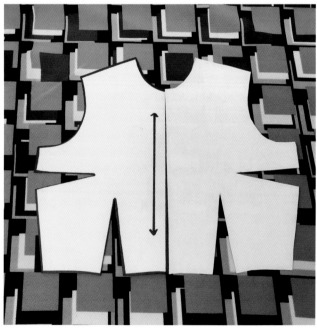

PATTERN LAYOUT: IRREGULAR CROSSWAYS PLAIDS

The heaviest horizontal lines of plaids and repeat prints are more attractive at or near hemlines. Similarly, a plaid's widest vertical stripes are best centered in front and back or balanced on either side, and diagonal stripes should be slanted in one direction only. Irregular plaids can have straight or curved hems. Align all hemlines of the pattern on the same horizontal stripe of a plaid or on lines of a bold repeat.

Irregular crossways plaid layout tips:

1. Lay out the entire piece of fabric right side facing up on a firm surface. Pin the original pattern piece for the skirt front to the fabric with the pattern markings facing up. Align it so that the center fold line of the pattern falls along the center of a narrow vertical stripe. If the hemline of the garment is curved, as in this example, align its center front edge with that of a narrow horizontal stripe.

2. Pin the duplicate pattern piece for the skirt front to the fabric with pattern markings facing down, aligning its center fold line with that of the original pattern piece and following the other placement instructions in step 1.

3. Pin the original pattern piece for the skirt back to the fabric with pattern markings facing up, aligning it so that the center back seam line—not the cutting edge—falls along the center of a narrow vertical stripe and the hemline falls along the edge of a similar narrow horizontal stripe as that of the skirt front. Make sure that the notch on the side seam falls in the same position on the plaid as its numbered counterpart on the skirt front.

continued on the next page

4. Pin the duplicate pattern piece for the skirt back to the fabric with pattern markings facing down, following the placement instructions in step 3.

5. Pin the original pattern piece for the bodice front to the fabric with the pattern markings facing up, aligning it so that the center fold line falls along the center of a narrow vertical stripe and the wide horizontal stripe falls above or below the bust line, which is at the apex of the dart.

6. Pin the duplicate pattern piece for the bodice front to the fabric with pattern markings facing down, aligning its center fold line with that of the original pattern piece, and following the other placement instructions in step 5.

7. Pin the original bodice back piece to the fabric, pattern markings up, so the center back seam line—not the cutting edge—falls along the center of a narrow vertical stripe and the notch on the side seam falls in the same position on the plaid as its numbered counterpart on the bodice front.

8. Pin the duplicate pattern piece for the bodice back to the fabric with pattern markings facing down, following the placement instructions in step 7.

9. Cut out the pattern pieces following the instructions for laying out a large floral print, steps 5 and 6 (page 127).

10. Pin and cut out any remaining pattern pieces according to the instructions for laying out a large floral print, step 7 (page 127), without attempting any further matching.

PATTERN LAYOUT: IRREGULAR LENGTHWISE PLAIDS

Irregular lengthwise plaid layout tips:

1. Lay the fabric right side facing up and pin the original pattern piece for the front of the dress to the fabric with the pattern markings facing up. Align the pattern piece so that any wide vertical stripe in the fabric falls at least 3" (7.6cm) in from the center front seam line or the armhole seam line on the pattern. If the hemline is curved, align its center front edge with that of a narrow horizontal stripe.

2. Turn the duplicate pattern piece for the dress front upside down and pin it to the fabric with pattern markings facing down, following the placement instructions in step 1. Make sure that the center front notches fall in the same positions on the plaid as on the original dress front.

3. Pin the original pattern piece for the dress back to the fabric with pattern markings facing up, aligning it so that the center back seam line, the hemline, and the notch on the side seam all fall in the same position on the plaid as their counterparts on the dress front.

4. Turn the duplicate pattern piece for the dress back upside down and pin it to the fabric with pattern markings facing down.

5. Pin the original pattern piece for the sleeve to the fabric with pattern markings facing up. Align it so that the wide vertical stripe falls down the center of the sleeve and make sure that the notch on the sleeve cap falls in the same position on the plaid as its numbered counterpart on the armhole of the dress front.

6. Turn the duplicate pattern piece for the sleeve upside down and pin with the printed side facing down.

7. Cut out the pattern pieces.

8. Pin and cut any remaining pattern pieces following the instructions for laying out a large floral print, step 7 (page 127).

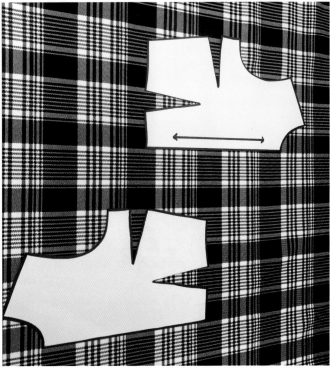

CHAPTER 4

SEWING CLASSIC GARMENTS

Before attempting to learn how to assemble the smaller details of a garment as shown in Chapter 6—the darts, zippers, pleats, pockets, etc.—you should first understand the correct order in which to sew these different details, whether it is for a dress, shirt, blouse, skirt, or pants (pants are featured in detail in Chapter 5). You can generalize the assembly sequence for these classic garments to most any pattern you will choose to sew.

Think of sewing garments together by first breaking them down into specific components. A component is an area of the garment such as a sleeve, bodice front, bodice back, or collar area. You should sew and apply any detail to these smaller areas before attaching them to another area. The assembly sequence is always a logical one. For example, the body section of a blouse is fitted and sewn before the sleeve is attached, otherwise the armhole in which the sleeve is inserted might not have the proper dimensions. Similarly, buttonholes and buttons are positioned after the garment is completed to ensure the closures will be smooth and neat.

If you have chosen the right size pattern (pages 72-74) and adjusted it properly for your figure, including polishing the fit with a muslin (pages 91-94), you should experience few fitting problems during the final assembly, and the result should be a finished garment that hangs properly and fits perfectly.

A Note about Step-by-Step Numbering

In this book, step-by-step instructions are broken down into small, bite-sized chunks for each phase of a project. Photos are given for some essential steps, but not all steps. Photos are almost always right next to the step text or mini section with which they correspond. If they're not, they have an extra caption clarifying what they're showing. So don't be confused if you see more than one step 1 on a page!

Detailed instructions for sewing elements such as darts, seams, hemlines, etc. are covered individually in Chapter 6.

THE CLASSIC DRESS

Although their styling varies from year to year and season to season, dresses are perhaps the most flattering garment a woman can wear. They skim the body, creating long, fluid lines that glide over any imperfections, and they can be designed to highlight a woman's best features—a short hem draws attention to the legs, a sweetheart neckline emphasizes the face, and short sleeves draw attention to arms. In addition, a well-fitted dress in a classic fabric is stylish and timeless, comfortable, and can be accessorized for day and evening wear.

The following is a generalized order of assembly that will work with most patterns. Add details and design elements to customize your dress and follow individual pattern guides for specific details related to that pattern.

SEWING THE DARTS AND SEAMS

1. Baste any darts on the dress front, back, and lower areas. Press down or toward the middle.
2. Baste the main seams of the dress body: the side, shoulder, and princess seams. Side pockets are attached to the side seam now.
3. Turn the dress right side out and try it on. Apply any refinements, such as contouring the side seam to your body.
4. If the fit is correct, stitch the seam with a regular seam allowance and stitch length. Pull out the basting thread, as necessary. Edge finish and press.

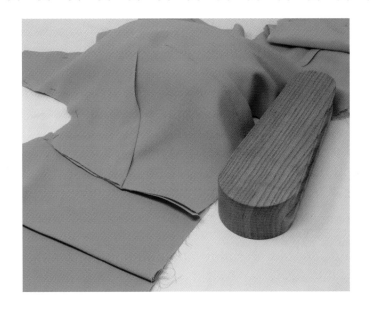

FINISHING THE NECKLINE AND CLOSURES

1. For dresses with back openings, insert the zipper, if any; press.
2. Attach the neckline facing to the dress with right sides together; clip, turn, and press. For dresses with full linings, repeat the steps for dress assembly and then attach to the neckline as you would the facing.
3. On the inside of the garment, hand tack the facing in place. Add a closure such as a hook and eye at the top of the zipper.

CHECK THE FIT

The bust points should point to the apex. Fabric will pool around the bust dart if too short and will pull if too long.

Shoulder seams should fall on the desired shoulder placement, angle to the shoulder point, and extend from the base of the neck outward.

Side seams should divide the front and back of the body with a visual vertical line. Contour to the desired amount of ease and fit.

Check the arm opening for correct placement on your body.

The neckline front and back should lay flat and hug the body naturally with no pulling or pooling of fabric.

SEWING THE ARMHOLES AND SLEEVES

1. On a sleeveless garment, attach the armhole facings to the garment; press.
2. On a garment with sleeves, stitch the sleeve seams; press. Then attach the sleeves to the armhole of the dress. For garments with a lining, baste it to the arm opening before attaching the sleeve. Once the sleeve is attached, hand sew the sleeve lining to the inside cap of the sleeve and then the hem.

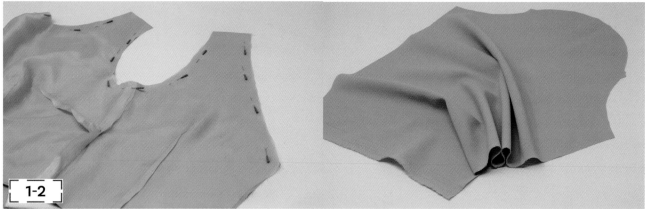

ADDING THE FINISHING TOUCHES

1. Baste any finished patch pockets to the garment; try on and pin fit to determine the best position. Pockets should not crowd the center front or be so low that you cannot reach them. Reposition as needed.
2. Stitch the pocket to the garment; press.
3. If desired, add a decorative line of machine topstitching along the edges and seam lines.
4. Try on the dress and mark the sleeve and skirt lengths; hem and press.

THE CLASSIC SHIRT

A classically styled, carefully fitted shirt is a staple of any wardrobe and a fundamental building block for many other garments. Coats, jackets, and even some women's dresses are simply variations on a tailored shirt. Learning to make this one garment can unlock your ability to make many others. The classic shirt is most often associated with fine cotton fabrics or stylized into denim and medium weight fabrics with impeccable topstitching on flat felled seams.

The component sewing concept is key when sewing a shirt. This fashion industry approach to sewing this common garment simplifies the complexity of some shirt patterns and will enable you to understand almost any design.

The following is a generalized order of assembly for a classic shirt. Generally, most shirt patterns consist of five basic components or areas of construction (listed in the sidebar on page 140). Within each component, you can add or subtract details such as darts, pockets, topstitching, fabric manipulation, and embellishments. Follow the steps in your pattern for specific details on things like the yoke, placket, and cuff assembly.

Detailed instructions for sewing elements such as darts, seams, hemlines, etc. are covered individually in Chapter 6.

SHIRT COMPONENT BREAKDOWN

1. Shirt front: pockets, darts, stabilizers, plackets, topstitching, buttons, and buttonholes

2. Shirt back: darts, topstitching, yoke, and pleat

3. Sleeve: elbow dart, side seams, placket, cuff, and topstitching

4. Shirt collar: interlining, collar band, upper collar, and topstitching

5. Finishing: joining front to back, joining collar to neckline, joining sleeves to arm opening, closure, topstitching, and hem

SEWING THE SHIRT BODY

1. Sew any yoke pieces to the shirt back and front. Topstitch if desired.
2. If there is no yoke, join the shirt front to the back at the shoulders. Edge finish and press.

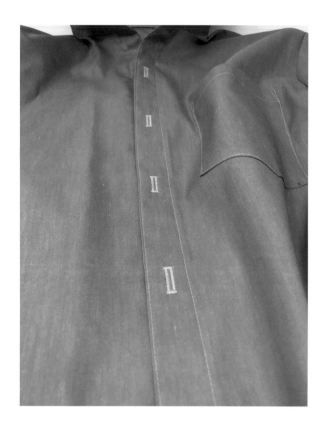

SEWING THE SLEEVES AND SIDE SEAMS

1. Make the sleeve placket on the wrist edge of the sleeve and attach it to the body section of the shirt; press.
2. Construct flat felled seams around the armhole of the shirt. Add decorative topstitching.
3. With right sides together, sew up the underarm and side seams of the shirt.
4. Attach the cuffs to the sleeves and topstitch if desired.

TIP

Sleeves can be attached fully assembled or partially. Some patterns will have you sew the entire sleeve, topstitch, and then add all the details prior to attaching to the shirt body..

ATTACHING COLLARS AND FACINGS

Shirt collars have several variations in assembly. Some may have you attach the collar to the collar band before attaching to the neckline, while others have the collar band attached to the neckline first. Reference your pattern for exact instructions.

1. Attach the front placket to the shirt front edges.
2. Sew the collar pieces right sides together, clip, turn, and press the points. Attach the collar to the upper edge of the collar band according to your pattern. Topstitch if desired.

MAKING BUTTONHOLES AND BUTTONS

1. Mark the buttonholes on the shirt body and cuffs.
2. Try on the shirt and pin it closed at the buttonhole markings.
3. If the fabric gaps at the buttonhole markings or bunches up in between, remove the pins and reposition them.
4. When the shirt closes smoothly and evenly, make the buttonholes and sew on the buttons.

ADDING POCKETS

1. Baste the finished breast pocket or pockets to the shirt and try the shirt on for positioning.
2. If the pocket is so high that it comes close to the tip of the collar and is uncomfortable to reach, reposition it on the shirt.
3. Sew the pocket to the shirt; press.

ADDING THE FINISHING TOUCHES

1. Try on the shirt and mark its length.
2. Hem and press.

FLAT FELLED SEAMS

The same seam easily recognized on a pair of jeans is also used on the classic shirt: the flat felled seam. This seam is made by placing the raw edge of one side of the seam inside the folded edge of the other, then stitching down, usually with a double row of topstitching.

Detailed instructions for sewing elements such as darts, seams, hemlines, etc. are covered individually in Chapter 6.

THE CLASSIC BLOUSE

A blouse is different from a shirt in that it is slimmer and shaped to a woman's more rounded body. Like a shirt, however, the blouse is also the basis for numerous other garments, including dresses. As with so many women's clothes, the effect of a blouse depends on the fabric you choose for it. The same pattern will look vastly different when made in shimmery silk, crisp cotton, or lightweight flannel, but all should fit well and be flattering regardless of the type of fabric. The classic blouse mimics a shirt but is sewn more like a dress when constructed from finer fabrics. Common details like the flat felled seam are replaced by fancier French seams and self-fabric bias bindings.

SEWING THE MAIN BODY

1. Baste the darts, if any. Press down or toward the middle.
2. Baste the main seams of the blouse body: the side, shoulder, and princess seams.
3. Try on the blouse and adjust the darts and seams, if necessary. Contour the shape of the side seam to your desired amount of ease and fit.
4. If the fit is correct, stitch the seams with a regular seam allowance and stitch length. Pull out basting thread, as necessary. Edge finish and press.
5. Check the fit. The blouse will have the same areas of fit as the classic dress. Check the fit guidelines on page 137.

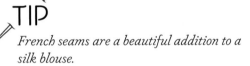

TIP
French seams are a beautiful addition to a silk blouse.

ATTACHING THE FACINGS AND COLLARS

1. Attach the facing or fold back the self-facing at the center front opening of the blouse; press.
2. Sew the collar pieces right sides together; clip, turn, and press the points. Attach the collar to the upper edge of the collar band according to your pattern. Topstitch if desired.

NOTE:
The classic blouse usually features the soft roll of a self-fabric facing rather than the crisp placket and topstitching of the cotton shirt.

ATTACHING THE SLEEVES

The blouse usually has set-in sleeves which are sewn completely prior to inserting into the arm opening.

1. Assemble the sleeve and cuff; press.
2. Attach the sleeve to the armhole of the blouse.

ADDING THE FINISHING TOUCHES

1. Mark the buttonholes and try on the blouse for positioning.
2. Sew the buttons on the blouse and cuff.
3. Baste any decorative pockets to the blouse and check their position. Stitch.
4. Try on the blouse for length; hem and press.

TIP

Bound buttonholes are a lovely finish on finer blouse fabrics.

THE CLASSIC SKIRT

Women have many clothing options to choose from for both style and function. Pants may be a wardrobe staple for many women (and are featured in Chapter 5), but it is the classic skirt that remains a versatile, flattering, and fashionable garment choice. Fitted at the waist and beautifully skimming off the full hip, the skirt creates a slimming silhouette that often enhances the figure more than pants. Despite the many design choices, most skirts are quite similar in their construction and one of the simplest and most enjoyable garments to sew. They can be made in a variety of lengths, cuts, fabrics, and styles—long or short, full to slim, sturdy material to lightweight, A-line, straight, and more. The variations are endless!

Skirt assembly has only four steps: front, back, waistband, and hem. This simplicity enables the sewist to focus on creating an impeccable fit combined with stunning fabrics and details—the versatility can expand the wardrobe in many creative ways. Once you have mastered the classic skirt, you can experiment with different fabrics and creative garment details, such as those featured in Chapter 6.

Detailed instructions for sewing elements such as darts, seams, hemlines, etc. are covered individually in Chapter 6.

SEWING DARTS AND SEAMS ON FITTED SKIRTS

1. Baste the waist darts, side seams, and any other vertical seam.
2. Try on the skirt. Check the dart position and fit.
3. Sew all darts and seams; press.
4. A skirt lining may be sewn to the top edge of the skirt at this time and finished off with the waistband or attached to a facing after the waistband has been attached.

TIP

Try sewing a kick pleat to the center back seam for an attractive finish.

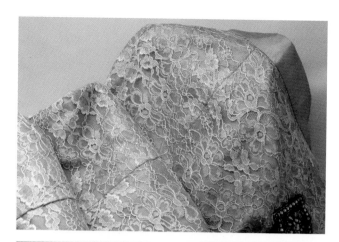

STITCHING DARTS AND SEAMS ON PLEATED SKIRTS

Most skirts include a basic waist dart or fitting element such as seams, pleats, or tucks to help contour the fabric around the curve of the figure. Darts are sewn on individual pieces before forming the shape of the skirt. Seams replace the dart and are formed when joining pattern pieces together, and pleats and tucks may be formed on the individual piece or after the skirt is formed, based on how deep the pleat/tuck is and its placement.

1. Form the dart on each skirt front and back piece. Fold and baste the pleats, if any, in place.
2. Baste the side seams and any additional vertical seams of the skirt and try it on.
3. If the pleat gapes or rolls open, remove the basting at the waistline and reposition the pleat until it falls properly. Re-baste. Pleats are not one-size fits all and need to be custom contoured to the body.
4. Stitch the darts, seams, and pleats in place; press.

CHECK THE FIT

Check the dart fit from the fullest part of the hip or abdomen. Your skirt should fit comfortably on the waistline and skim the fullest part of the hip or abdomen before flaring or tapering the silhouette of the lower edge. If the dart angles and points away from the fullest part of the hip or abdomen, remove the dart basting and reposition the dart to the natural vertical placement. If the dart is too short, it will pucker at the tip and have excess fabric in the hip or abdomen. Correct this by pinning and lengthening the dart by stitching further down on the skirt to approximately 1½" (4cm) from the fullest part of the body or to the point where the dart looks flattering and is not pulling and the excess fabric is removed. If the dart is too long, the skirt will fit tight over the upper hip or abdomen and the dart will pucker at the tip when tried on. Horizontal drag lines will be present. Correct the fit by shortening to approximately 1½" (4cm) from the fullest part. Make sure all darts are the same length from left to right side of the body.

INSERTING THE ZIPPER AND WAISTBAND

Skirts can have a variety of closures, including a lapped zipper, invisible zipper, fly closure, and hook and eye, along with various waistbands. The top edge of a skirt may have a simple bias binding, facing edge, elastic band, or traditional fitted waistband. Follow your specific pattern for exact application. If the skirt has been properly fitted, then basting the zipper may be omitted.

Inserting the Zipper and Waistband

1. Attach the zipper according to the style in the pattern.
2. Baste the waistband to the skirt and try on.
3. If the skirt fabric pools or droops below the waistband, it is because the band is too high on the back. Mark a new stitching line lower on the skirt with pins or chalk to the desired width. Remove the waistband, then trim the skirt seam allowance to ⅝" (1.5cm) above the new stitching line. Reattach the waistband.

ADDING THE FINISHING TOUCHES

Before hemming, do any of the following as needed for your specific skirt:

- Attach the skirt facing or lining to the waistband if part of the pattern.
- Mark the buttonhole positions and sew the buttonholes and any hook and eyes or snaps.
- Baste any decorative patch pockets to the skirt and try on for position.
- Stitch the pockets to the skirt; press.

Once you're ready to finish the skirt, try it on, mark its length, hem, and press.

Adding the Finishing Touches

THE CLASSIC TAILORED JACKET

Padded and lined, shaped and fitted, the tailored jacket is a classic fashion icon that is all about the inner structure and impeccable fit. The cut of the lapels may alter subtly from decade to decade and the shoulders may require slightly more or less padding, but the basic look endures. In fact, almost every jacket in a woman's wardrobe remains a variation on a tailoring theme that has been essentially constant for a century or more.

Detailed instructions for sewing elements such as darts, seams, hemlines, etc. are covered individually in Chapter 6.

When the modern hip-length jacket first appeared in 1859, it was dubbed a "sack coat" and sold to men only. Shortly, it proliferated into dozens of variations that today are the predominant sellers in everyday wear: the suit jacket, sports jacket, blazer, riding jacket, and tuxedo coat.

Cut from solid-colored or striped fabric, adorned with metal buttons and perhaps a braid edging, the sack coat becomes a blazer. Add box pleats front and back, put a belt around the waist, and it is a Norfolk jacket. Lengthen the skirt and flare out the bottom from a fitted waist, and the sack coat is a hacking or riding jacket. Fashioned from black or white mohair or worsted with matching satin or grosgrain lapels, the sack becomes a dinner jacket—or a tuxedo, as it came to be called after it first appeared as a less formal replacement for white tie and tails at a fancy ball in Tuxedo Park, New York, in 1886.

The sack coat has long since been adopted by women. Unlike a skirt that may be assembled in a timely fashion, a true tailored jacket does require some time and dedication, but the results are well worth the effort. Although a well-made sack coat may represent the epitome in tailoring, the basic art of jacket making is as straightforward as any other aspect of custom sewing. The methods described on the following pages are well within the capability of any accomplished needlecrafter and make for a satisfying sewing experience.

The following is an in-depth look at the jacket, which is a more involved garment and therefore has more pages dedicated to it than the classic garments featured earlier in this chapter. Make sure to follow all the specific details of your individual pattern.

From full, traditional tailoring to the drape of a lightly structured jacket, the classic jacket is a must in every sewing wardrobe. Mastering the foundation is truly the start to sewing success!

UNDERSTANDING INTERFACINGS

Beneath the surface of every classic tailored jacket is a carefully considered arrangement of structuring materials that help determine the garment's ultimate shape. Think of interfacing as the garment's skeleton, a hidden component with visible benefits that provide shape and support and prolong the life and shape of the garment. The beautiful silhouette of a tailored jacket begins with planning how the interfacings will be added. These underpinnings include the fabric interfacings that sculpt a jacket's front, the shoulder padding, and the curved linen band that gives a collar its graceful roll. Like the garment fabrics, these foundation materials should be of top quality.

A traditional tailored woman's jacket is supported in front with two layers of wool interfacing fabric, one large and one small, and one layer in back. For the larger front pieces, measure from the neckline to the hem, and then use scraps from this material to cut out the smaller front pieces. The back interfacing extends from the shoulder to just below the armhole. Its width should be equal to twice the distance from the top of the side seam line to the center back line.

Interfacing Selection

Interfacing gives you the control to engineer your fabric and change its properties. You should choose the best type of interfacing for the garment and consider the time, money, effort, and materials involved in tailoring a jacket to achieve the optimal results. Better interfacings are usually purchased on a bolt by the yard just like tailoring fabrics. Tip: Avoid precut pieces in plastic wrap from big box stores.

Interfacings are used in areas such as the shaped neckline, facings, hems, collars, and pockets, and to reinforce buttons. Component areas may require different types of interfacing, which are available in a range of choices: natural, blends, and synthetics in a variety of weights and textures, woven to knit, low- and high-heat sensitive.

There are both sew-in interfacings and fusible interfacings available. With advantages in technology, fusible interfacings have improved dramatically in their quality and selection. Fusibles can shorten the tailoring process by replacing hand stitching with an iron. Some tips for using fusibles include: test on fabric scrap before applying; fuse the whole fabric piece, then cut out the garment piece; overlap raw edges; warm the fabric before joining the fusible; and use multiple layers of lighter interfacing. Heavier fusibles have more glue and take longer to adhere. If the glue leaks out, it is too heavy. Fusibles can also be preshrunk. All of this said, sew-ins have several distinct advantages over fusibles. They can be easily tested with your fabric in the store before purchase, preshrunk by machine laundering and drying, and are easy to remove. Misapplication of a sew-in will not ruin the fashion fabric, and they are necessary for traditional couture techniques such as pad stitching.

Interfacings, both of the fusible and sew-in types, come in a wide variety and will allow your jacket to hold its structure throughout the life of the garment.

Sew-in interfacings like this one are necessarily for traditional couture techniques such as pad stitching.

TYPES OF INTERFACING

Wool Interfacing: A strong, highly resilient fabric made of a mixture of cotton, wool, and/or goat hair. Also called hair or foundation canvas. The interfacing is used on a jacket to help shape and support the fabric, and to keep the jacket from stretching, wrinkling, or sagging. Use medium-weight interfacing with most suit fabrics, and lightweight for summer tropicals. Select the best quality interfacing available, made of natural fibers only. Test the quality by crushing the fabric in your hand; when released, it will spring back to shape and not show any wrinkles. Avoid burlap interfacing, which is scratchy and stiff.

Haircloth Interfacing: A wiry, extra-resilient interfacing fabric that is a mixture of strong cotton fibers and tough horsehair, used over the wool interfacing to reinforce the chest and shoulder areas of a jacket. Select haircloth made of natural fibers only, if available.

Cover Cloth: A loosely woven material, preferably cotton flannel, with a slightly fuzzy, or napped, surface; sewed over haircloth to prevent the sharp ends of the horsehair from protruding. The fabric adds extra padding that helps round out the shape of the jacket. If flannel is not available, substitute soft, lightweight felt.

Collar Interfacing: Stiff, firmly woven linen interfacing material sewed between the collar surface and the undercollar. It helps give the collar shape and firmness, allowing it to turn over smoothly at the roll line, and permitting it to set neatly and accurately at the neck. If linen canvas is not available, use wool interfacing. In fact, some tailors prefer wool, to achieve a softer effect. Avoid cotton canvas treated with a chemical finish called sizing; it will not stand up to dry cleaning.

Undercollar Fabric: Sewed to the collar interfacing to form the underside of the collar. For most women's jackets the garment fabric itself is used. For men's jackets, which are usually of heavier material, a strong, durable wool fabric called melton cloth is preferable. Melton cloth gives the collar extra reinforcement and longer wear. And because it is less bulky than most heavy garment fabric, melton allows the collar to be shaped and to roll more easily. It is also used with loose weaves to provide sharp collar edges. Melton cloth comes in a variety of colors to match, contrast or harmonize with the suit fabric color.

Wigan: A loosely woven, durable interfacing fabric used around the bottom of sleeves to reinforce the hem. (It is named after the town of Wigan, England, where it was first produced.) Select pure cotton wigan, if available. If not, substitute a polyester and cotton blend, jacket pocketing, or a lightweight, nonwoven interfacing fabric.

Pocketing Fabric: Tightly woven twilled cotton fabric, treated with a satiny finish to make the material soft. Pocketing fabric is available in different weights and is used to form not only pockets on jackets and pants, but also to reinforce the crotch and to make the fly and waistband facing. It may also be substituted for wigan to reinforce sleeve hemlines. The softest and most durable pocketing material is a pure cotton twill called silesia. If silesia is not available, substitute a polished cotton or a blend of cotton and polyester. Avoid stiff cotton pocketing treated with sizing.

Twill Tape: A thin, extra-strong strip of twilled linen or cotton fabric, also called stay tape; sewed along the lapel roll line of the jacket to prevent stretching and to keep the jacket front from buckling away from the chest. The tape is also used to reinforce the edges of the lapels and to ensure flat, sharp edges that do not pucker or stretch. The narrowest width of tape available—preferably ⅜" (1cm) wide—will produce the neatest lapel roll and edges. Before using, preshrink the tape by dipping it in water. Avoid non-twilled seam binding and tape treated with sizing.

Waistband Interfacing, Facing, and Trousers Curtain: Waistband interfacing is a strip of strong, canvas-like fabric sewn to the waistband to reinforce it and to help hold its shape. The waistband facing is another strip of softer fabric that covers the interfacing and forms the waistband's lining. The trouser curtain is an extra piece of fabric that extends below the waistband to keep the waist area from stretching, to cover the waistband seam, and to hold trouser pleats in place. Ready-made waistband parts, sold by the yard, are available, some already joined. If you make your own, select firm but pliable linen canvas for the interfacing. (Avoid harsh nylon and sized, or chemically treated, cotton stiffening.) For the facing and the trouser curtain, select soft, durable cotton such as pocketing fabric or a cotton and polyester blend.

Shoulder Pads and Sleeve Heads: Shoulder pads are usually made of triangular pieces of muslin or cotton wadding, which is a kind of nonwoven cotton fabric. The triangles form the outer layers of a cloth sandwich, which is filled with lamb's-wool fleece or raw cotton batting. The pads are used to shape and build up the shoulders of a jacket and must be carefully fitted before they are inserted. Sleeve heads are 2" (5cm)-wide strips of cotton wadding or lamb's-wool fleece placed around the top of the sleeve to create a smooth line and to support the roll at the sleeve cap. They will also improve and help maintain the hang of the sleeve. Ready-made shoulder pads and sleeve heads are available. If you make your own, shape the pads carefully and join the layers using hand padding stitches or machine zigzag stitches.

Preshrinking Interfacings

Better quality interfacings should not need to be preshrunk, but interfacings that have a little more open weave may need preshrunk because the fibers may retract toward each other.

For washable woven fabrics, wefts, and knits:

1. Fold in half with the resin (glue) side inward and place in tub of hot tap water.
2. Let the water come to room temperatures.
3. Let soak with no agitation.
4. Remove and gently squeeze out excess water or towel dry—do not wring.
5. Unroll, then place over a hanger or shower rod to dry. Place knit interfacings on a flat towel so they do not distort. The interfacing is defective if the glue comes off in your hand. Discard and select a better product.
6. Just before using, preshrink once more by steam shrinking.

For nonwovens and dry clean only fabrics:

1. Place cut pieces over fabric pieces.
2. Hold iron 1"–2" (2.5–5cm) above the fabric and hover.
3. Give shots of steam for 7–10 seconds. The interfacing may draw up as you steam. This is shrinkage. Smooth out and fuse as usual.

General preshrinking guidelines:

- Natural fibers will shrink more than synthetics.
- Knits shrink more than a woven. Both shrink more than nonwovens.
- The more fusibles used in a garment, the more the likelihood of potential problems with shrinkage.
- Pre-shrinking is important for fully-fused garments and those laundered often.

How to Test Fuse Interfacing

1. Select interfacing based on the project requirements.
2. At minimum, cut a 4" x 4" (10 x 10cm) or larger piece of fabric and fuse with interfacing.
3. Select the iron temperature according to the fabric and preheat. Part of the testing process is to find the right combination of fabric, heat, and fusible.
4. Press the fabric to remove wrinkles and warm up.
5. Position the fusible glue side to the wrong side of fabric. Steam shrink, then cover the sample with press cloth and fuse.
6. Apply firm, even pressure for 10–15 seconds until completely fused. Do not glide the iron over the fabric. Press by lifting the iron, moving into position, and pressing down.
7. Let the sample cool, turn right side up, cover with a press cloth, and fuse again for a smooth and secure bond.
8. Let the fabric cool completely before moving it.
9. Examine the bond. See how the fabric feels. Take a note of the fusing time, settings, cutting direction, and any other reference notes for future use.

TIP

Fuse a large circle to test the interfacing with various angles.

CREATING CUSTOM INTERFACING

Many patterns have interfacing pieces as part of the pattern, or you may need to cut the main pattern pieces from interfacing. You can achieve a more custom-tailored effect by creating custom interfacing pieces. It is important that the pattern is refined and pre-fitted in muslin before creating the custom interfacing pieces.

Trace the Front Pattern

1. Using a tracing wheel and dressmaker's carbon paper, mark the shoulder and armhole seam lines and the side seam line along the marked part of the side cutting line on a large piece of interfacing.
2. Mark the lapel roll line, the top point of the waistline dart, and the shoulder-dart stitching lines if there is a shoulder dart.
3. Lightly mark any remaining pattern markings such as the grain line, waistline, pocket placement, and hem. Use a ruler to join edges together.
4. Remove the pattern.

Cut Out the Front Interfacing Pieces

5. Cut out the interfacing along the cutting lines.
6. If you marked a shoulder dart, cut it out along the marked stitching lines to reduce bulk as you sew. You will not need to sew a dart in the interfacing.

Mark and Cut the Armhole Reinforcements

7. Using a piece of interfacing fabric large enough to cover the armhole area, fold the fabric in half so that the selvage edges are together or arrange two layers of scrap fabric so that the grains are aligned.
8. Place the armhole section of one of the front interfacings, marked side up, on the fabric and align the grains. Pin.
9. To mark the shoulder cutting line for the reinforcement, use a tracing wheel and dressmaker's carbon paper to transfer the shoulder seam line of the interfacing between the armhole seam line and a point about 4" (10cm) beyond it, depending on the size of the jacket. If necessary, extend the line across any shoulder dart opening.
10. To mark the armhole and side cutting lines, transfer the armhole and the side seam lines of the interfacing.
11. Remove the interfacing.
12. To mark the front cutting line, begin by finding the point on the armhole cutting line where it starts to curve sharply. This will be approximately two-thirds of the way down. Starting at that point, measure in about 3 ½" (9cm) along the crosswise grain of the fabric and make a mark.

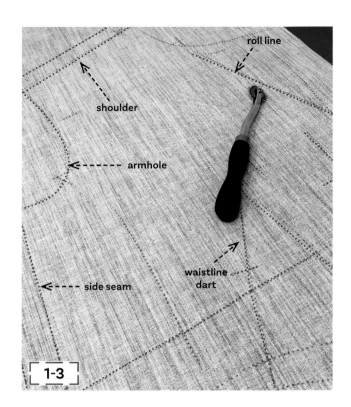

1-3

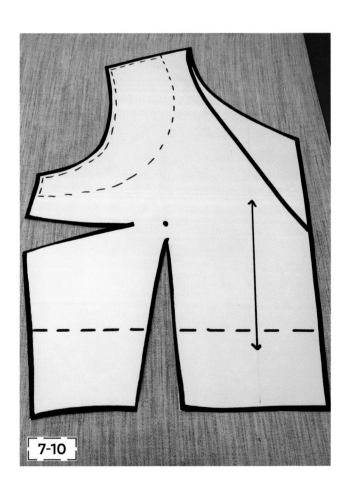

7-10

13. Draw a gently curved line to connect the end of the shoulder cutting line with the mark you made in step 13 and the end of the side cutting line.

14. Cut out the armhole reinforcements along the cutting lines.

Mark and Cut the Back Interfacing Piece

15. Fold the fabric in half, lengthwise, so that the selvage edges are together.

16. Place the upper half of the jacket back pattern piece on the fabric so that the upper part of the center back seam line is along the fold. Pin.

17. Along the center back seam line, measure down 5" (12.5cm) from the neck seam line and make a mark on the folded edge of the fabric as a guide for drawing the bottom cutting line.

18. Use dressmaker's carbon paper to transfer the neck and shoulder seam lines on the pattern to the interfacing. Then, transfer the side seam line from the armhole cutting line to a point 3" (7.6cm) below it.

19. To mark the armhole cutting line, trace the pattern armhole cutting line.

20. If there are markings for a shoulder dart, use dressmaker's carbon paper to transfer the stitching lines—even though you crossed them out and did not use them on the garment.

21. Remove the pattern. If you marked a shoulder dart, skip to step 26.

22. To determine the position of the shoulder dart if you did not mark one, measure in along the shoulder cutting line 1 ½" (4cm) from the neck cutting line and make a mark.

23. Starting at the mark, draw a line 3" (7.6cm) long, parallel to the upper part of the armhole cutting line. This is the center line of the dart.

24. On each side of the center line—and ¼" (0.5cm) away from it—make a mark on the shoulder line. Draw lines to connect the marks with the end of the center line.

25. To mark the bottom cutting line, begin by drawing a straight line (at a right angle to the folded edge) from the mark you made on the folded edge above to a point even with the end of the dart.

26. Continue the line by curving it downward so that it is parallel to the lower armhole line. Curve it around to the end of the sideline. The shape may be approximated because the interfacing will not be visible on the finished jacket.

27. Cut out the interfacing along the lines, cutting out the dart as you go.

11-14

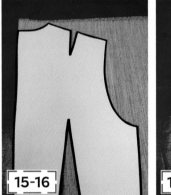

15-16

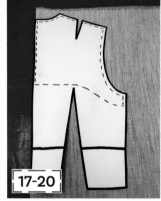

17-20

This is the finished back interfacing piece.

THE JACKET FOUNDATION

The first step in tailoring a jacket is to construct the contoured foundation of the custom interfacing pieces that will give shape to its body. When these structuring materials have been stitched together, the jacket body is assembled temporarily for its initial fitting (page 158). For best results, do not skip the time-saving step of muslin fitting before assembly. This will enable you to begin assembly with the fit issues already refined, so you can enjoy the art of sewing and tailoring your classic jacket.

Customize your interfacing with hand pad stitching or the use of fusibles. The following is a generalized outline of the steps in tailoring a jacket, and they can also be used for creating outer coats and other jacket style garments.

To join the custom interfacing to the jacket, hand basting stitches are used. These stitches will be removed in the finished garment, so placing multiple lines up the front, the lapel, and other areas ensures there is no shifting as the garment is assembled.

ASSEMBLING THE FRONT INTERFACING

1. Assemble the interfacing pieces you already cut out: two front interfacings, two front armhole reinforcements, and one back interfacing.
2. If your jacket front does not have a shoulder dart, skip to step 4. If there is a shoulder dart, cut out two bias strips from pocketing fabric (see page 152). Make each strip 2" (5cm) wide and 2" (5cm) longer than the shoulder dart.
3. Place one of the main interfacings marked-side down. Close the dart opening by placing a piece of bias tape underneath and position the dart edges so they are next to each other, as if forming a dart. Pin to the bias tape to hold in place. Hand or machine stitch up one side and down the other to hold the dart edges to the bias tape.
4. Turn the interfacing marked-side up. Place one of the armhole reinforcements on it. Then align the shoulder, armhole, and side edges of the reinforcement with the corresponding seam lines of the interfacing. Pin.
5. Starting at the shoulder edge, run a curved line of basting through the center of the reinforcement to the side edge. Remove the pins.
6. Again starting at the shoulder edge, cover the reinforcement with ½" (1.3cm)–long padding stitches (page 23), sewing along the crosswise grain of the fabric. Make sure to sew through both layers of fabric. Remove the basting.
7. Steam press the padding stitched area.
8. Turn the assembled interfacing over, reinforcement side down, and press the other side of the padding stitched area.
9. Repeat steps 3–8 to assemble the other interfacing.

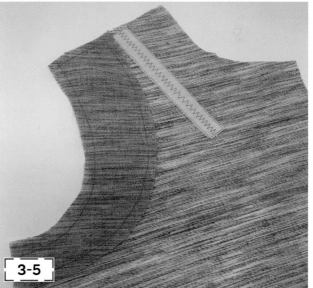

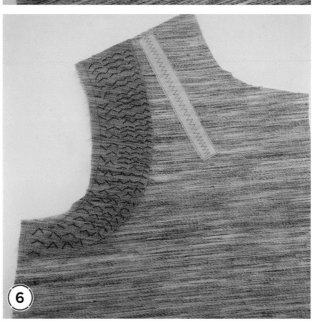

FINISHING THE BACK INTERFACING

1. Cut two bias strips from pocketing fabric. Make each strip 2" (5cm) wide and 2" (5cm) longer than the shoulder dart.
2. Close the shoulder dart openings, following the instructions for closing the front dart in step 3 of the previous sequence.

FITTING THE JACKET

Fitting the tailored jacket is a multi-step process. It begins with taking custom body measurements, making basic pattern adjustments, and refining the fit in a muslin. The first fitting involves basting all main garment seams and darts, trying the garment on, and refining any additional fitting needs. The garment is then taken apart, adjusted, and the permanent seams and stitches are sewn to create the garment. If the fitting muslin has been refined prior to assembly, then the first fitting can be eliminated. This decision is based on the final fashion fabric, the cost of the garment, the end use, and personal preference. No matter how careful the initial preparation, the tailored jacket must be fitted during construction.

These tailoring jacket adjustments can be made on ready-to-wear jackets if special care is taken. Keep in mind, when the pattern is custom fitted almost all these fit adjustments can be eliminated with 99 percent accuracy.

Adjusting a Loose Neckline

1. If the collar and neckline are loose, raise the collar above the jacket back to reveal the center back seam.
2. Starting at the neckline, pinch the excess fabric into a vertical tuck at the center back seam and pin.
3. Pin the tuck evenly up the collar to its top edge, then taper and pin the tuck down the center back seam.
4. To mark the new center back seam, draw chalk lines on both sides of the adjustment tuck.

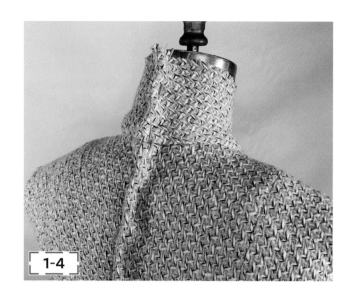

Adjusting a High Collar

1. If the collar is too high—less than ½" (1.5cm) lower than the shirt collar—remove it from the jacket body.
2. Re-pin the collar to the neckline below the original neckline seam allowance markings, starting at the center back and tapering it into the gorge line.
3. Mark the new seam line with chalk on the jacket body.

Adjusting a Low Collar

1. If the collar is too low—more than ½" (1.5cm) below the shirt collar—remove it from the jacket body.
2. Pin the collar to the neckline above the original neckline seam allowance markings, starting at the center back and tapering it into the gorge line.
3. Mark the new seam line with chalk on the jacket body.

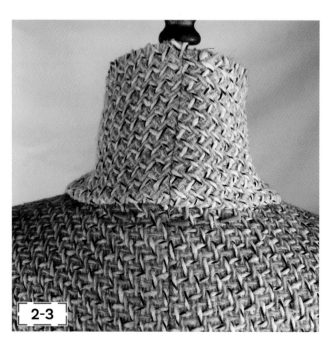

Adjusting a Sloping Shoulder

1. Check the fit at both shoulder seams. Often only one shoulder slopes.
2. Raise the collar above the jacket and open the shoulder seam at the armhole.
3. Pin the folded jacket back shoulder seam allowance inside the jacket front seam allowance, taking in more fabric in the back seam allowance than on the front, and taper the adjustment into the original seam at the neckline, inserting pins as you go.
4. Distribute the adjustment along the shoulder seam until it lies flat along the center of the natural shoulder.
5. Mark the new seam lines on the jacket back and front with chalk.
6. Re-pin the collar.

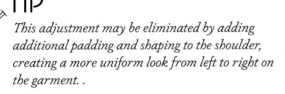

TIP

This adjustment may be eliminated by adding additional padding and shaping to the shoulder, creating a more uniform look from left to right on the garment. .

3-5

Adjusting a Square Shoulder

1. If the shoulder is square, remove the collar and open the shoulder seam at the armhole.
2. Partially unfold the jacket back shoulder seam allowance and pin it to the jacket front seam allowance, letting out more fabric from the back seam than the front and tapering the adjustment into the original seam at the neckline. Insert pins as you go.
3. Distribute the adjustment along the shoulder seam until it lies flat along the center of the natural shoulder.
4. Mark the new seam lines on the back and front with chalk.

2-4

Adjusting a Loose Back

1. If the jacket back is too loose across the shoulders, raise the collar above the jacket. Starting on the center seam, pinch the excess fabric into a vertical tuck and pin.
2. Extend the tuck on the center back seam. Taper it into the original seam to a point at the waistline, inserting pins as you go.
3. Mark the adjusted seam line with chalk down the length of both sides of the tuck.

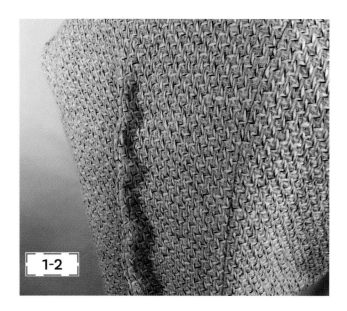

1-2

Adjusting a Narrow Back

1. If the jacket back is too narrow across the shoulders, raise the collar above the jacket. Open the center back seam in the shoulder area from about 3" (7.5cm) below the neckline to the underarm.
2. Partially unfold the seam allowance on one side of the back opening. Pin the folded edge to the other side, up to ⅜" (1cm) outside the original seam allowance markings. Distribute the adjustment evenly on both sides.
3. Taper the adjusted seam into the original seam, inserting pins as you go.
4. Mark the adjusted seam lines on both sides of the adjustment with chalk.

Adjusting a Long Back

1. If the jacket back is too long, remove the collar and open the shoulder seam from the neckline to the armhole.
2. Starting at the neckline, fold under the excess fabric in the jacket-back shoulder seam allowance. Pin the folded edge to the jacket front along the original shoulder seam markings.
3. Re-pin the collar to the jacket below the original neckline seam markings. Start at the center back and taper it into the gorge line.
4. Draw a new collar seam line on the jacket back with chalk.
5. Mark the new shoulder seam on both sides of the folded edge with chalk.

2-5

Adjusting a Short Back

1. If the jacket back is too short, remove the collar. Open the shoulder seam from the neckline to the armhole.

2. Starting at the neckline, partially unfold the jacket back seam allowance at the shoulder, letting it out. Pin the folded edge to the jacket front along the original seam allowance markings.

3. Re-pin the collar to the jacket above the original neckline seam allowance markings, starting at the center back and tapering into the gorge line.

4. Draw a new collar seam on the jacket back with chalk.

5. Mark the adjusted shoulder seam on both sides of the folded edge with chalk.

2-5

Tapering the Waist

1. If the jacket body is too loose at the waistline, determine which seams should have the adjustment, either the side seams, or the back.

2. To reduce fullness in the back, place a pin in the fullest part at the side back seams or the center back seam. Pin above and below to remove the excess blending into the original seam line.

3. To reduce fullness in the side seam at the waist, place a pin in the fullest part of the excess at the side seam. Pin out remaining excess above and below the seam, transitioning to the original seam line.

4. The reductions can be made in all the seams, or a select seam based on where the fullness needs removed.

5. If a jacket is snug around the waistline, the seams can be let out in the same areas. Determine where the garment is snug. On the inside stitch a new seam closer to the edge of the seam allowance. Let out the seam allowance by carefully removing the stitches of the original seam line.

1-2

Adjusting a Loose Jacket Body

1. If the jacket body is too loose at the side seams near the intersection of the seam and the arm opening, begin at the armholes and pinch the excess fabric.
2. Mark and distribute the adjustment on both side seams vertically down the sleeve and transition into the original seam line; pin.
3. Mark new seam lines on both sides of the tucked seam with chalk.
4. If the sleeve is already sewn to the arm opening, open the seam to about 2" (5cm) on either side of the sleeve seam. This will allow access to the entire length of the sleeve. If the reduction is taken into the arm opening, the same amount must be removed from the upper seam of the adjoining sleeve.

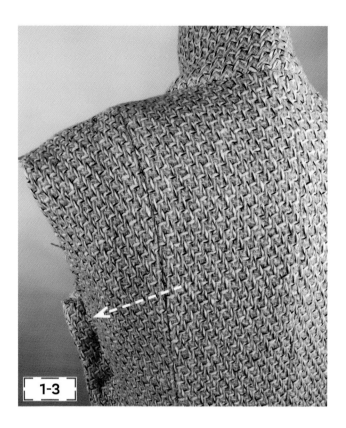

1-3

Adjusting a Narrow Jacket Body

1. If the jacket body is too tight at the side seams, open the side seams from the armhole to the waist.
2. Starting at the armhole, unfold the jacket back side seam allowance. Pin the folded edge to the jacket front outside the original seam allowance markings.
3. Taper the adjusted seam into the original seam at the waist, inserting pins as you go.
4. Mark the new seam lines on both sides of the adjustment with chalk.
5. If the adjustment intersects the arm opening then the same amount will need let out of the upper sleeves, so they sew back without a pucker.

2-4

ASSEMBLING THE JACKET

With the pattern refined and the first fitting complete, the next step is to take the fit sample apart and mark the pattern pieces precisely. Jacket assembly begins with the front of the jacket. The first steps include putting in waistline darts, stitching the underarm seam, and assembling the pockets.

Of all work on the jacket front, putting in pockets is the most demanding. The classic welt pocket is named for the wide welt, or doubled-over strip of fabric, that edges the opening. The two flap pockets on the sides have edgings of narrow welts, which tailors call piping, one below at the lip of the pocket opening and another one above where the flap is attached to the jacket.

After the pockets are on, the interfacing is permanently attached to the front. Then the jacket body is temporarily reassembled for the jacket's final fitting, but this time the sleeves are included.

Preparing the Jacket Front

1. On the wrong side of the jacket fronts, align the seam line of the dart. Stitch the waist darts. Cut open the fold of the dart to within ½" (1.5cm) of the tip.

2. On the wrong side, press open the body of the dart. Press flat the tips of the dart. Using a press cloth, carefully steam press the dart on the right side.

3. If the jacket has underarm darts, finish them as you did the waistline darts.

4. If the jacket has an underarm seam or side front panel, place the side panel on the jacket front right sides together. Align the seam and stitch. Press open.

1-2

3-4

Making the Jacket Front Pockets

For jackets that feature the classic welt pocket or a pocket flap, attach these to the front of the jacket next. Follow your specific pattern instructions or the welt pocket guide on page 261.

INTERFACING THE JACKET FRONT

Basting the Sew-In Interfacing to the Jacket Front

1. Place the two custom jacket front interfacing assemblies, cover cloth sides down, on a flat surface.

2. Position the left jacket front, wrong side down, over one of the interfacings so that the front edges and the lapel roll lines are aligned.

3. To baste the jacket front to the interfacing assembly you will be making several lines of 1" (2.5cm)–long basting stitches, here and in steps 4 and 8, which should not be removed until the jacket is finished. Begin the first line of basting about 4" (10cm) below the shoulder edge midway between the lapel roll line and the armhole and end about 4" (10cm) above the hem. The basting line will pass close to the center of the welt pocket and run about 1" (2.5cm) in front of the waistline dart and directly over the front of the flap pocket.

4. Run a second line of basting stitches parallel to the first, beginning halfway between the first line of basting and the lapel roll line. This line of basting will cross the front edge of the welt pocket.

5. Turn back the jacket front edge to the second line of basting, exposing the front edge of the welt pocket.

6. Fold back the reinforcement patch on the welt pocket to expose the seam allowances of the pocket assembly.

7. Fasten the welt pocket seam allowances to the interfacing with hemming stitches (page 28). Turn the edge of the jacket front down again over the interfacing.

8. Run a third line of basting stitches along the length of the lapel roll line, smoothing the garment fabric toward the front edge of the jacket as you proceed.

9. At the lower edge of the lapel roll line continue the basting about 1 ½" (4cm) from the front edge until you reach the hemline. So that the front of the finished garment will curve to the contours of the body, be sure to ease the garment fabric back from the interfacing edge as you baste. Ease the fabric ⅛" (3mm) for firm fabrics or ¼" (0.5cm) for soft fabrics.

1-2

3-9

Basting the Armhole to the Interfacing

1. Run a line of basting stitches about 2" (5cm) from the armhole edge, starting 4" (10cm) below the shoulder seam and ending at the underarm dart or seam. Smooth the fabric layers toward the armhole as you proceed.
2. Turn back the jacket front at the armhole edge and pull back the reinforcement patch of the welt pocket. Attach the seam allowances of the pocket assembly to the interfacing with hemming stitches.

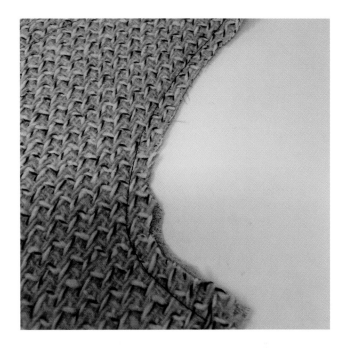

Padding the Lapel Interfacing

1. Place the jacket front wrong side down and fold back the lapel to the roll line. Hold the lapel in a curved shape so that the interfacing fabric eases in slightly toward the roll line.
2. Starting at the edge of the lapel next to the roll line, cover the entire lapel with rows of ⅜" (1cm)–long padding stitches (page 23). To keep the stitches from showing on the underside of the lapel, pick up only one thread of jacket fabric with each stitch. Do not stitch beyond the lapel roll line on the jacket fabric.
3. Place the lapel, wrong side up, on an ironing board, with the roll line at the edge of the board. Steam press thoroughly.
4. Turn the jacket assembly over, wrong side down, and steam press the lapel with a pressing cloth, holding the rest of the jacket front up so that the curve at the lapel roll line is not disturbed.
5. Repeat on the right front lapel.

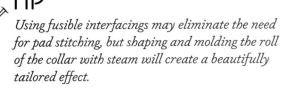

TIP

Using fusible interfacings may eliminate the need for pad stitching, but shaping and molding the roll of the collar with steam will create a beautifully tailored effect.

THE SECOND FITTING

Assembling the Sleeves

1. Working on one sleeve at a time, place the undersleeve piece on a flat surface wrong side down. Position the upper sleeve piece over it, wrong side up and aligning the inside seam lines, i.e., the seam that will be at the underarm when worn. Pin.
2. Baste and remove the pins.
3. Align and pin the outside seam lines. Then baste from the top edge, through the vent opening if there is one, to the lower edge. Remove the pins.
4. Turn up the hem allowance at the bottom of the sleeve and pin. Baste ½" (1.5cm) from the folded edge. Remove the pins.
5. On the top of the sleeve, run a line of machine basting stitches (about six stitches to the inch [2.5cm]) between the notches, ¼" (0.5cm) above the seam line. Leave enough loose thread at each, approximately 4" (10cm), so that you can grasp it firmly when you ease the material.

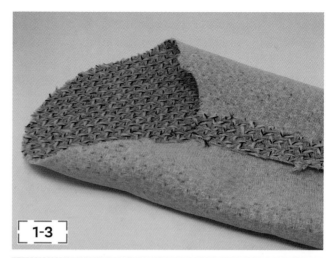

1-3

4

Finishing the Preparatory Assembly

1. Finish the jacket assembly as you did for the muslin by first fitting and stitching the shoulder and side seams forming the jacket. Then turn the jacket wrong side out.

2. Turn one of the sleeves right side out. Insert the sleeve into its corresponding armhole. Then align the seam lines, matching and pinning at the pattern markings.

3. Pull the loose threads gently to ease in the fullness on the top of the sleeve. Pin. Baste and remove the pins.

4. Repeat steps 2 and 3 on the other sleeve.

5. Turn the jacket right side out. Attach the shoulder pads.

6. Try on the jacket to check the fit and make appropriate adjustments. Pin the front jacket together, overlapping the button marks. Be sure the hem of the jacket is even all the way around. If the jacket wrinkles at the underarm, build up the shoulder pads. Adjust the position of the sleeve if necessary.

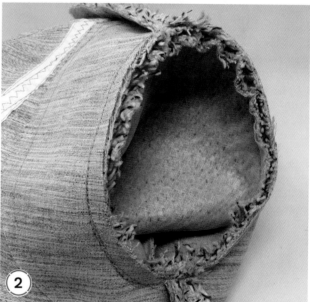

FINISHING THE JACKET FRONT

After the jacket's second fitting adjustments have been made, the remaining work on the front should be completed. This means adding the facings—lengths of garment fabric that run down the inside of each front section and, when turned outward, form the surface of the lapels. Attached correctly, the facings help the jacket front keep its shape. A woman's jacket, which uses lighter weight, more delicate lining fabrics, is lined only after it has been fully constructed.

1. On the inside, trim the lapel and front edges of the interfacing from the hemline to the front end of the gorge line (upper edge) so that the interfacing is flush with the seam lines on the jacket front.

2. Continue to trim the interfacing just inside the seam lines along the gorge line and around the neck edge. Be careful not to trim off the twill tape on the lapel roll line.

3. Hand sew along the trimmed gorge line and neck edge with a catch stitch (page 27). Pick up only one or two threads of the jacket fabric with each stitch. Note: The gorge line is the area where the body of the lapel attaches to the collar.

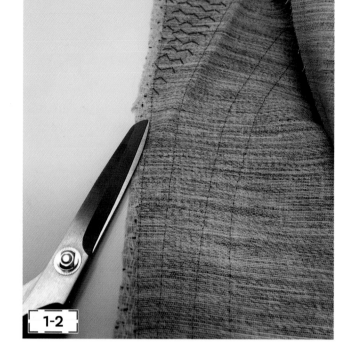

1-2

The Front Reinforcement Tape

1. Place twill tape so that its outer edge is aligned with the gorge line and its end overlaps the tape already on the lapel roll line. Pin at the roll line. Pull the tape taut. Pin along the gorge line.

2. At the upper corner of the lapel, clip the tape to, but not through, the outer edge. Then turn the tape so that the outer edge is aligned with the front edge of the interfacing. Keep the outer edge of the tape aligned with the front edge of the interfacing. Continue pinning the tape flat until you are 1" (2.5cm) above the curved edge at the bottom of the jacket or, if the bottom of the jacket is square, 2" (5cm) above the corner.

3. If the jacket bottom is curved, pull the tape taut and pin at ½" (1.5cm) intervals around the curve. If the edge is square, clip and pin to the corner the same as step 2.

4. Pin the tape flat along the hemline to 2" (5cm) beyond the end of the interfacing. If you are working with loosely woven material, continue pinning the tape as far as the side seam line to reinforce the entire front hemline.

Sewing on the Reinforcement Tape

1. Run a line of basting stitches along the center of the tape and remove the pins.
2. Using small hemming stitches, sew the inner edge and the clips of the tape to the interfacing layer. When you reach the end of the interfacing at the hemline, sew the inner edge to the jacket, picking up only one or two threads of garment fabric as you sew.
3. Attach the outer edge of the tape to the interfacing along the gorge line. Then sew the rest of the outer edge to the jacket, again picking up only one or two threads of garment fabric. Remove the basting and steam press the tape.

Attaching the Facing to the Jacket Front

1. With right sides together, place the jacket front facing on the jacket front.
2. Locate the ends of the lapel roll line and the button placement lines on the jacket and transfer the marks to the facing with chalk.
3. On the facing only, run a line of 1" (2.5cm) basting stitches on the roll line. Run a second line of basting ½" (1.5cm) inside the front seam line. Begin at the top button mark. As you baste, ease the facing fabric ⅛" (3mm) in from the front edge between the top and bottom button marks. This easing will provide for extra fabric that will be needed when you make the buttonholes and attach the buttons.
4. Continue the basting below the bottom button mark, this time keeping the edges of the facing and jacket front aligned.
5. As you baste around the edge, pull taut the facing fabric so that the edge will curve slightly toward the body when the jacket is worn. If the front edge of your jacket is square, begin to pull the facing taut about 1" (2.5cm) above the corner. End the basting at the inner seam, or edge, on the facing before the lining.
6. Make a third line of basting, this time starting at the top button mark and sewing 1" (2.5cm) inside the lapel edge up to the shoulder edge. For the first 2" (5cm), ease in the facing fabric ⅛" (3mm) from the front edge. Align the front edges and continue basting until you are about 3" (7.5cm) from the top of the lapel. Next, ease in the facing fabric again ⅛" (3mm) from the edges and baste around the corner for about 3" (7.5cm). Align the edges again and continue the basting up to the shoulder edge.

Stitching the Front Edge

1. Turn over the assembled jacket front so that the interfaced side is up. Machine stitch on the front seam line just outside the twill tape. Stitch between the front end of the gorge line and the inner edge of the bottom of the facing.

2. At the point where the stitching meets the gorge line, make a diagonal clip in the seam allowances, angling the clip toward the armhole. Clip up to, but not into, the stitching.

3. Remove the tailor tacks and the bastings. Press open the front seam, using a sleeve board or point presser.

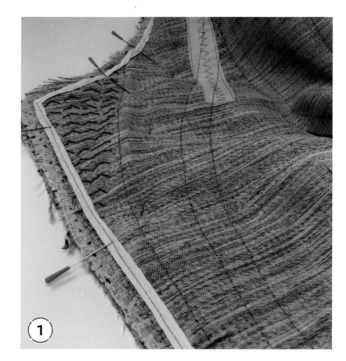

Trimming

1. Trim the seam allowances diagonally at the lapel corner. If you are making a jacket with a square lower corner, trim the lower corner too.

2. Trim the jacket front seam allowance to a width of ⅛" (3mm) between the clip and the front edge of the hem allowance.

3. Trim the seam allowance of the facing between the same points to a width of ¼" (0.5cm).

Shaping the Front Edge

1. Turn the assembled jacket front right side out.

2. Using a point turner, carefully push out the lapel corner and the lower corner if your jacket has a square corner.

3. Starting at the center front, gently roll the seam between your fingers, bringing the stitches to the edge.

4. Starting at the upper edge of the lapel, roll the seam again so that the stitching is turned ⅟₁₆" (2mm) toward the jacket front. To keep the seam in that position while the jacket is being completed, run a line of ¼" (0.5cm) basting stitches ¼" (0.5cm) from the edge. Continue rolling and basting in this manner until you are 2" (5cm) above the top button mark.

5. For the next 2" (5cm), keep the seam directly on the edge as you baste.

6. When you reach the top button mark, roll the stitching in the other direction so that it is turned ⅟₁₆" (2mm) toward the facing. Baste. Then continue in this manner to the hem end of the seam.

7. Now run a line of 1" (2.5cm) basting stitches 1" (2.5cm) inside the first line, smoothing out the fabric from the first line as you proceed. Do not remove this basting and the first line of basting until the jacket is completed.

8. Turn over the assembled jacket front so that the facing side is down. Turn back the lapel along the lapel roll line and, holding it in a curved shape, make a row of 1" (2.5cm) diagonal basting stitches along the roll line. Do not remove this basting also until the jacket is completed.

9. Use a catch stitch to attach the inner edge of the facing to the interfacing, ending 3" (7.5cm) above the hem edge. Be careful not to catch the jacket front fabric in your stitches. Repeat on the other jacket front.

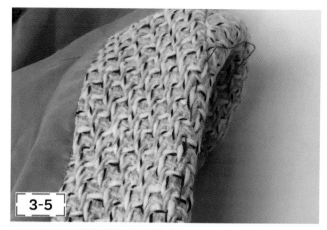

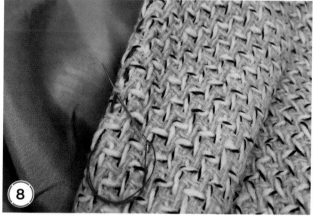

JOINING THE JACKET BACK TO THE FRONT

Styling details of the jacket back dictate slightly different assembly procedures. For example, a man's jacket is almost always vented, its back skirt split to provide easy access to the pants pockets. The slit must be reinforced with twill tape before the vent and center seam can be stitched.

After this step is completed, the jacket back is sewn to the fronts along the side seams. Because the finishing of the hem is easier if the jacket sections can be spread out flat, the shoulder seams are not sewn until later. If the fabric is a soft one, such as camel hair or a novelty tweed, the hem must also be reinforced with twill tape to keep it from stretching. Once hemmed, the lining is inserted.

A woman's jacket may or may not have vents and is not lined until it has been fully constructed. But the back does require interfacing around the shoulders. And if its fabric is soft, the hem, too, must be reinforced with interfacing cut on the bias.

Assembling the Jacket Back

1. To join the jacket backs if there is no vent, place the two backs together, right sides together. Pin and baste along the center back seam line. Remove the pins. Then machine stitch and remove the basting. Steam press the seam open.

2. Place the jacket back wrong side up and lay the upper back interfacing over it, making sure that the side with the bias strips on the darts faces up. Align the edges of the interfacing with the shoulder seam lines on the jacket back, then pin.

3. To create the same fullness in the interfacing as you have in the jacket at the shoulders, ease in the interfacing slightly away from each armhole edge. Pin.

4. Baste 1" (2.5cm) inside all the edges of the interfacing, except the lower edge. Remove the pins.

5. Hand sew along the shoulder and sew the neck and side edges with a catch stitch. Pick up only one or two threads of the jacket fabric with each stitch.

6. Remove the bastings except for those along the armholes.

(1)

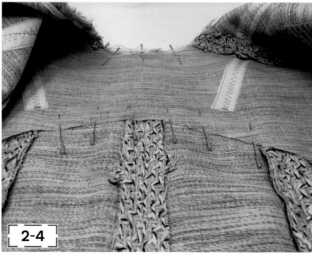

2-4

TIP

For jackets with a vent, follow the pattern guide, making sure you reinforce the vent opening with twill tape.

Closing the Side Seams

1. Place the right sides of the jacket together and align the side seams. Pin and slightly ease the fabric between the waistline and armhole. Baste and remove pins.
2. Machine stitch, being careful not to catch the edge of the back interfacing. Remove the basting. Press the seam open.

Reinforcing the Hem

If you are using a soft jacket fabric such as camel hair or some tweeds, you need to reinforce the hem.

1. From interfacing material, cut a bias strip the length from one facing edge to the other and 1" (2.5cm) wider than your hem allowance.
2. Place the strip along the hem, so that the lower edge of the strip extends ½" (1.5cm) below the hemline. Pin.
3. Baste along the center of the strip and remove the pins.
4. Hand sew along the hemline with running stitches. With each stitch, pick up only one or two threads of the jacket fabric. Remove the basting.

1-2

Hemming the Jacket

1. Turn up the hem allowance along the hemline and pin. Baste ¼" (0.5cm) from the folded edge and remove the pins.
2. If you did not reinforce the hem, hand sew along the unattached edge of the hem with small hemming stitches. With each stitch, catch only one or two threads of the jacket fabric. Remove the basting and the tailor tacks.
3. Steam press the hem edge with a pressing cloth.
4. If you reinforced the hem with a bias strip, hand sew the unattached edge of the hem to the bias strip with small hemming stitches, being careful not to catch the jacket fabric. Remove the basting and the tailor tacks. Then steam press the hem edge with a pressing cloth.
5. Use a catch stitch to sew the edge of the bias strip to the jacket fabric. With each stitch, catch only one or two threads of the jacket fabric.

SEWING THE JACKET COLLAR

A jacket's body assembly becomes complete when the shoulder seam is stitched and the collar put on. Tailored collars have three layers: an undercollar, a reinforcing layer of interfacing, and the upper collar, the only layer that is visible when the jacket is worn.

In a woman's jacket, the undercollar is cut from the same fabric as the jacket itself and the whole collar is completed before being attached to the jacket.

Sewing the collar to each lapel also demands particular care. The seam between them, known as the gorge line, is the most prominent seam in the entire jacket, and it is finished by hand so it will be as smooth and inconspicuous as possible. .

Sewing the Shoulder Seam

1. With right sides together, align and match the front shoulders to the back shoulder seams. A light amount of easing the back into the front may be required if the back shoulder dart was not formed. This easing should be placed 1" (2.5cm) away from the neckline.
2. Pin. Baste along the seam line and remove the pins.
3. Machine stitch, being careful not to catch other layers of fabric. Remove the basting in the seam only, not the ease basting on the back shoulder seam allowance.
4. Press open the seam, being careful not to stretch the fabric. The seam should curve slightly toward the jacket front at the armhole edge; do not try to straighten it.
5. Turn the assembled jacket right side out.
6. Smooth the front interfacing over the shoulder seam toward the jacket back and baste along the shoulder seam.

1-4

Assembling the Collar

Once the shoulder seam has been sewn, the lapel collar is the next step when making a tailored jacket. The collar component is featured in garment details on page 246.

Adding Sleeves

Following the collar, the tailored sleeve is the last main component to attach before the finishing touches. Reference page 233 in the garment detail chapter for complete sleeve instructions.

Attaching the Shoulder Pad

1. Lift the jacket, but not the sleeve, wrong side out so that the shoulder falls in a rounded shape.
2. Place the shoulder pad over the interfacings so that the pad's straight edge is aligned with the armhole seam allowances with its widest point centered over the shoulder seam. Approximately two-thirds of the shoulder pad should be on the back interfacing. If the pad is too large, trim the edges.
3. Pin the pad at its three corners.
4. Put your hand between the front interfacing and the jacket fabric and make several 1" (2.5cm) long padding stitches on the front third of the shoulder pad, catching it to the front interfacing. To sew through the pad, insert the needle with a stabbing motion, then pull it through from the other side. If you want to reduce the thickness of the pad, pull the stitches tight. Remove the pins.

Sewing the Buttonholes

The most important last touches on a tailored jacket, and the most visible, are the hand sewing of the buttonholes and the final pressing. A buttonhole is simply a slit outlined with tiny stitches, but practice is needed to make sure the stitches are identical in size and spacing. Do not start directly on the jacket. Practice on two layers of garment fabric with interfacing between them to simulate the actual jacket. Remember, women's buttonholes are on the right. To learn how to create hand buttonholes, turn to page 267.

ADDING THE FINISHING TOUCHES

1. Remove all remaining basting and tailor tacks on the jacket.
2. Press the entire jacket to bring out its shape.
3. For a woman's jacket, assemble and attach the lining (page 272) and touch up the pressing using a pressing cloth and clapper.
4. Sew on the buttons. You have a finished jacket!

CHAPTER 5

ULTIMATE PANTS WORKBOOK

With simple lines and proportions, an accurately fitted pants pattern will help you make most trousers and casual pants, which can then be stylized into jeans, shorts, leggings, and other creative designs. If you can master the front fly and side pockets, then you can confidently sew a variety of pants and fabrics to suit any occasion.

Many sewists experience unique challenges with pants fitting that can be easily resolved with the right strategy and approach. However, there is a functional aspect to sewing and fitting pants that is not learned from traditional instruction, because the typical solutions are limited in scope. The key to success in fitting pants is to make the pattern match the unique dynamics of the leg. The diversity in figure types, shapes, and sizes can create challenges when trying to achieve a perfect fit, yet rewarding when you understand how to address and resolve the cause of the problem. Common fitting issues you may encounter include leg twist, binding in the seam, or excess fabric below the derriere.

By following this chapter step-by-step, you will be guaranteed great success in your next pants fitting.

How to use this chapter: This chapter features a complete step-by-step systematic approach to pant fitting. Instead of seeking multiple fit methods, focus your approach on learning how to adjust a classic trouser pant pattern to your unique body shape. Once you have a pattern that matches your body proportions, you'll learn the common core pant adjustments used to refine the fit and then how to modify the pattern to create any style of pant.

straight   skinny   boot-cut   flare   wide leg   pegged   stirrup

5-pocket jeans   bush pants   cargo pants   sailor pants   jodhpurs   hot pants   skort   sweatpants

Pants come in a variety of styles to fit any shape, contour, or body type. The pant leg may be slim fitting, straight and tailored, or baggy and full.

harem   palazzo   carpenter / overall   jumpsuit

LEG CHARACTERISTICS

The first step in fitting a pair of pants is evaluating the leg so that you better understand how the pattern will interact with the body and leg movements. The front is distinctively different than the back, so the corresponding pattern pieces need to be measured separately. A single full hip measurement, for example, does not tell you how much space is needed in the front and how much in the back. If the pattern does not match your body correctly, then a fit issue will occur. The following are leg dynamics that impact how you fit, style, and sew a pant. They also illustrate why most pant patterns require customization to attain that priceless, perfect-fitting pair of pants.

ABDOMEN AND HIPS

- High or low hip
- Rounded or flat abdomen
- Hip span with wide or narrow bone structure
- Saddle bags on the front low hip
- Low buttocks across the back
- Pelvic tilt and waistline placement
- Saddle contour of the crotch curve
- Swayback

BODY MASS

- Solid muscle placement
- Pliable soft tissue
- Loose body mass
- Loss of muscle tone

LEG SHAPE

- Fuller thighs
- Thin and narrow leg
- Thin, but wide leg
- Chubby legs
- Athletic leg
- Fuller calves
- Legs spaced apart
- Inner legs touching
- Knock-knees

Which of these characterize your figure and how might they affect fit? Take a look at an unaltered pant pattern and see if it would match your figure. You might be surprised at the difference.

In this model evaluation, we see a wide hip span with thin, yet full, legs. The waist to hip has a natural hourglass contour, the tummy is flat, the legs fill the distance from the side seam to center front, and the thighs touch. Overall, the model is symmetrical from left to right.

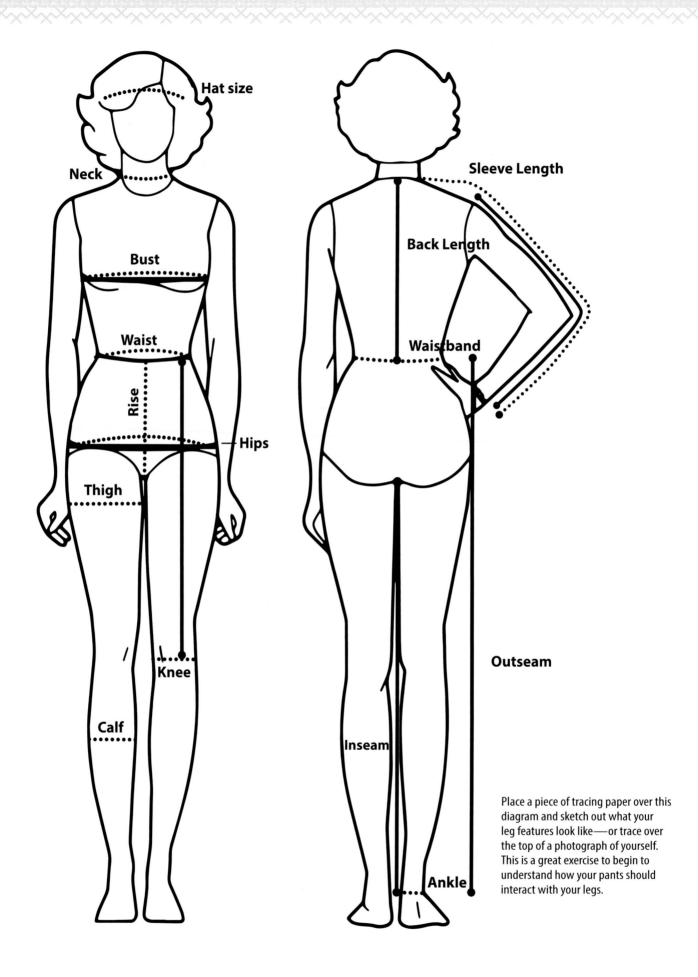

Hat size

Neck

Bust

Waist

Rise

Hips

Thigh

Knee

Calf

Sleeve Length

Back Length

Waistband

Outseam

Inseam

Ankle

Place a piece of tracing paper over this diagram and sketch out what your leg features look like—or trace over the top of a photograph of yourself. This is a great exercise to begin to understand how your pants should interact with your legs.

MEASURING THE BODY

Once you have evaluated your leg, the next step is to take your body measurements using the areas listed on the measurement chart as a guide. You can always take more measurements that are unique to your body.

Use adhesive dots to mark start and stop points for accuracy. Taking smaller areas of measurement is always more accurate and allows you to adjust in the correct part of your pattern rather than simply on the edge. For example, the full hip measurement is only used to determine a pattern size for a starting point. On the actual pattern piece, you will measure smaller areas on the front separate from the back.

Always measure from your natural waistline even if the final garment will sit lower on your body. For consistency, also sew your fit sample to match your natural waistline when placing the pants on your body as you are refining your fit. Once the fit sample is polished to perfection you can crop and restyle the height of the waistband.

FITTING THE PANTS PATTERN

The pants pattern includes the waist, abdomen, thigh, and crotch areas. The abdomen area is located approximately a third of the way between the waist and the hip, and the hip area extends through the widest part of the upper part of the pants. The thigh is placed 3" (7.5cm) below the fork of the crotch, and the crotch depth is marked from the natural waist down to a point directly over from the fork of the pants.

Correctly fitting pants requires a crotch shape that has a more natural and flattering fit. The European cut pattern is the standard for a more tailored fit. The front curve is shorter than the back. The front seam is straight while the back is curved, using the bias of the fabric to refine the fit. The style of the pants happens in the front, while the fit happens in the back. Sewing this type of crotch curve is not achieved in one single half circle type of seam. Instead, the front is sewn to the front and the back to the back. The intersecting crotch seam is pinned and each inseam is stitched separately toward the crotch seam, rather than in a continuous U-shape.

More pattern designers feature the European cut, thus making it relatively easy to find, and this style of pants crotch curve is recommended to proceed with the following instruction. If your pattern is different, or you are not sure, you will want to pay close attention to the instructions for fitting the crotch curve on page 190.

POPULAR PANT FABRICS AND HOW FABRICS AFFECT FIT

The perfect pair of pants occurs when there is a successful combination of the style/silhouette, the fit, and, of course, the fabric. Each is important, but the fabric is the most functional and tactile element that may visibly indicate a fit or style issue. Fabric selection is more than picking your favorite color from a list of suitable fabrics on the back of a pattern envelope, although the pattern envelope is a good place to start. This guide will suggest certain fabrics that the designer had in mind when creating the pattern, but the same pattern made from different fabrics will have different results in fit, feel, and overall aesthetics.

Take a pair of jeans for example. The horizontal drag lines across the rise are a sought-after characteristic of this fashion staple, but those same lines on a wool trouser indicates a fit issue. The only difference in these pants may be the fabric. One worked well for the intended look while the other did not. So how do you select the best fabric for a pair of pants?

Your fabric selection should meet the needs of the final pant. First, is the fabric suitable for the style of pant? Should the fabric be drapey and soft for a palazzo pant, structured yet pliable for a trouser, or stiff and durable for a pair of jeans? Will you feel comfortable with the fabric against your skin? Will the fabric bend, drape, or retain its shape based on how the pant will be worn? If the fabric has stretch, what is the stretch recovery? The seat or knee area of pants stretch with the body, but the fabric should recover to the original shape after movement. Saggy knees and seats are unattractive and will cause the pant to stretch out.

Is the fabric flattering? If the fabric will not look good on your body, shape, or size, then select a different option. Lastly, what is the care of the fabric? If you are spending the time to fit and sew a beautiful pair of custom pants, then test the fabric before sewing. Does the color fade or retain vibrancy? Does the fabric shrink? A fabric that shrinks may still be suitable, but you may need to hand wash and lay flat to dry to avoid shrinkage from heat. Once your fabric is chosen, preshrink and wash it just like you would the final pant. It is recommended that custom trousers and pants be washed in cool water and line dried or laid flat to dry.

With a few well-thought-out decisions, your fabric selection will complement your pant design. Following is a quick guide to some common pant fabric choices to consider.

- **Fine wool suiting:** lightweight, stable grain, no stretch, sews beautifully. Perfect for trousers.
- **Stretch gaberdine:** stable grain, slight stretch in the crossgrain, great for trousers, slight stretch provides comfort, easy to care for. The stretch adds ease in the pattern, so you may need to take deeper side seams to tighten up the fit.
- **Stretch cotton poplin:** moderate degree of stretch allows for fit around curvy figure, flexible, used in capri or chino type pants, can be styled for jeggings. Also great for trousers with a more casual look.
- **Twill:** cotton twill pants have a little more structure than the stretch cotton, sews beautifully, great for embroidery and decorative stitching, available in a lot of colors. Stretch twill will have a small amount of spandex to create the stretch.
- **Shantung:** this delicate fashion fabric comes in just about any color. By backing the fabric with fusible knit interfacing, you can stabilize the fabric and make dressy trousers, or capri pants for a more fashionable look.
- **Georgette:** this sheer fabric makes for a beautiful, flowy, elegant pant. Available in many colors.

FRONT

Vertical   Horizontal Half Body

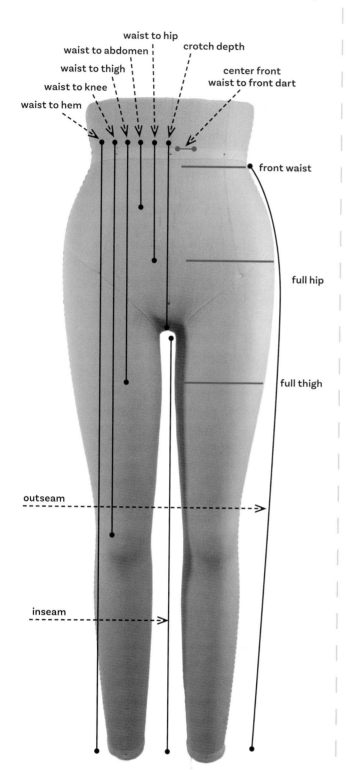

waist to hip
waist to abdomen
waist to thigh
waist to knee
waist to hem

crotch depth

center front
waist to front dart

front waist

full hip

full thigh

outseam

inseam

BACK

Vertical   Horizontal

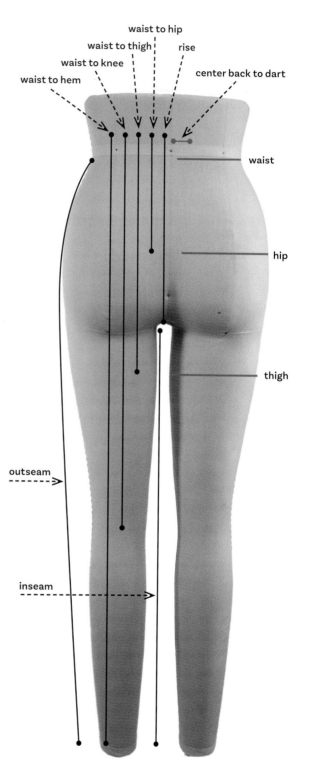

waist to hip
waist to thigh
waist to knee
waist to hem

rise

center back to dart

waist

hip

thigh

outseam

inseam

BODY MEASUREMENTS FOR PANTS FITTING: APPLY TO YOUR BASIC PANT BLOCK

MEASUREMENTS

(always use natural waistline for measuring and fitting; then you can style it lower)

VERTICAL

- Front Waist to Abdomen_____
- Front Waist to Hip_____
- Back Waist to Hip_____
- Waist to Full Thigh_____
- Waist to Knee_____
- Waist to Hip at Side Seam_____
- Back Rise_____ Crotch Depth Front_____
- Back Waist to Knee_____
- Total Crotch Curve_____
- Inseam_____
- Outseam_____
- Waist to Floor Front_____
- Waist to Floor Back_____

HORIZONTAL

- Full Waist_____
- Abdomen Front_____
- Full Hip_____
- Front Hip_____
- Back Hip_____
- Center Front to Side Front at Waist_____
- Side Front to Side Seam at Waist_____
- Center Back to Side Back at Waist_____
- Side Back to Side Seam at Waist_____
- Left Thigh Full_____
- Right Thigh Full_____
- Front Left Thigh_____
- Front Right Thigh_____
- Back Left Thigh_____
- Back Right Thigh_____

CROTCH DEPTH: Sit in a chair with arms to your side. Measure from the waist to the chair. Take the measurement plus ½" (1.3cm) or a little more for fuller hips.

THIGH: 3" (7.6cm) below crotch point or at fullest area

EASE: What amount do you need to add in addition to body measurements?

EASE: Quadrant (4 quadrants per leg); distribute according to leg dynamics

PLUMB LINE DOWN LEG: Use tape or string to create a plumb line to divide the quadrants

PLUMB LINE DOWN INSEAM: Attach a string with a weight to the crotch and let it hang down the inseam to divide the pant

ADJUSTING YOUR PATTERN

There are a few guidelines to understand before you adjust your pattern to match your custom body shape. This is a slightly non-traditional approach to pants fitting, so understanding the protocol of how to address the pants pattern will ensure you achieve the intended results.

Body Prep

1. Begin with a pattern that fits closest to your full hip. It is not custom and will need adjusted; however, this will serve as your guide to get started.
2. Always wear correct foundation garments for each fitting.
3. Shoes and heel height affect your posture and how pants hang on the body. Wear the same shoe for each fitting.
4. Apply body contouring such as a hip pad to level out the hip and other padding if necessary.

Pattern Prep: Apply to Unaltered Pattern

1. Draw a horizontal balance line (HBL) across the upper part of the pants pattern. A hip line will also serve as an HBL.
2. Remove the seam allowance so you can see the exact areas on the pattern that will interact with the leg.
3. **Make a crotch curve template (see template lesson on page 190).**
4. Draw the horizontal abdomen line on the pattern about one-third of the way down from the waist if not already marked.

Pattern Adjusting Protocol

1. Adjust top to bottom.
2. Apply vertical adjustments first.
3. Apply horizontal adjustments second.
4. Treat the front separately from the back.
5. Use the smaller areas of measurement.
6. Never adjust on the edge of an area of fit. Always adjust your pattern within the area you are measuring, so the adjustment is distributed throughout the entire area.
7. Adjust the pattern to match your body measurements, and then apply ease.
8. Do not include seam allowance or fitting elements, such as darts, when measuring your pattern. Darts and fitting elements are meant to be sewn up and add no space to the pattern.
9. You are not making your body fit the pattern—you are making the pattern fit your body.

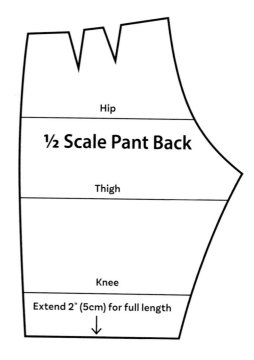

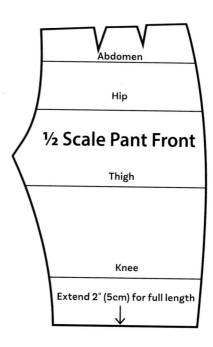

How to use a half-scale pant pattern: Use this half-scale pattern (downloadable for free in the store at *www.designerjoi.com*) to practice pant fitting and the adjustments before you apply them to a full-size pattern. You can even use the half-scale pattern with your own measurements. Simply divide your measurements in half and apply all the fitting lessons to the half-scale pattern. Once you have made a perfect proportion half-scale template, you can take it to a copy center and have it enlarged 200 percent, which will make it a full-size pattern. You will still need to follow the crotch curve fitting lesson and make a muslin fit sample for final refinements. The half-scale pattern is also ideal for practicing creative style design in the proportion of your body.

AREAS OF MEASURE ON THE PATTERN

Adjusting the Pattern

The process for altering is to take your body measurements and adjust the pattern to match, resulting in a custom-graded pants pattern. This step eliminates major fit issues due to inaccurate pattern proportion in relation to the body.

1. Measure you/measure your pattern: Measure an area of the body and compare to the same area on the pants pattern. If they are the same, do nothing. If the pattern is smaller than your body measurement, then you need to increase the pattern to match your body. If the pattern is bigger than your body measurement, decrease that area of the pattern.

2. Increase or decrease: Draw a cutting line on your pattern in the middle of the area to be adjusted. For example, if the waist to hip needs to be longer, do not cut on the hip line. Adjust in between. It may seem counterintuitive to add to an area and then decrease to another in that they may balance each other out. But the result is a perfect proportion pattern to your body mass.

3. Refine the pattern: As you modify your pattern, you will need to true up the edges. Take your ruler and connect any edges that have been cut to create a continuous line.

These horizontal and vertical adjustments are very systematic and meant to grade the pattern to your own body proportions. Some adjustments may cause the front and back to have different side seam lengths. Temporary discrepancies from front to back are to be expected because we are treating them separately. They will be joined together in the muslin. Remember: It is still a flat 2D paper pattern and will need final polishing in a muslin fit sample.

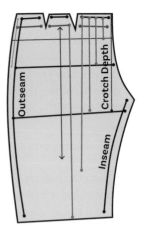

The front pattern with lines illustrating areas of measure that correspond to the same areas on the body.

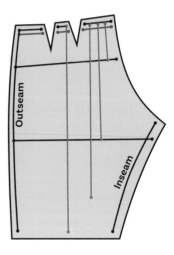

The back pattern with lines illustrating areas of measure that correspond to the same areas on the body.

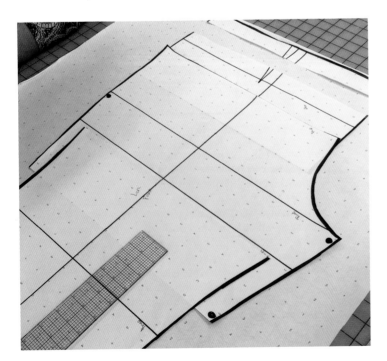

This pattern has been adjusted vertically to match the student's custom measurements. The waist to abdomen has been increased to match a longer front tummy. The waist to hip has a reduction so the length matches the body. Even though one area has been increased and the other decreased, it is important to make the adjustments in the areas of fit for the ultimate custom pattern. The final length adjustment is shortening the waist to the full thigh. The outer edges of the pattern are temporarily uneven during the pattern adjustment. Once the vertical areas are fitted, and the horizontal areas are corrected, then the outer edges can be connected and refined using a ruler. The final step will be adding the custom crotch curve template before creating a muslin fitting sample.

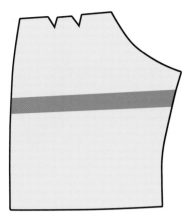

To adjust vertical areas of measure on the back pattern, a line will be drawn on the pattern in the areas being fitted. Cut the line and add to lengthen or overlap to shorten.

To adjust vertical areas of measure on the front pattern, a line will be drawn on the pattern in the areas being fitted. Cut the line and add to lengthen or overlap to shorten.

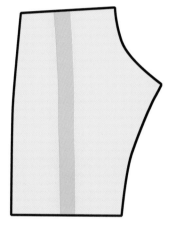

To adjust horizontal or circumference areas of measure on the back pattern, space can be added to the side seam or a line will be drawn vertically on the pattern in the areas being fitted. Cut the line and widen to make larger or overlap to narrow the pattern.

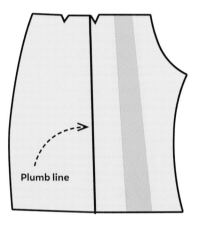

Plumb line

To adjust horizontal or circumference areas of measure on the front pattern, space can be added to the side seam or a line will be drawn vertically on the pattern in the areas being fitted. Cut the line and widen to make larger or overlap to narrow the pattern.

Before You Begin

Before you begin, match the side seams of the pattern and make a notch on the front and back side seam approximately 4" (10cm) down from the natural waist. This will be used to help line up the pants after adjustments have been made, and it may be adjusted in the muslin fitting. Make an additional notch 4" (10cm) down the inseam on the front and back pant pattern.

Also, trace the unaltered crotch curve on the front and back of the pants pattern onto a separate piece of paper to use as a template in the next step.

The crotch depth measurement is a final check in the upper area of the front pattern. Once the waist to hip has been adjusted, re-measure the waist to the fork of the front crotch curve and compare. Adjust the upper area of the pattern to match if necessary.

The waist to hip at the side seam is the last area to adjust. Measure from the hip line on the front up toward the waist at the side seam. Add or reduce length by extending the side seam upward or downward. Blend toward the center front. Those with a high hip will use the adjustment. Because the side seam is shared from the front to back, this area will be adjusted the same front to back.

Once all adjustments have been made, measure down the side seam from the top to the bottom and compare to your body outseam measurement. Add or reduce near the hem of the pattern.

Draw an imaginary plumb line down the leg from the side front, the area where the waist would line up with a dart on the torso, and evaluate your leg characteristics and placement of body mass. Once all the adjustments on the pattern are made, the proportion of the pattern will match your leg.

FITTING THE CROTCH CURVE TEMPLATE

The crotch curve is often referred to as the saddle of the pants. Just like customizing the armscye, the crotch curve on the pants may need to be custom-shaped to match your unique curves. Before you customize this shape, you first want to scale your pattern using the tips listed previously. Once the body of the pattern matches your body, you can address the crotch curve, which is on the edge of the pattern. Fitting a crotch curve template eliminates having to fit multiple full pants muslins. A template is free to make and quick to fit and results in numerous fitting issues being eliminated.

How to Make a Template

Take the tracing of the front and back crotch curve from the unaltered pattern and trace onto muslin with no seam allowance included. To make the template fit the body, and because the edge of the pattern is simply a line, trace about 3" (5cm) out from the edge of the pattern. Cut the template in a double layer of muslin to help stabilize the edges of the template. Stitch the layers together on the front separate from the back. Next, stitch the templates together at the crotch seam. If your pattern is a true European cut, the template may not lay flat on your cutting table—this is normal. The seam may also be at an angle.

Place a plumb line on the template using a ribbon or a string. Tie a weight on the bottom and stitch to the crotch seam. It may look a little funny, but the results are priceless.

Fitting the Template

Put on your prettiest skivvies, a leotard, or swimsuit and fit the template to your unique body shape. Place the front curve next to your front and wrap the template around the back. Raise or lower until you reach a comfortable position. Rotate the template forward or toward the back until the plumb line hangs down the inseam. Determine how close you want the curve to fit your body. On woven fabrics and on standard trouser pants, approximately 1" (2.5cm) is a guide for how far the template should sit away from your body. Avoid a snug fit as it may cause your pants to bind. Once you have a comfortable position, pin the template to your natural waist on the front and the back. If you are fitting yourself, you should be able to pin the front and reach around and mark the back with chalk.

A fitting template is a tracing of an area of a pattern made from the unaltered pattern. The template is then used to draw back an area of the pattern if the pattern has been modified. In the pant pattern, a tracing of the crotch curve helps refine fit in an area of pant that often has subtle fit issues.

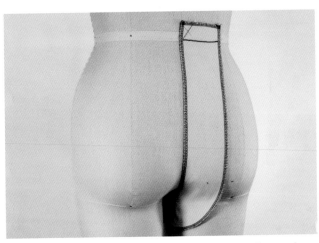

The paper tracing of the pattern used in the fitting template can be sewn in a double layer of muslin. The muslin can then be fitted and contoured to the body and fitted. This is a wonderful technique that saves time from making a fit sample and having to redo the sample because you did not fit the crotch curve prior to sewing.

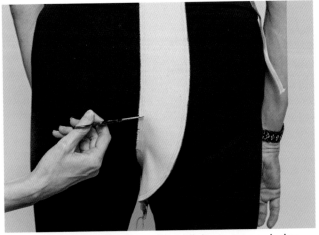

To custom shape your template, take small clips to open and relax the curve to add space to the crotch curve. If the template sits away from the body, then measure the distance and trace that space into the curve to lessen the angle. Once the final shape has been matched to the body, you can pin tiny horizontal angles on the template to remove any horizontal excess.

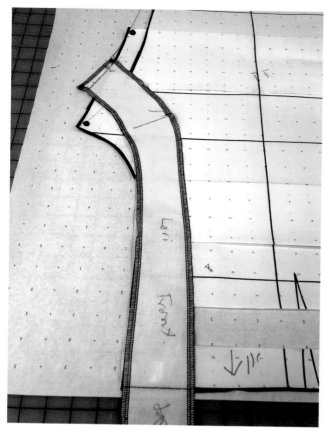

At first glance, the correctly fitted muslin crotch curve template may look dramatically different when placed on the original edge of the pattern, but this will reflect the correct contours of the front and back of your body. Make sure you are only tracing the center front edge of the template. It is normal for the fork (lower edge of the curve) to have a different angle than the unaltered pattern. Resist the urge to use the original, because it will not fit correctly.

Test the Fit
- Is it comfortable?
- Does it bind?
- Is it baggy?
- Can you sit, stand, walk, or do yoga?

Using the Template
Place your template on your altered pattern by matching the natural waistline. Trace the template shape onto your pant. Using the template allows you to make custom adjustments to the body of the pants pattern that may initially intersect the crotch curve, and then allows you to replace that with a curve that fits your body according to your preferences. Can you see why the natural waist is a key area for achieving the best fit? Trace the edge of the template.

Troubleshooting the Fit
- If pants sit away from the body, then add to the crotch curve.
- If pants sit close to the body, then cut away, creating space in the curve.
- If the seat drops down, then add to crotch curve length.
- If the template has any wrinkles or folds, pin those out.

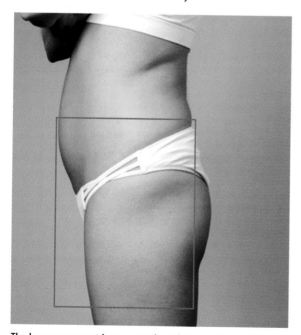
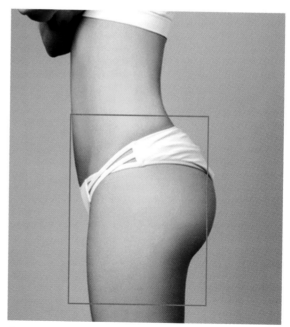

The boxes represent how an unaltered pant pattern will lay against the contours of the body. In this example you can see why a custom curve template would be beneficial in achieving the correct fit. The same unaltered pattern placed on either figure would create many fit issues. How might the same unaltered crotch curve fit differently on the front or back of either model? Where would the finished pant or crotch curve bind on the body if the pattern is not fitted prior to sewing? Where would the pant or crotch curve hang too far away from the body if sewn without fitting?

PATTERN MARKINGS, EASE, AND SEAM ALLOWANCE

Pattern Markings

Add the following markings to your pattern:

- Vertical grain line: This may be altered in the muslin fitting.
- Horizontal balance line (HBL): Make sure you have a horizontal line across the front and back.
- Side seam notch: Add below the abdomen and above the hip line for matching the side seams. The knee can also be used to match the front to back.

Ease and Seam Allowance

Ease is any amount you add to a pattern in addition to your body measurement. Up to this step, you have adjusted the pattern to match only your body measurements. Most designs and fabric will need additional ease for style and comfort—knits are the exception.

Wiggle room ease is the amount of ease needed for body movement within the garment. This is where the quadrant principle is helpful. Avoid simply adding inches to the side because that may not be the correct location to distribute the amount, especially in an unaltered pattern. Instead, build ease into the body of your pattern. You can do this in two ways:

- Add the ease increment to your body measurement so that it is already included.
- Add the ease to your pattern pieces after you adjust it to fit your body.

Design ease is the amount of ease added on top of body measurements and wiggle room ease that creates a new silhouette or simply makes the garment even looser. This will be added in creative design.

Ease is unique to everyone; some like a loose fit while others prefer a snug fit. Ease can also be customizable in different areas of the pattern and from front to back. You may have no ease at the waist, wiggle room at the hips, and very flowy pant legs with lots of design ease toward the bottom, or less ease in the front and more in the back. As a result, it is imperative you make a fit sample—after all, that is what the pros do!

For this test pant, add:

- 2" (5cm) at each side seam
- 2" (5cm) at the inseam
- 2" (5cm) at the hem
- 1" (2.5m) at the center front and center back seam
- 1" (2.5cm) at the waist

When sewing the seam and inseam, you will sew a 1" (2.5cm) seam allowance, leaving 1" (2.5cm) ease on each side for a total of 4" (10cm) of ease. You may add more if additional space is desired. The center front and center back will not need adjusted at this point. They should lay directly on the center front and back of your body. Additionally, the waist only needs seam allowance for attaching the waist band. The generous seam allowance will be trimmed down after the fitting.

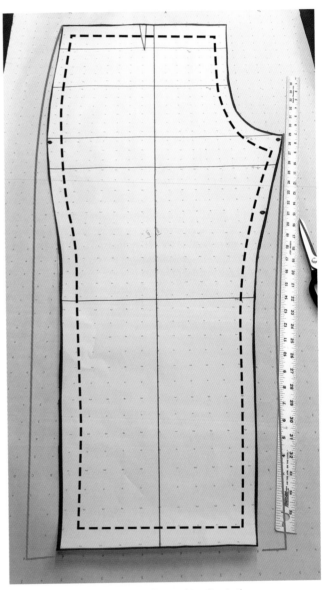

The area of the pattern beyond the stitching line is the seam allowance. This does not add any space to the pant for fitting, but simply allows the formation of the seam. The ease is any excess beyond body measurements that forms a specific style or excess room in the pattern.

SEWING THE MUSLIN PANTS FITTING SAMPLE

The muslin fit sample is all about refining the shape of the pattern to match the body. Omit sewing things like decorative pockets and the fly front. These will be added in the final sewing. Focus on the main body of the pants.

1. Baste any darts on the front and back of the muslin.
2. Baste the center front seam using a 1" (2.5cm) seam allowance.
3. Baste the center back seam using a 1" (2.5cm) seam allowance. Leave an opening from the waist down approximately 6"–9" (15–22cm) for an opening.
4. Baste the side seams using a 1" (2.5cm) seam allowance.
5. Baste the inseam using a 1"–2" (2.5–5cm) seam allowance.

Waistband

Add a waistband, binding, or twill tape to the waist of the pants after assembling the muslin.

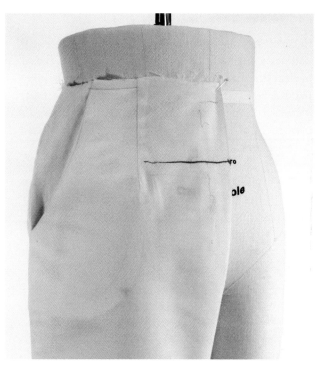

The muslin pant is easiest to fit if the waist of the pant goes to the natural waist of the body, creating a consistent location for placing the pant on the body during multiple fittings. Adding the pockets and design elements are optional in the fitting muslin, but do help with scale and proportion as well as how they lay on the curve of the body.

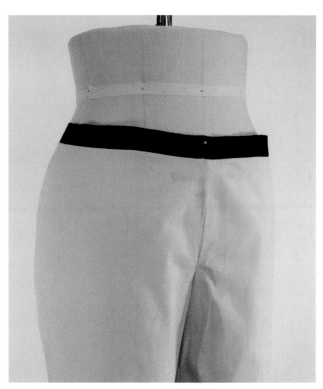

If the pant design does not go to the natural waist, more care and attention is needed to make sure the same placement line is used for each fitting. If you prefer a lower "rise" or cropped pant, the upper part of the pant may be trimmed down from the natural waistline after all fitting has been completed.

FITTING THE PANTS SLOPER

Regardless of how you have created your pants pattern, a muslin fitting is crucial for finalizing the perfect fit. The goal of pattern fitting is to scale the pattern to match your body. The art of fitting comes from sculpting the 3D fabric sample. If you scaled the pattern following the previous steps, then the details such as darts and waistband will rest correctly on the body. The fit may be loose due to the additional ease. This is normal and will be resolved in the fitting. Wearing the correct foundation garments and shoes, place the pants on and fit the waistband to your natural waist.

Fit your pants sloper following these steps:

1. Position the waist.
2. Position the crotch curve and rise (fork area of the pants).
3. Level the balance lines if they are drooping.
4. Check the plumb lines and grain lines.
5. Fit the front.
6. Fit the back.
7. Refine as needed.
8. Contour and refine the side seams.
9. Bend your leg to check the crotch curve fitting.
10. Mark carefully any place you have marked with a pin, remove pins, and carefully take apart the fitting muslin and true up the adjustments. Make sure not to stretch the crotch curve on the bias.
11. Press.
12. Trace the muslin onto oak tag or pattern paper and add all markings and notches making your final pattern. Avoid going backward to the previous paper pattern. You want to continually progress forward in this method.
13. Use your sloper to design different styles of pants.
14. One muslin is usually sufficient, but you may make an additional one if you need to polish off any final details.
15. Once the muslin is fitted, adjust any details such as side pockets to match the contours of the polished pattern.

Pins can be repositioned, so experiment until you have your best fit. Evaluate function. Can you sit, stand, bend, and walk comfortably?

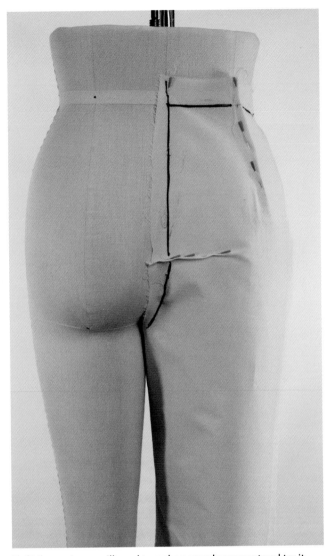

To fit the pant, you will need to make a sample garment and try it on. The test pant will have both the left and right side. By pinning or shaping the fabric, you can custom fit how the pant interacts with your unique body shape.

TIP

Make a fit sample from this pattern in a few different types of fabric such as denim, gabardine, or point knit. See how the pants fits differently. Use your crotch curve template to adjust for different fabrics too. Make the template in matching fabrics to the weight of fabric you will be sewing on.

By tackling fit issues during the development of your pants pattern, you avoid future frustration.

FITTING ISSUES

In studying the process presented earlier in this chapter, you will recognize the value in customizing your pant pattern prior to the fitting. Most of the following illustrated fit issues are prevented or minimized by simply adjusting the pattern to the scale and proportion of your body.

There is no need for guessing and playing fit detective. Instead, your fitting process will include simple things, such as contouring side seams to your body curves, marking the hem, and making subtle refinements.

In the event you are fitting an unaltered or non-customized pattern or are altering a current pair of pants, the following fitting solutions are commonly used to address these fit issues and how to fix them.

FITTING TIPS

High Center Waistline

Sometimes the waistline is not perfectly straight across the front or back, and it may contour up toward the center. Simply extend the height of the waistband at the center to match the difference. Transition across into the side seam. Important: The very center of the pattern must form a right angle and not come to a point.

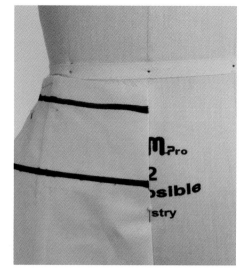 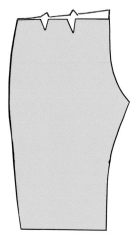

Sway Back

The sway back is a common fit issue in the small of the back. It is actually an issue with the length of the pattern being too long in the upper part of the pant. Simple adjusting of the pattern will prevent this; however, if you have pooling of fabric above the seam and right below the waistline, pinning a horizontal tuck across the back will remove the excess.

 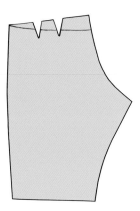

Dropped Front Waistline

If the waistline dips down in the center front or center back, place a string or elastic around the waist until it falls naturally around the body. Mark the new waistline. The center should form a right angle. Option: Make a hinge by cutting from the center front to the side seam and take the reduction near the waist but in the body of the pattern.

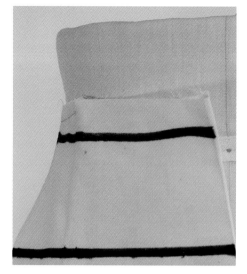 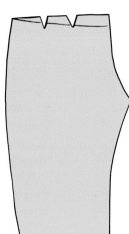

Front Excess Crotch Fullness

If the pant features horizontal wrinkles and the front crotch curve is not resting flush on the body, the crotch curve is too deep and space needs to be added to the pattern. Raise the curve ¼" (0.5cm) and blend into the center front. Repeat if more is needed.

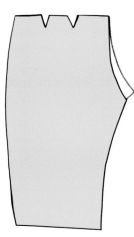

Front Crotch Binding

When the front crotch curve is too shallow, it will bind and create vertical drag lines. To add space to the pattern, deepen the crotch curve and remove space. Begin by removing ¼" (0.5cm) in the crotch curve and repeat until the front curve matches the body exactly. Of course, following the crotch curve template eliminates this problem before it happens.

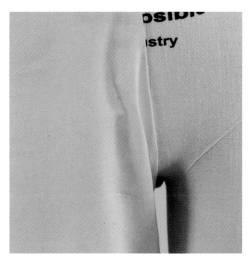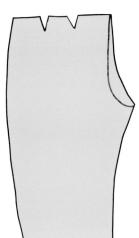

Front Frown Lines

When the crotch line is too far below the natural contour of the body, it will droop and drag lines will radiate angling down, often referred to as frown lines. This area is the front rise of the pant. The solution is to remove space and narrow out the fork in the pant. Remove ¼" (0.5cm) from top of the inseam and blend down the leg. Repeat again if more reductions are needed.

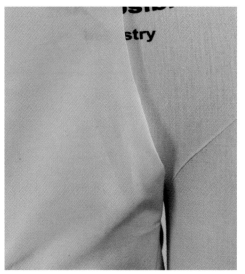

Front Smile Lines

When the crotch line is too short and binds into the body, forming smile lines, space is added to the pant making more room for the body. Extend the front inseam, adding ¼" (0.5cm) to the fork of the pant, and blend into the leg. Repeat again if more space is needed.

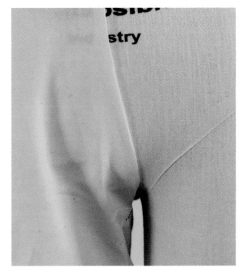 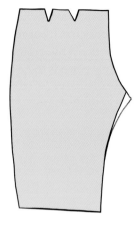

Drooping Seat or Back Drag Lines

Horizontal lines below the seat is a result of either excess length in the upper pant leg or not enough space in the center back crotch curve. Pin a horizontal tuck across the back of the leg. If the issue is excess length, then no other adjustments are necessary. If the seat feels snug or this does not remove the problem, then space is needed in the back crotch curve. Add space by deepening the back crotch curve by ¼" (0.5cm) so it sits below the seat. Repeat if more space is needed.

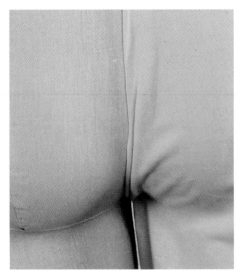 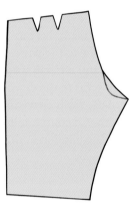

Flat Seat

When the back rise at the top of the inseam is too far away from the body, the pattern is not resting on the body. A flat seat will have this problem. There simply is too much space. Remove space from the rise by deducting ¼" (0.5cm) at the top of the inseam and blend into the pant. Repeat if necessary.

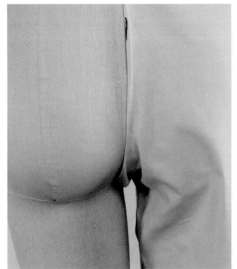 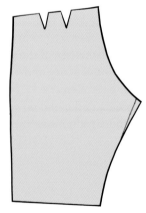

Full Seat

Drag lines pulling toward the crotch seam indicate the back rise is not long enough for the bottom. Add length by extending the top of the inseam outward ¼" (0.5cm) and blend into the inseam. Repeat if more space is needed.

Thigh Fullness

Fuller back thighs are a common fitting issue near the seat of the pant. Drag lines pointing toward the crotch seam clearly identify this problem. The rise of the pant is too short. Extend the inseam out ¼" (0.5cm) and blend into the inseam. Repeat if drag lines still exist until the pant fits comfortably.

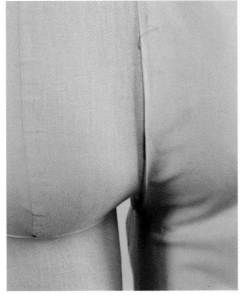 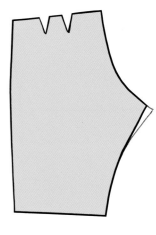

Narrow Thigh

Narrow thighs often do not fill out the pant and the excess space unsupported by the body simply hangs with vertical lines near the seat. Remove space in the rise by taking a reduction from the top of the rise and blend down the inseam. Begin with ¼" (0.5cm) and repeat if more excess needs removed.

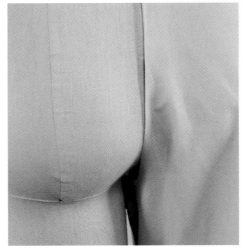 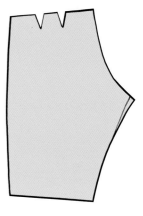

General Fullness Take in or Let Out

General fullness between the waist and crotch area near the center front or center back may be removed by taking in the center seam. If the pant is snug across the abdomen, then space may be added down the center area. Additionally, if the fullness is positioned near the side seam area, then take in or let out the side seam area, contouring to your unique hip curve.

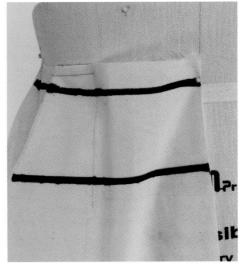 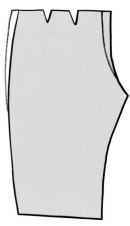

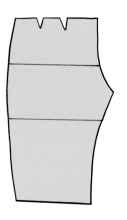

Horizontal Balance Lines

As you are fitting pants, the horizontal lines, such as the hip, thigh, or abdomen, should always remain parallel to the floor. These balance lines will dip down if there is not enough space in the crotch curve. The fitting solutions will address this issue by simply adding space to the back lower crotch curve.

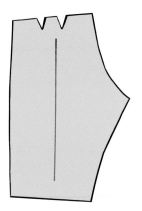

Grain Modification

How easy it is to place the grain of a paper pattern to a leg that is perfectly straight up and down! If you are lucky enough to have this figure feature, then grain modification is unnecessary. However, the generic grain of the pattern often does not correspond to the figure with posture issues caused by spinal contours, knock knees, or other leg posture variation. The pant can be fitted correctly and still hang off grain in the back. Collapsing near the outer knee, leg twist, or pulling to the inseam at the knee clearly illustrate that the pant is not draping on the body correctly.

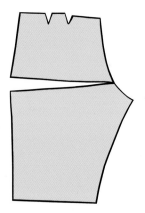

Tuck in the Pant

When the grain of the pant angles slightly, it is easy to correct by taking a tuck in either the upper pant or the leg just below the seat. A horizontal tuck at the side seam blending across the leg will lift the pant for issues affecting the outer edge of the pant. Taking the horizontal tuck near the inseam below the thigh area will lift the leg for issues affecting the inseam.

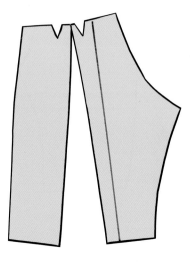

Vertical Grain Reposition

For major leg twist or large adjustments, a direct correction of the grain includes cutting up the pant leg from the hem up the pant until it spreads open and relaxes the fit. The result is the pant will drape correctly on the body and to the dynamics of the pant leg. Place a tape measure or string down the center of the back leg and let it hang naturally. This will be the grain on your body. Cut. Measure the width of the opening at the hem and knee. Because the pant leg is hanging open, it may be necessary to remove some fullness from the inseam, and this fullness may not be the same amount from the front to back. Repin the inseam as needed. Remove the pant. Trace a corrected pattern and draw the new grainline on the pattern. It is completely normal for the new grainline of the paper pant pattern to look slightly off grain compared to the unaltered pattern. Remember, you have now created your own custom grain that will match your body and be reflected in how the fabric drapes and hangs.

SEWING CLASSIC WOMEN'S PANTS

If you wear clothing, you know that a truly custom fitted pair of pants is worth the time and effort to perfect, since it is almost impossible to find that sort of fit off the rack. From classic neutrals to a pop of color in fashion fabrics, the custom tailored trouser will certainly find its way into your sewn wardrobe at some point if you have not already taken the time to sew a pair. Did you know that with the right fit and a bit of flair at the hem, combined with the right shoe, you will look taller in your classic pant? When you custom shape and fit the crotch curve too, your pants will also look great and move with ease and comfort.

Use the basic pant assembly sequence on the next page as a guide along with your own commercial pattern.

Once you draft a classic pants pattern that fits your figure, you will be hard pressed to buy a pair off the rack again. One key is a fitting template to make fast work of refining the crotch curve for a comfortable fit. I wrote about this method for *Threads* magazine #216, Winter 2021.

FLY ZIPPERS, DARTS, AND CENTER SEAMS

1. If you are inserting a fly-front zipper, mark the length of the zipper opening and reinforce the crotch at the bottom. Follow your pattern instructions for individual steps.
2. After stitching the center front seam, stitch the back pieces together at the center back.
3. Baste the waist darts, if any, and try on to adjust the fit if necessary. Stitch the darts in place.

POCKETS AND SIDE SEAMS

1. Side pockets are inserted into the side seam with a facing and custom pocket bag. Different patterns will have subtle variations on the side pocket.
2. Add topstitching as desired.

INSEAM

1. It is normal for the inseam to have a different length from the front to back. Pin the inseam at the hem up to the knee. The upper part of the back inseam will be stretched to fit the front. Match them at the top, stretch, and pin together. Baste.
2. Baste the side seams. Try on the pant. Contour to your leg, mark, and stitch.

FINISHING TOUCHES

1. If you are making pants without a waistband, baste and finish off the waistline with a facing or binding.
2. For pants with a waistband, follow your specific pattern instructions, but attach the finished band to the top of the pant and enclose the top edge.
3. Make buttonholes and sew on buttons, snaps, or hooks and eyes, if any, to the pant closure.
4. Try on the pants and mark the length; hem and press.

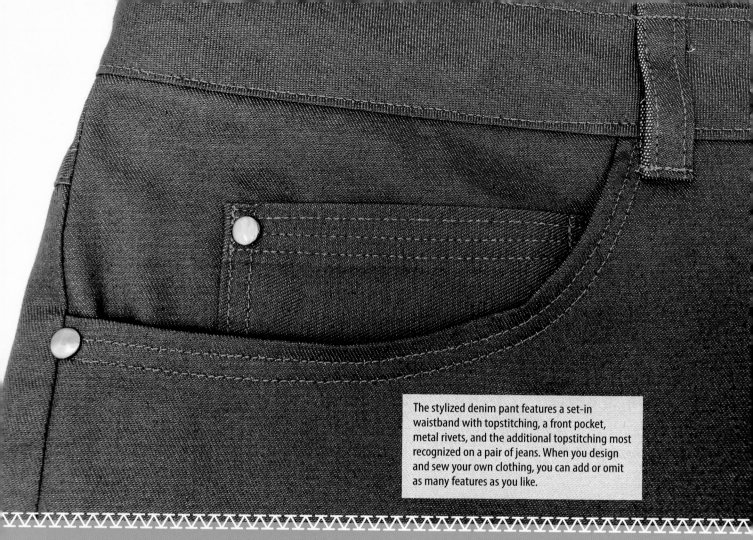

The stylized denim pant features a set-in waistband with topstitching, a front pocket, metal rivets, and the additional topstitching most recognized on a pair of jeans. When you design and sew your own clothing, you can add or omit as many features as you like.

CREATIVE PANT DESIGN

Once you have a classic trouser pant that is custom fitted to your body shape, size, and leg characteristics, the pattern can be redesigned using a flat pattern to create any style of pant. The stylized pant is created by the combination of fabric, fit, and style. The perfect garment is like a recipe with the right combination of ingredients, including the overall style; the fitted pattern; the custom body contours; the fabric drape, weight, and characteristics; and the intended use or function of the garment. For example, horizontal drag lines in a pair of jeans might be part of the design, but when they are visible in a pair of trousers, they are considered a fit issue. A perfectly fitted wide leg pant on a fuller figure will look slimming when sewn from a flowy crepe fabric, but the same pant sewn from a heavy twill will add unflattering fullness on the body. A designer tip is to make a finished pant that you wear and test the fit. It may take one or two to determine your final refinements, because day-to-day use is different than in the fitting room. You are the designer. Experiment with a few different fabrics and types of fit to gain confidence and experience, and you will be well on your way to pant mastery in your wardrobe.

THE PALAZZO PANT

Cut up from the hem to the waist or angle the cut toward the side seam to make a hinge. Spread the pattern to create fullness in the pant leg. As the designer, you can place this fullness in specific areas of the pant to accentuate your figure. If you have a fuller inner thigh, avoid adding excess toward the inseam. Instead, place the fullness toward the center front. Different fabrics will look different with fullness added. Select fabric that drapes and hangs well. For example, a rayon or ponte knit would make a lovely palazzo pant. A heavy denim would make a bottom–heavy pant that would be unflattering. As the pant lengthens, the drape widens.

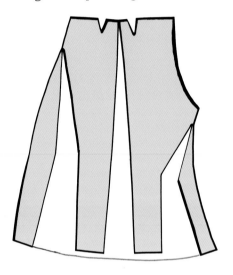

PLEATS AND SEAMS

Pleats and seams come and go in fashion in ladies' pants. To create a pleat, simply cut down the vertical length of the pattern from the top to bottom. Cut to, but not through, making a hinge. Spread the pattern to the depth of the pleat. For seams, draw a line on the pattern in the desired location and shape. Cut your pattern apart. Make sure to add seam allowance for sewing back together. Use seams to your advantage for flattering your figure.

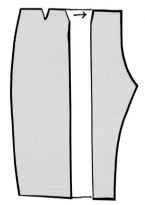

YOKE

The yoke is common in the back of jeans, but can be added to the front as well. Darts can be rotated and eliminated by being absorbed in the yoke seam. Yokes also provide bias for fitting around the contours of the body.

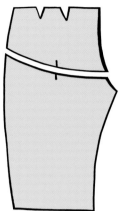

SLIM FIT/JEGGINGS

Contouring the pant leg to create the slim fit is most successful when starting with a classic pant already scaled to the proportion of your body, shape, and curves. Pin fit the pant to match the contours of your body to your desired fit. Slim fit pants need to be created from a fabric with slight stretch or a knit in order to get them on the body.

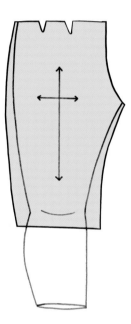

JEANS

There are a variety of types of fit and fabrics used to create jeans. When making your own jeans, use the formula: 1) the pant style, 2) the fit, and 3) the fabric that will create that look. A classic trouser pant can be sewn in denim and result in a classic fit jean. By using the jegging pattern and adding stretch denim, you get a jegging. Some jeans have intentional drag lines in the crotch area. By taking an intentional reduction in the crotch curve, the pant will create drag lines, the often sought-after feature of jeans.

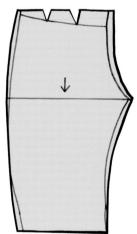

CHAPTER 6

DETAILS OF GARMENT CONSTRUCTION

Now that you know the construction sequence for your project, it is time to review the instructions for assembling specific elements of your garment that give you a truly custom experience—the seams, pockets, zippers, sleeves, etc. As you follow the workflow in Chapter 4 or 5 for your selected garment, return to these step-by-step instructions to complete each phase of assembly.

These instructions might be more detailed and demanding than those you are used to seeing or those you found in your pattern envelope. However, the result will be a perfectly fitted, soundly constructed, custom-tailored garment that will last for years and stand as a testimony to your sewing skills.

A Note about Step-by-Step Numbering

In this book, step-by-step instructions are broken down into small, bite-sized chunks for each phase of a project. Photos are given for some essential steps, but not all steps. Photos are almost always right next to the step text or mini section with which they correspond. If they're not, they have an extra caption clarifying what they're showing. So don't be confused if you see more than one step 1 on a page!

SEAMS

Seams not only join pieces of a garment together, they are also the most obvious indicators of whether a garment is well made and enhance the fit and style. Seams are used to ease a longer piece of fabric into the seam line of a smaller piece, reduce bulk, and finish the raw edges of fabric. They have a functional use, such as adding strength to an area of a garment, like a man's shirt or a flat-felled, denim side seam in which the raw edges are folded over and encased inside.

Essential to the success of all seams, whether decorative or functional, is careful marking and basting followed by machine stitching with the proper needle, thread, and stitch size for the fabric and garment. Even more important is smoothly pressing each seam as soon as it is completed—not even the most thorough pressing of the finished garment can substitute for pressing each seam as it is sewn. With the techniques shown here, you can sew a flat, smooth, and finished seam as well as any professional designer or tailor.

SEAM ALLOWANCE

Seam allowance is the distance from the stitching line to the edge of the fabric. Traditionally, in home sewing the seam allowance is ⅝" (1.5cm), and then it is trimmed down with a serger, a specialized seam, or trimmed down to reduce bulk. In factory sewing, a different width is used for different areas of a garment and the trimming step is eliminated. If you find a particular width that works for you, feel free to modify the seam allowance on your pattern accordingly.

THE PLAIN SEAM

Basting and Stitching the Plain Seam

1. With the wrong sides of the fabric facing outward, pin together the pieces to be seamed, inserting the pins at right angles to the stitching line. Match and pin first where the seam line markings intersect. Some sewists prefer to place the pins parallel to the seam allowance, which is fine for straight seams and fabrics that will not shift as you stitch. Fabrics that are slippery or seams that have a curve are best pinned at a right angle to the seam.
2. Add pins at 1"–2" (2.5–5cm) intervals on a straight seam and at intervals as short as ¼" (0.5cm) on a curved seam.
3. Baste just outside the seam line markings and remove pins.
4. After trying on the garment for fit, machine stitch directly along the seam-line markings; remove the bastings. An added step for knit fabrics: To reinforce the seams, machine stitch a second line ⅛" (3mm) outside the first seam.
5. Press open.

> **TIP**
>
> *To help keep consistent seam width, use the markings on your sewing machine as a guide. Additionally, place a piece of tape on the machine as a guide or use an adhesive seam guide. To gain even more accuracy on your seaming, trace the stitching line with fabric chalk on the wrong side of the fabric and stitch over the line.*

TRIMMING THE SEAM

Because home sewing patterns traditionally have a wider seam, it is necessary to trim it down to allow for the fabric and seam to contour better to the curve of the body. Examples are the neckline, armscye, and the waistline. Clipping is a technique where you cut a right angle to the seam allowance but do not cut through the seam, which helps the fabric to lay flat on the body.

A plain seam

A plain seam
after pressing

Finish with shears or pinking shears for non-raveling fabrics.

Finishing Seam Edges with a Standard Sewing Machine

For a simple finish on tightly woven fabric that will not fray, trim the seam allowance to ½" (1.5cm), using dressmaker's shears. For a more decorative cut edge on a tightly woven fabric, use pinking shears.

For a simple finish on knit and woven fabrics that may ravel, machine stitch ½" (1.5cm) from the seam, then trim with dressmaker's shears. Or use pinking shears for a more decorative cut edge on woven fabrics. Make sure you do not cut into the machine stitching.

Finishing Seam Edges with a Serger

A serger is a common option for home sewists who want a great way to finish off the edge of a plain seam. Sergers provide many seam finish options with a variety of stitches that are both decorative and functional along with width and length adjustments. Use a matching or contrasting thread color to further customize your project.

Serge the seam allowance together or stitch either side of the seam allowance for a decorative finish. Make sure you are only serging the edge of the seam allowance and not stitching on the fabric. Since sergers do have a blade and cut the fabric, make sure you do not catch any of the garment under the blade when finishing off.

Finish with an additional stitch line for fabrics that may ravel.

Finish with an overlock seam using a serger.

INTERSECTING SEAMS

1. To be sure that stitched seams on two sections of a garment will intersect accurately when joined together, match the two sections with the wrong sides facing outward. Insert a pin at the point where the new stitching line crosses the stitched seams; bring the pin up at right angles to the new stitching line.

2. Once the intersections are marked, add more pins at 1"–2" (2.5–5cm) intervals on a straight seam and at intervals as short as ¼" (0.5cm) on a curved seam, making sure that all seam allowances are pinned flat.

3. If necessary, baste stitch for fitting or holding the seam together and machine stitch as sewn for the plain seam.

4. Trim to ½" (1.5cm) and diagonally clip the four corners of the joined seam allowances or finish with desired seam finish.

TIP

This is a great technique to use on the waistbands, pockets, crotch seams, and anywhere a perfect right angle or seam intersection is desired.

EASING SEAMS

1. On the longer piece of fabric, run a line of basting ⅛" (3mm) outside the stitching line sewing between the pattern markings that indicate the area to be eased. Use a short basting stitch—six stitches per 1" (2.5cm)—and leave 4" (10cm) of loose thread at both ends (use thread the color of your final stitching—this basting will remain inside the finished seam to help keep it flat).

2. Pin the seam together between the ends of the seam and the ease markings, leaving open the area to be eased.

3. Pull the loose thread basting thread on either side and ease (draw up) the excess until the seam matches the shorter seam. The excess should be evenly distributed on the seam.

4. Baste if needed, then machine stitch the entire length of the seam.

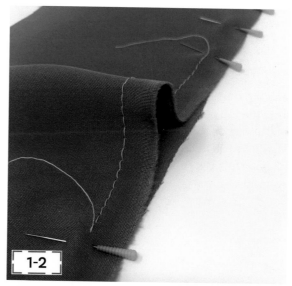

1-2

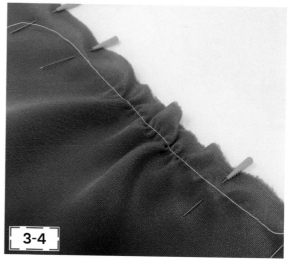

3-4

Easing the Curved Seam

1. After machine stitching a seam with a curve, using a stitch slightly smaller than usual because of the curve, trim the seam allowance to ½" (1.5cm).
2. Clip for concave seams or notch for convex seams at ¼"–½" (0.5–1.5cm) intervals; the sharper the curve, the shorter the intervals. Cut to within ⅛" (3mm) of the machine stitching, making sure not to cut through the stitching. Press open.

Clip for concave seams.

Notch for convex seams.

THE FLAT FELLED SEAM

Preparing to Make the Flat Felled Seam

1. With right sides together, stitch the plain seam using the desired seam allowance on the pattern as normal. Press the seam open. Then fold and press both seam allowances in the direction indicated on your pattern.
2. Trim the underneath seam allowance to ⅛" (3mm).
3. Trim the top seam allowance to ½" (1.5cm).

Folding the Flat Felled Seam

Fold the top seam allowance over the underneath one, lining up the edge of the top seam allowance along the machine stitching of the original plain seam; this encloses the underneath seam allowance.

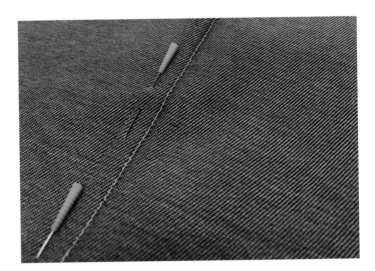

Basting and Stitching the Flat Felled Seam

1. Turn the fold to the side on which the felled seam should fall.
2. Pin the felled seam, inserting the pins from the folded edge toward the seam at right angles.
3. Baste if needed ⅛" (3mm) from the folded edge.
4. Machine stitch midway between the basting and the folded edge. Remove the basting and press.

GRADING SEAM ALLOWANCE

1. To reduce the bulk of seam allowances where there is a facing (a layer of fabric backing at garment edges) and an interfacing, trim the seam allowance of the interfacing to ¹⁄₁₆" (2mm) from the stitching.
2. Trim the seam allowance of the facing to ⅛" (3mm) of the stitching.
3. Trim the seam allowance of the outer fabric to ¼" (0.5cm) of the stitching.
4. To reduce seam bulk at corners that have been faced, and perhaps also interfaced, trim both sides of the corner, starting 1 ½" (4cm) from the corner on the outer fabric and cutting through all layers. Do not cut closer to the stitching line than ¹⁄₁₆" (2mm).

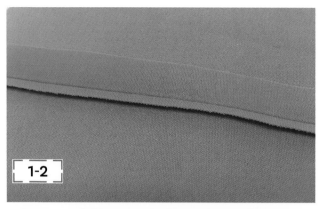

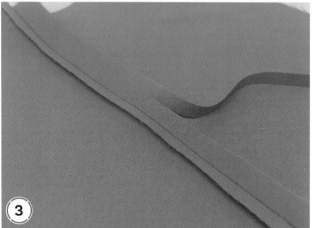

MAKING A CHANNEL SEAM

A channeled seam is ideal for boning, sheering (drawing up) a design, or simply adding a decorative effect.

Joining the Garment Sections

1. Pin the two pieces of fabric right sides together at 1" (2.5cm) intervals along the seam line, matching seam intersections, notches, and any other pattern markings.
2. Hand or machine baste at 6 stitches per 1" (2.5cm) directly on the seam line, stitching over the pins. Leave 4" (10cm) long loose threads at each end. Remove the pins.
3. If you machine basted, clip the upper basting threads at 1" intervals along the length of the seam, but leave intact the thread on the underside of the seam.
4. Open the garment pieces and press the basted seam open on the wrong side. Turn and press on the side that will be visible on the finished garment (the right side).

Attaching the Channeling

1. Cut a 2" (5cm) wide strip of fabric, the length of
   the seam to be slotted, along the lengthways grain.
   Use either fabric left over after cutting out your
   pattern, or for a dramatic effect, choose a fabric of
   a similar weight and texture but contrasting color.
   Bias strips and decorative ribbon can also be used
   for channeling.
2. Baste a row of stitches lengthways down the exact
   center of the channeling to aid you in correctly
   positioning the strip over the seam.
3. Finish the edges of the underlay with an
   appropriate finish for the fabric and garment. If
   the channeling is cut on the bias, it will not fray
   and no finish is necessary. This will reduce bulk in
   the seam.
4. With the wrong side of the garment pieces facing
   up, center the underlay, wrong side up, over the
   basted seam. Match the bastings along the center
   of the underlay to the seam. Pin carefully on each
   side of the bastings through all layers of fabric.

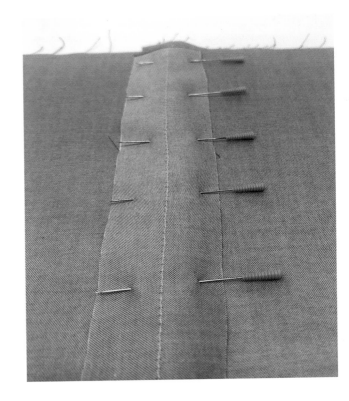

Completing the Channel Seam

1. Place the garment wrong side down. Working
   from the right side, the side that will be visible on
   the finished garment, hand baste the underlay to
   the garment pieces. Use a tape measure to guide
   the basting, which must be equidistant from
   the seam line. It is usually ½" (1.5cm) on either
   side, but it can be set slightly narrower or wider,
   depending on the effect desired. Remove the pins.
2. Machine stitch at the normal 12 stitches per
   1" (2.5cm) as closely as possible to the outside
   of the bastings made above. If you wish to add
   emphasis to the seam, make larger stitches—six per
   1" (2.5cm)—or use contrasting thread.
3. Remove all bastings, which opens up the slot. Press
   on both sides of the completed seam.

DARTS

Darts are the foundational fitting element that help to shape flat pieces of fabric to the contours of the human body. When used decoratively, their placement and manner of stitching often add to the design of a garment.

There are only two kinds of darts, and both are based on triangular shapes. The most common type begins with the wide part of the fold at a seam and narrows to a point on the contour of the body, such as the full bust. This is the single-pointed dart and is placed at the waist, bust, elbow or shoulder seams. The sides of the dart are called the legs. The vertical double-pointed dart is less common; it is used to give contour to a waistless dress or long blouse or jacket.

You might not consider a tuck, pleat, gather, or seam line to be defined as a dart; however, in the design of a garment, these are considered dart equivalents because they are created from the basic dart shape. Invisible darts also exist in the side seam where the front joins the back near the waistline.

Although darts are basic, making them look perfectly smooth and flawless requires careful adjustment to the pattern, precise marking, stitching, and pressing. It is worth the few extra minutes needed to make extra markings, which prevent an off-center or misplaced dart. In addition, a seemingly small step—sewing a few stitches off the fabric edge at the dart tip—can eliminate a puckered point.

THE SINGLE AND DOUBLE DART

Getting Ready to Make Darts

1. In addition to the pattern markings traced on the wrong side of the fabric, draw in a vertical line marking the center of the darts where they will be folded.
2. Place short horizontal markings at the tips and at the widest parts of the darts and at the midway points between the two.

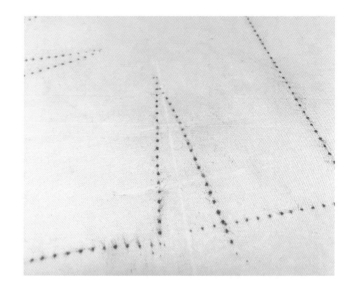

Pinning the Darts

1. Fold back the body section along the center line of each single dart, matching the horizontal markings.
2. Pin the single dart first at the seam line, next at the tip and then at the midpoint. Add intervening pins at 1" (2.5cm) intervals.
3. Pin the double dart first at the widest point, next at the tips and then at the midpoints. Add intervening pins at 1" (2.5cm) intervals.

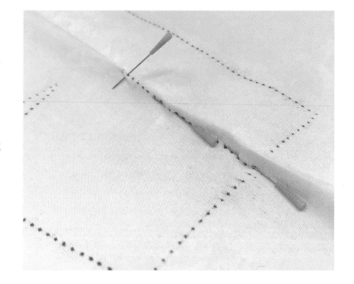

Basting and Fitting

1. Baste just inside the stitching line, securing the thread with a fastening stitch at both ends.
2. Baste the seams of the garment together just outside the stitching line. Try on and adjust the garment for fit.

Finishing the Single Dart

1. Remove only enough of the seam basting around the dart to permit you to stitch the dart.
2. Machine stitch, beginning at the widest end.
3. Sew a few stitches off the edge of the fabric at the tip end. Then cut the thread and hand knot. Remove the dart bastings.

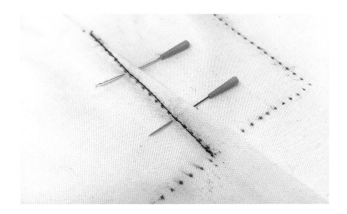

Pressing the Dart

1. Press average-sized vertical darts on medium-weight fabric so that the fold is toward the center of the garment.
2. Press down horizontal darts, such as the bust dart.
3. On very wide darts or heavy fabrics, cut along the center fold line to within 1" (2.5cm) of the tip and trim seams to ⅝" (1.5cm). Press the dart open as shown. Press the tip toward the center.

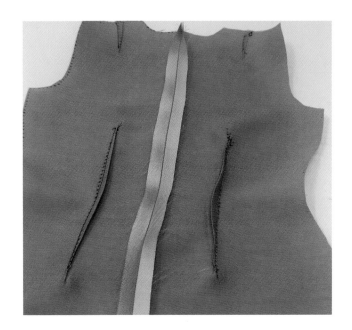

Finishing the Double Dart

1. Beginning at one tip, machine stitch at the very edge of the fold. Sew a few stitches off the fabric edge at the other tip, then cut the thread and hand knot the threads at both tips. Remove bastings.
2. Clip into the dart at 1" (2.5cm) intervals to within ⅛" (3mm) of the stitching line.
3. Press toward the center of the garment.

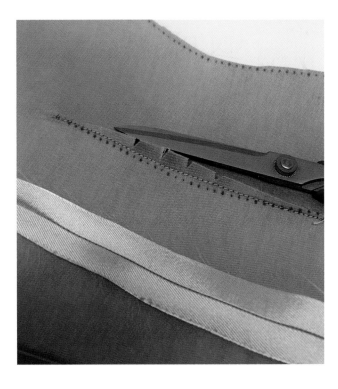

TIP

Darts are the foundation for fitting a flat fabric to a three-dimensional body shape. Many patterns have minimal darts for fitting; however, if adding an additional dart to a garment polishes the fit and removes excess fabric, then pin in additional darts to achieve fitting mastery.

PLEATS

The secret to making a perfect pleat is to take the time to mark and fold it accurately—a small price to pay for the grace, movement, and controlled fullness that pleats can add to a garment.

   The classic pleat is a straight pleat. It can be used singly or in a series in which each pleat is folded to lie in the same direction. It can also be used to form an inverted pleat in which two pleats are turned toward each other to meet in the center. Pleats can be left unpressed for a soft, draping effect, or firmly pressed along their folds for a crisp, tailored look. For an even more tailored look, pressed pleats can also be stitched on the side of the fabric that will be visible when the garment is completed, from the top edge to a point partway down the pleat.

   The actual steps in making a pleat are few and simple. To ensure evenly spaced, straight pleats, work on a flat surface large enough to lay out the entire piece to be pleated and keep all basting stitches in until you reach the stage recommended in the instructions opposite. Fit the pattern to the full hip prior to forming pleats.

MARKING THE PLEATS

1. Run a line of basting along the waistline seam marking.
2. Unless you have done so already, run a line of basting following pattern markings for the fold line (the line along which the pleat will be folded).
3. Using a different colored thread, run a line of basting following pattern markings for the placement line (the line against which the folded pleat will be placed).
4. If you plan to press the pleat and topstitch it partway closed, use a horizontal running stitch to mark the position on the fold line where the topstitching should end.

CONSTRUCTING THE PLEATS

1. With the fabric wrong side down, fold each pleat on its fold line and pin it against its placement line. Begin to pin at the bottom to ensure an even hemline, and make sure to catch all layers of fabric. The number of pleats and the direction in which they are folded will depend upon your pattern.
2. Baste the folded pleats, stitching from the bottom of the garment to the top, ¼" (0.5cm) from the fold. Stitch through all layers of fabric.
3. Machine stitch along the waistline seam, a fraction above the basted markings, to hold the pleats in place.

FINISHING UNPRESSED PLEATS

Remove the bastings after the garment has been assembled and is ready to hem. The pleats will then fall in soft folds from the waistline.

FINISHING PRESSED PLEATS

After pressing the pleats on both sides of the fabric and assembling the garment, remove only enough of the bastings to enable you to hem the skirt. Do not remove the remaining pleat bastings, including the placement line, until the garment has been assembled, hemmed, and pressed again.

FINISHING TOPSTITCHED PLEATS

1. After pressing the pleats and assembling the garment, add a line of machine stitching on the right side of the fabric, the side that will be visible when the garment is completed, ⅛" (3mm) from the edge of the fold of each pleat.
2. Stitch from the waistline down to the horizontal marker or to the point most becoming to you. Follow the instructions for hemming, removing bastings, and final pressing.

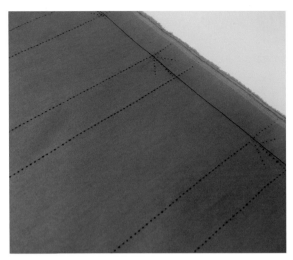

Marking the Pleats

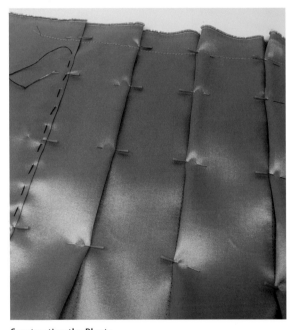

Constructing the Pleats

Finishing Topstitched Pleats

THE GODET: A PLEAT VARIATION

Inserting in a Slashed Opening

1. With the garment wrong side out, stitch and press open the garment seams.
2. Mark the position for the point of the godet with a line of small horizontal basting stitches running through the pattern dot indicating point.
3. Run a line of vertical basting stitches along the pattern marking for the slash line of the godet, the line along which the garment section will be cut, in order to insert the godet.

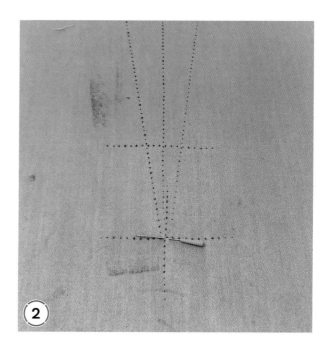

Reinforcing the Slash Point

1. Make a reinforcement patch from a 3" (7.5cm) square of organza, underlining, or lining fabric cut on the bias, diagonally across the weave.
2. Turn the garment right side out. Center the reinforcement patch over the point of the godet, using basted markings as a guide.
3. Pin the patch to the garment fabric and baste it in place. Remove the pins and the basted slash-line marking.
4. Turn the garment wrong side out and machine stitch the patch to the garment outside the godet seam markings, setting your machine at 15 to 20 stitches per 1" (2.5cm). Begin at the lower end of the patch and stitch along one side of the godet seam marking. At the point of the godet, pivot and take one stitch across the point; then pivot again and continue stitching along the other godet seam line to the end of the patch. Remove basting holding patch.
5. Slash the godet along the slash line markings. Cut through both garment and patch, up to the horizontal machine stitch at the point of the godet.
6. Turn the garment right side out and press the edges of the patch toward the slash.
7. For godets stitched into a seam line, stitch the seam line closed to the point where the godet will be attached. Reinforce the seam line with backstitching at the point where the godet is attached. Stitch a piece of twill tape into the seam allowance to reinforce.

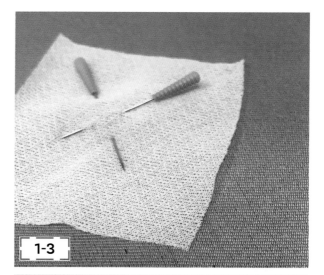

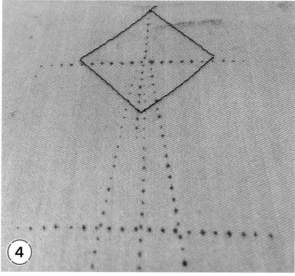

Inserting the Godet in a Slash

1. Turn the garment wrong side out, spread open the slash, and turn the patch to the wrong side of the garment. Push a pin from the wrong side of the garment fabric through the point of the slashed godet opening.

2. Place the godet wrong side up in the slashed godet opening of the garment.

3. Match the seam line markings of the garment and the godet along one side and push the pin inserted at the tip through both the godet and the garment fabric parallel to the seam line.

4. Align the other matching seam lines of the garment and the godet.

5. Pin the garment to the godet at ½" (1.3cm) intervals along the seam lines to a point about 1" (2.5cm) below the end of the reinforcement patch. Insert pins at right angles to the seam lines.

6. Baste the garment to the godet just inside the seam lines.

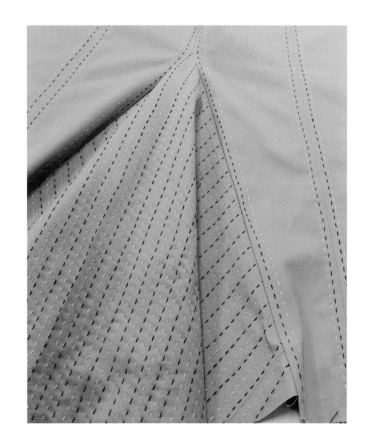

Stitching the Godet

1. Machine stitch at the normal 12 stitches per 1" (2.5cm) along the seam line, joining one side of the godet to the garment. Stitch toward the point, stopping once the first side is complete. Flip your fabric and stitch up to the point on the other side.

2. Hang up the garment overnight to set the bias, that is, to allow for any stretching in the godet.

3. Press the seam allowances toward the garment. Trim all extended edges of the reinforcement patch so that they are even with the seam allowances.

ZIPPERS

The zipper can be fun and fashionable with many variations that are useful for creating more than a properly fitting garment and an ease of dressing. Style options for zippers consist not only of numerous colors and materials, but also custom zipper teeth and pulls. Gone are the days of minimal options. Today our zipper choices are as vast as our fabric options.

Although zippers have intimidated the home sewer for years, it is perfectly possible to make a neat, smooth zipper without an unsightly gap or bulge. Only by fitting the garment and making the necessary adjustments to darts and seams, including the zipper seam before putting in the zipper, will you ensure a perfect fit.

The most common way of inserting a zipper is the centered application, which is used in neckline and center back and front closings where the zipper is concealed under two flaps and has two rows of stitching visible. In the lapped application, as used in the side seam closings for skirts and women's pants and dresses, the zipper is concealed beneath a single, wide lap with only one line of stitching visible. The fly-front zipper, which provides a wide lap of fabric over the zipper, is used on the front of the trouser, jeans, and skirt fly.

Select a zipper in the color of your fabric and the length specified on the pattern.

THE FLY-FRONT ZIPPER

Preparing the Pants Front and Fly

Before you begin, lay out the pant pieces with right sides facing up. Place a safety pin near the waist on the right pant leg (as though you were wearing the pants). As the left or right leg is referenced, this will help prevent confusion in the fly assembly. Put an edge finish on the right side of the fly. A woman's pant opens on the right side, the opposite of a man's pant.

1. The front skirt or pant pattern will have a fly extension as part of the center front. Chalk mark the stitching lines and the zipper dot marks from the pattern to the wrong side of your fabric.

2. Apply any interfacing to the fly as suggested by your pattern. Optional: Just inside the seam allowance attach a piece of twill tape to stabilize the fly.

3. With right sides together, baste along the center front seam line from the top down to the zipper dot where the fly stops, and the seam continues.

4. Change your stitch length to a shorter length, back stitch, and sew the curve of the lower crotch seam. Clip to, but not through, the stitching line at the dot.

5. Reinforce the crotch curve with an additional row of stitching or serge the edge. Press the fly open.

1-4

Attaching the Zipper

1. Place the zipper face down with the right zipper tape on the seam allowance. The zipper stop should fall approximately ¾" (2cm) above the clipped curve. The zipper teeth will be ½" (1.5cm) just to the left of the seam line.

2. Pin the left zipper tape to the left fly. Stitching only through the fly extension, stitch the left zipper tape down using a zipper foot.

1-2

ZIPPER TIPS

- For bias garments, stabilize the seam with twill tape and use a zipper longer than the opening. The zipper will weigh the seam and prevent curling at the bottom of the opening.

- For zippers that extend into the waistline or areas with a facing, also use a zipper longer than the opening. Once the zipper is attached, place a new zipper stop on the zipper and trim.

- Before inserting the zipper, press it flat, especially when using an invisible zipper.

Making the Fly

1. Continuing with the left zipper fly, flip the fly allowance under and topstitch next to the zipper teeth. Make sure to only catch the fly allowance.

2. Lay the fly open with the zipper resting in the center position.

3. Slide the right edge of the zipper tape (the unsewn edge) over onto the right fly facing. Pin and stitch. Position the fly extension so that you are only stitching the zipper to the fly.

4. Turn the pant over with the right side facing up. Locate the zipper stop on the bottom of the zipper. Use the topstitching guide provided with your pattern and chalk mark the topstitching line. Make sure the stitching will catch the fly extension. Do not stitch over the zipper stop. Topstitch just above.

5. Baste just inside the topstitching to hold all layers together. Topstitch along the stitching line and remove all basting.

6. Optional: On the wrong side of the fly opening, hand stitch the edges of the zipper tape to the fly extension. For lined trousers, attach the lining by hand around the fly opening. For trousers and jeans with a fly shield, stitch the shield to the left fly and finish off the left fly edge.

7. Finish the fly with a bar tack on the front side of the pant at the bottom of the curve of the fly. Stitch through all layers.

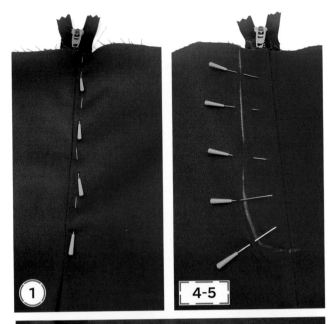

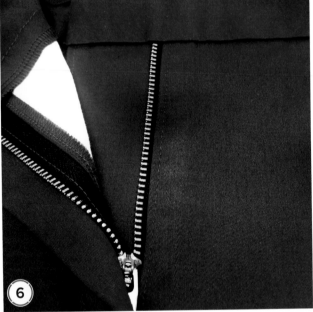

THE CENTERED ZIPPER

Determining the Length of the Zipper Opening

1. Pin the center back seam of the garment closed after the garment has been fitted and all darts and other seams have been sewn and pressed.
2. Place the open zipper face down on the center back seam line so that the zipper's top stop is ¼" (0.5cm) below the markings for the neck seam line.
3. Mark the position of the top and bottom stops of the zipper on the center back seam line with chalk or a pin.
4. Re-mark, using a horizontal running stitch. Extend these marks across the two center back seam allowances.

Preparing the Seam

1. With right sides together, baste the center back seam from the bottom of the garment pieces to the marking for the bottom stop; remove the pins. Machine stitch and remove the basting.
2. Baste closed the remainder of the center back seam, stitching on the seam line marking from the bottom stop to the neck edge. Press seam allowance open.
3. Fold the garment in half vertically with the left side facing up. Extend the seam allowance of the right back so that it lies flat.

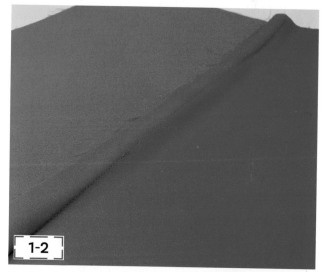

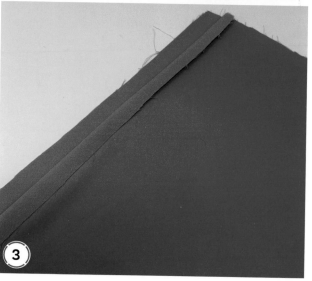

Basting the Zipper to the Garment

1. Place the open zipper face down on the extended right back seam allowance with the top stop at the horizontal marking and the teeth flush against the center back seam. Pin the left tape to the back seam allowance.

2. Baste the zipper tape to the extended seam allowance, using short stitches placed ¼" (0.5cm) from the teeth and remove the pins.

3. Close the zipper and turn the garment right side out.

4. Hold the zipper inside the garment so that it is centered on the seam; pin it across both of the center back seam allowances.

5. Hand baste along both sides of the zipper ¼" (0.5cm) from the center seam line, catching all layers—the garment fabric, the seam allowance, and the zipper tape. Remove the pins.

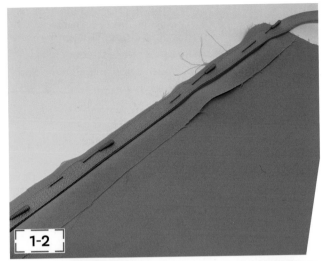

1-2

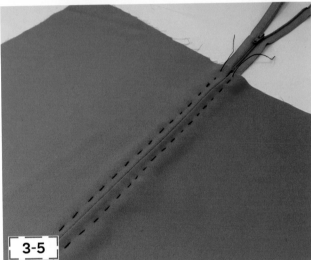

3-5

Stitching the Zipper

1. Turn the garment wrong side out.

2. Slide the right side of the fabric—the side that will be visible when the garment is completed—into the machine and, using a zipper foot, stitch down the right-hand side of the zipper, just outside the basting line, from the neck edge to ⅛" (3mm) below the bottom stop marking.

3. Making sure not to catch anything other than the zipper, continue stitching across and up the left side of the zipper to the neck edge. Snip open the center seam basting, remove all other bastings and press.

4. For a garment with a lining, it may be hand stitched down, or you may catch the lining when topstitching the zipper.

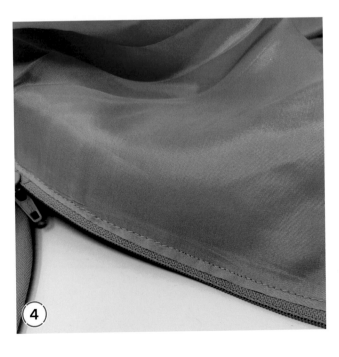

4

THE LAPPED ZIPPER

Preparing the Side Seam for Inserting the Zipper

1. If your pattern does not provide an extra-wide seam allowance of 1" (2.5cm) for the side zipper, add it to the side seam as you cut out the fabric.
2. With wrong sides facing out, pin closed the left side seam, then mark the length of the zipper as shown for the centered zipper (page 225, steps 1–3).
3. Baste if needed, then stitch the side seam from the hemline up to the marking for the bottom stop.
4. Baste closed the remainder of the side seam directly on the seam line marking from the bottom stop to the waistline edge. Press open the side seam.

Sewing the Zipper to the Seam Back

1. Lay the garment down on the back section and extend the back seam allowance so that it lies flat.
2. Place the open zipper face down on the extended back seam allowance, with its top and bottom stops at the horizontal markings. The teeth should be flush against the closed side seam. Pin the left tape to the back seam allowance.
3. Baste the zipper tape to the extended back seam allowance close to the teeth. Work from the bottom of the zipper tape to the top, machine basting with a zipper foot or using short hand stitches. Remove the pins.
4. Fold the seam allowance under the garment along the line of basting.
5. Using a zipper foot, machine stitch along the narrow strip of folded seam allowance from the bottom of the zipper tape to the top. Remove the pins.

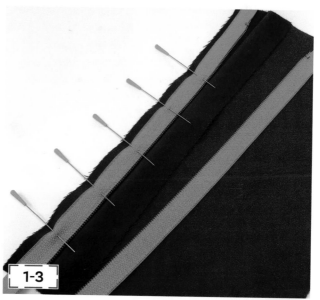

1-3

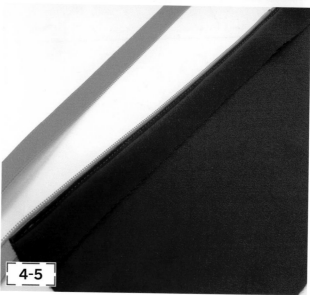

4-5

Sewing the Zipper to the Skirt Front

1. Turn the skirt right side out.

2. Position the zipper inside the skirt so that it lies flat on the seam. Pin it in place across both seam allowances.

3. Hand baste the seam from the bottom stop marking to the top edge, sewing through all layers: the skirt front, front seam allowance and the zipper tape. Remove pins.

4. Slide the skirt front, wrong side down, under the zipper foot. Beginning at the side seam and following a line ⅛" (3mm) outside the marking for the bottom stop, stitch across the bottom and up the length of the zipper to the top edge of the garment. Snip open the side seam basting, remove all other bastings, and press.

TIP

For a decorative and couture effect, use hand-pick stitches to attach the zipper. To make it even dressier, attach a tiny bead or crystal with each pick stitch.

WAISTBANDS AND WAISTLINES

The waistline may stylize the bottom edge of a blouse or jacket as a decorative hem, emphasize the top edge of a skirt or trouser pant, support the weight of a ball gown, or accentuate the curve of the body as part of a dress. In all cases, your garment should be fitted perfectly to your figure at the basting stage before you begin work on the waistline finish. Only if this is done in advance can you avoid two common pitfalls: a waistline seam that does not fall precisely at the wearer's waist or a seam that droops or puckers because the bodice and skirt are not the same size at the waist.

There are two marks of a well-made waistband: It lies flat without wrinkling or buckling, and it has a soft, rolled edge at the top. The secret to this look is in the way you handle the interfacing.

Waistbands are fastened by hooks and eyes or buttons that are attached to an extension of the band called the lap. Many patterns call for an extension that overlaps at least ¾" (2cm) across the opening of the pants or skirt. Some patterns, however, have an extension that underlaps the opening; the visible edge of the opening runs, then, in a straight line all the way up to the top of the waistband. The basic method of construction remains the same for both.

ATTACHING THE INTERFACING

1. Attach interfacing to the wrong side of the waistband. Cut fusible interfacing ½" (1.5cm) narrower along all sides. Center on the band and affix.

2. Baste the interfacing to the waistband along the notched side and both ends. Remove the pins and trim. For sew-in interfacing, trim after basting to the band.

3. Hand stitch the interfacing to the waistband ⅛" (3mm) above the center fold line, using thread the same color as the fabric. Make ½" (1.5cm) stitches on the interfacing side, but do not stitch through the waistband material; pick up only a thread of the waistband fabric.

4. Trim the interfacing close to the bastings along the three outer edges. Do not trim along the center fold line.

5. Turn under one long edge of interfacing ½" (1.5cm) and press.

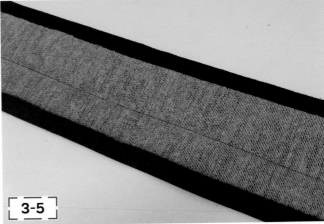

SEWING THE WAISTBAND

1. Fold the waistband in half lengthwise, right sides together. Press.
2. With right sides together, stitch the unfinished edge to the waistband of the pant or skirt. Make sure the extension for the button closure is extended beyond both edges unless the band matches exactly at the opening. Press the seam allowance toward the band.
3. Fold the band in half with right sides together. Stitch vertically on the button lap extension on the right side of the band. For the left side with the longer overlap, stitch down and over to the opening. Stitch and trim.
4. Turn over the long unstitched folded edge of the waistband to the inside of the garment.
5. Pin it to the garment, then baste and remove the pins.
6. Hand stitch the folded edge of the waistband to the garment with a slip stitch. Do not stitch into the garment fabric, but pick up only a few threads of the seam allowance. Remove all bastings and press.

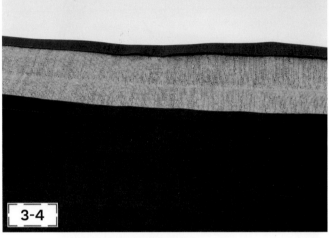

SLEEVES AND CUFFS

Two classic sleeves are the tailored sleeve for shirts and the soft sleeve for blouses, and they can be distinguished by their cuffs. The tailored cuff is made of two separate pieces crisply stitched together along the outside edges, whereas the blouse cuff is cut in one piece and folded under at the edge. Regardless of the type of sleeve, nothing is more important than a smooth set-in look at the armhole.

The smooth armhole attachment is easiest to achieve with the tailored sleeve. It goes into its body section quite simply because both are cut full to allow for freedom of movement. Because there is little difference between the size of the sleeve and the armhole, the sleeve can be attached in one long seam before assembling sleeve or body section.

The body section of a blouse fits more closely, and its armhole is therefore relatively smaller than its sleeve, which needs enough fullness to allow the arm to move freely. This fullness must be reduced, or eased, as the sleeve is sewn into the armhole of an assembled garment.

The key to a smoothly set-in sleeve is the ease basting. Make double lines of machine basting rather than a single line to guide you in controlling the fullness at the sleeve cap.

In addition to the tailored sleeve, the jacket sleeve also has its own set of techniques for the perfect hang from the shoulder to hem.

THE FITTED SLEEVE

Preparing the Sleeve

1. To mark the center line of the sleeve, spread the sleeve open, wrong side up, and measure halfway in from the underarm seam lines at the hemline. Draw a chalk line connecting this point to the pattern marking indicating the center of the sleeve cap. Run a line of basting stitches along the chalk-marked center line.

2. Run a line of basting stitches horizontally across the sleeve, joining the two points where the markings for the underarm seams meet the markings for the seam along the top curved edge of the sleeve.

3. Run a line of basting along the hemline at the bottom of the sleeve, if one is indicated on your pattern.

4. Run a line of basting stitches along the seam line around the top curved edge of the sleeve or cap.

5. Make two parallel lines of machine basting—six stitches to the 1" (2.5cm)—along the cap of the sleeve between the pattern markings indicating where the sleeve will be eased into the armhole. One line of basting should be ⅛" (3mm) outside the seam line marking and the other ⅛" (3mm) outside the first. Leave 4" (10cm) long loose threads at each end.

Joining the Underarm Seam

1. Fold the sleeve in half, wrong side out, matching the intersection between the underarm seam and the cap seam, then matching the notches. Pin along the underarm seam at 1"–2" (2.5–5cm) intervals. Baste and remove the pins.

2. Machine stitch at the normal 12 stitches per 1" (2.5cm) along the underarm seam. Remove the bastings and press the seam open.

Easing the Sleeve Cap

1. Turn the sleeve right side out and press the underarm seam again, using a press cloth.

2. With the sleeve right side out, gently pull the loose threads of the basting stitches first from one end, then from the other, to adjust the fullness of the sleeve cap and easing it to fit the armhole. As this action gathers the fabric, push it into small, even ripples on each side of the lengthways basting.

3. Continue easing, working the fabric and the threads until the sleeve cap is approximately the size of the armhole of the body section.

Aligning the Sleeve

1. Test the alignment of the sleeve by holding it up with the crossed bastings facing you. The lengthways bastings must hang exactly vertical and the crossways bastings must cross the lengthways ones at a precise right angle. If either line is askew, redistribute the easing of the sleeve cap.

2. Smooth away all the ripples in the eased cap ½" (1.5cm) on each side of the lengthways basting.

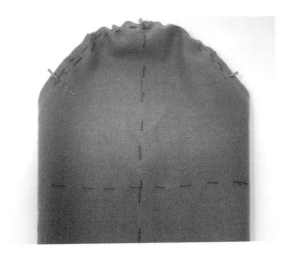

Attaching the Sleeve

The bodice must be correctly fitted to the body prior to attaching the sleeve.

1. Turn the assembled body section of the garment wrong side out. If you have not already done so, baste a row of stitches around the pattern markings for the armhole seam line.

2. Slip the sleeve into the armhole of the body section and align the lengthways bastings of the sleeve with the shoulder seam of the garment.

3. Roll the sleeve cap over the armhole of the body section. Align the center marking on the garment shoulder seam with the lengthways sleeve bastings at the cap end of the sleeve; insert a pin at the seam line. Match the underarm seam of the sleeve to the body section side seam and pin there. Then match and pin the notches.

4. If tailoring a jacket with shoulder pads, turn the front interfacing out of the way so you will not catch it in the front seam.

5. Starting at the top of the sleeve cap, pin around the armhole in both directions, matching seam lines and placing pins at ¾" (2cm) intervals.

6. Hand baste the sleeve to the armhole, sewing along the seam line. Remove the pins.

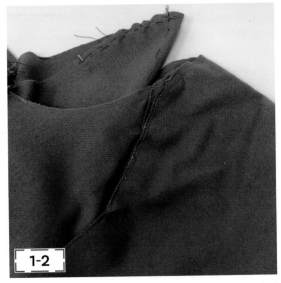

1-2

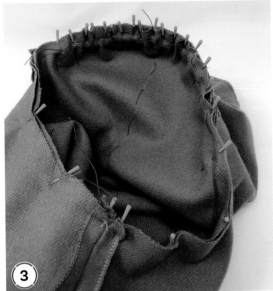

3

TIP

For tailored jackets with shoulder pads, place the pad over the interfacing so that the straight edge is aligned with the armhole seam allowance with the widest point over the shoulder seam. Pin the pad at its three corners. Turn the jacket right side out and stitch several basting stitches from the shoulder to armhole and over the shoulder pad. Turn the jacket wrong side out. Using long running stitches, stitch the front interfacing and the shoulder pad to the seam allowance around the armhole. Optional: Attach a sleeve head.

Trying On the Garment

1. Turn the garment right side out and try it on to be sure the basted-in sleeve fits perfectly at the armhole.
2. The basted alignment lines must be perpendicular and parallel to the floor, and the ease gathering at the armhole should be evenly distributed. If either line is askew, re-set the sleeve.

Stitching the Sleeve to the Body

1. Turn the body section wrong side out. Tuck the sleeve into the armhole.
2. Partially smooth the easing of fullness of the sleeve cap seam allowance by pressing it lightly with the tip of the iron. Do not press beyond the seam line.
3. Starting at the underarm seam, machine stitch the sleeve to the garment all around the armhole, sewing on the side of the bastings away from the seam allowance.
4. Reinforce the underarm seam of the sleeve with a second row of the machine stitches between the notches, stitching into the seam allowance ¼" (0.5cm) away from the machine stitching. Remove all bastings.
5. Clip into the underarm seam allowance at the notches. Cut up to, but not through, the reinforcement stitches, then trim along the machine stitching. Taper the ends so that the rest of the seam allowance is trimmed to ½" (1.5cm).
6. Press the underarm seam allowance over the reinforcement stitches. With the tip of the iron, press the remaining seam allowance.

Finishing the Sleeve Hem

1. Pull the sleeve out through the armhole so that it is wrong side out and enclose the raw edge at the bottom of the sleeve with a classic hem.
2. Turn the hem up along the basting line and pin. Hand baste close to the fold. Remove the pins.
3. Pin and baste the finished edge to the sleeve. Remove the pins.
4. Hand stitch the hem to the sleeve with a blind hemming stitch. Remove all bastings and press on the wrong side.

THE TAILORED SHIRT

Preparing the Cuff Opening

1. The order of sewing steps for a shirt cuff or sleeve may vary slightly from one pattern to another based on the designer, the style of sleeve and the details. However, sleeves and cuffs of tailored shirts are basically the same.

2. To reinforce the area around the cuff opening, called the placket, machine stitch without backstitching from the bottom right edge of the pattern marking for the placket to the placket point, using 15 stitches per 1" (2.5cm).

3. Raise the presser foot on your machine, turn the sleeve slightly, lower the presser foot and take one stitch across the placket point or 2–3 stitches for plackets with a wide overlap. Then raise the presser foot again, turn further, lower the presser foot, and continue stitching down the other side of the placket.

4. Cut a straight line up the middle of the V formed by the stitching, cutting to the placket point.

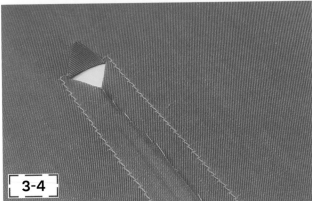

Attaching the Strip of Fabric to the Placket

1. From fabric left over after you cut out the pattern, cut a binding along the lengthwise grain 1½" (4cm) wide and twice the length of the closed placket.

2. With wrong sides together place the binding over the placket, aligning the ends of the placket with the outer corners of the strip.

3. Pin the binding to the placket, with the point of the placket ¼" (0.5cm) in from the outer edge of the strip.

4. Baste the binding to the placket and remove the pins.

5. Machine stitch, resetting the machine to the normal 12 stitches per 1" (2.5cm), in a straight line along the placket just inside the reinforcement stitches, pausing at the placket point to move the bunched-up fabric out of the way. Remove the basting.

6. Pull the unstitched edge of the binding from under the placket so that the strip projects wrong side up.

7. Press the seam allowance over the projecting binding.

8. Fold in the outer edge of the binding ¼" (0.5cm) and press toward the front.

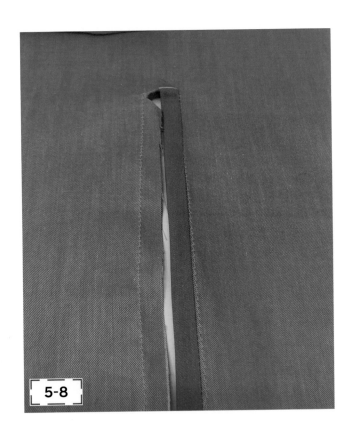

Enclosing the Placket

1. Pin the folded outer edge of the binding to the placket so that it just covers the lines of machine stitching.
2. Baste and remove the pins.
3. Machine stitch along the folded edge, spreading the placket farther open as you go; pause at the point of the placket to redistribute the bunched-up fabric. Remove the basting and press.
4. Turn the sleeve over so that it is wrong side up. Repeat on the other side according to the cuff style and pattern.
5. Overlap one side of the placket over the other and bartack across the top or house, holding it in place. The top is called a house; often the formation of the top looks like a house.
6. For patterns with continuous single narrow binding, fold one side under along the placket line. Without backstitching, machine stitch on a diagonal from the point of the placket to a spot ¼" (0.5cm) down on its outer edge.

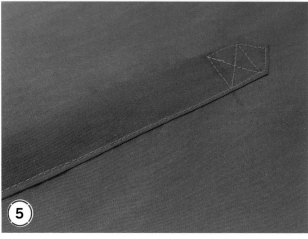

Pleating the Bottom of the Sleeve

1. To make pleats at the places indicated on the pattern, turn the sleeve right side up on to the side that will be visible in the finished garment and open it out flat.
2. Fold the pleats along their markings toward the placket, then pin.
3. Turn under the front lap of the placket—that is, the side closest to the pleats—and hold it and the pleats in place by basting along the bottom stitching line. Remove the pins.

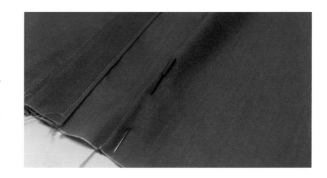

Attaching the Sleeve to the Body

1. Sleeves can be attached to the body of the shirt before the cuff has been added, or after. Sleeves can also be attached flat followed by a continuous seam from shirt hem to sleeve hem, or a finished sleeve can be inserted into the circular opening of the garment body. Reference your pattern for the corresponding layout
2. Turn the sleeve wrong side out. Machine baste between the pattern markings that indicate where extra fabric will be eased, making two parallel lines of basting ¼" (0.5cm) apart along the top of the sleeve.
3. Pull the loose threads gently, first at one end and then at the other, in order to distribute the easing evenly.
4. Pin the sleeve to the armhole of the shirt body, all sections wrong sides out, matching dots, notches, and seam intersections.

Stitching the Sleeve to the Body

1. Distribute the eased fabric evenly until the sleeve fits smoothly into the armhole. Add pins as necessary.
2. Baste the sleeve to the body section, remove the pins, then machine stitch. Remove the basting but leave in the ease lines.
3. Press both seam allowances toward the body section. Turn the garment right side out and press again.
4. Turn the garment wrong side out and construct an optional flat felled seam around the armhole.

Making the Side Seam

1. With the wrong sides of the fabric facing out, bring the side and underarm seams together and pin the front of the body section to the back at the intersection of the armhole seam.
2. Pin the underarm seam of the sleeve, then pin the side seam of the body section, matching the notches.
3. Baste along the underarm seam and the side seam in one continuous line. Remove the pins.
4. Machine stitch from the bottom of the sleeve to the shirttail in one continuous line. Remove the basting.
5. Press both seam allowances toward the back of the garment and construct a continuous flat felled seam along the sleeve and body section.

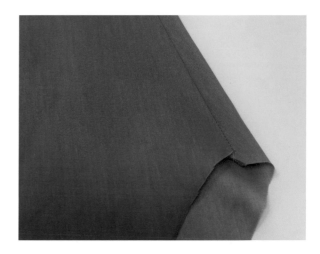

Attaching the Interfacing and Facing to the Cuff

1. Lay the cuff down wrong side up. Place the interfacing on top and pin together.
2. Baste just outside the stitching line. Remove the pins.
3. Trim away the interfacing all around the basting.
4. Fold in the top edge of the cuff along the stitching line and press.
5. Trim the folded edge to ¼" (0.5cm).
6. Place the cuff facing wrong side down and cover with the interfaced cuff wrong side up. Pin together.
7. Baste along the three outer sides, leaving the folded edge open. Remove the pins.
8. Machine stitch along the three basted sides.
9. Trim the seam allowance to ¼" (0.5cm) around the three stitched sides; the facing will extend on the fourth side of the cuff. Remove the basting.
10. If the cuff is rounded, clip into the corners.
11. Turn the cuff right side out and press it and its extended facing flat.

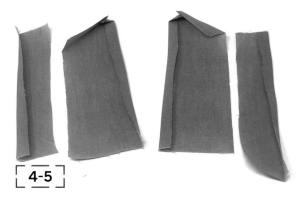

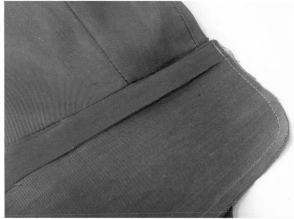

Attaching the Cuff to the Sleeve

1. Turn the sleeve right side out and curl up the bottom edge.
2. Holding the cuff so that the wrong side of the facing is toward you, pin the extension of the cuff facing to the curled-up bottom of the sleeve. Match notches.
3. Hand baste the cuff facing to the sleeve, then remove the pins.
4. Machine stitch the facing to the sleeve, following the stitching line. Remove the basting.

Completing the Cuff

1. Slip the bottom seam allowances between the cuff facing and interfacing. Press, then trim to ¼" (0.5cm).
2. Pin the folded edge of the cuff just over the stitching line of the sleeve.
3. Hand baste, then remove the pins.
4. Machine stitch along the folded edge sewing at the top of the cuff from one edge of the placket to the other. Then pivot the cuff in the machine and stitch all along the outer edge of the cuff. When you reach the top edge of the cuff again, secure the last stitches by backstitching. Remove the basting.
5. Machine stitch a second line all around the cuff ¼" (0.5cm) in from the stitching line made above.
6. Following the basted pattern markings for buttonhole positions, make buttonholes and attach buttons.

COLLARS

All collars fall into one of three basic shapes: standing, rolled, or flat. Within each of these categories, you can create size, shape, and edge variations to accent your body and enhance your selected fabric for the ultimate custom sewing experience.

The standing collar rises crisply from the shirt front to encircle and sometimes conceal the neck. The closely fitting standing collar can open in the front or back. The rolled collar folds over softly, adding height to the neckline; the shape is provided by diagonal basting along the top edges of the collar. As its name suggests, the flat collar lies against the blouse, providing interest to the front neckline. The tie collar is a variation on the basic flat shape; it should be made in a soft fabric, such as silk, that will hold a bow attractively.

THE SHIRT COLLAR

Interfacing the Collar

1. Assemble the collar pieces according to your pattern: the upper collar, the under collar, and the interfacing. Some patterns have the collar attached to the band prior to attaching to the shirt neckline, while others have the band attached, then the collar, followed by the collar band facing. While some find they have a preference, either method is correct and will give you the same results.

2. Pin and baste the collar interfacing to the wrong side of the undercollar, matching the pattern markings. Remove the pins. If using a fusible, remove the seam allowance and center the interfacing on the undercollar.

3. Trim the interfacing just above the basting along the neckline only.

4. With right sides together, pin the collar to the undercollar matching pattern markings. Stitch, leaving the neck edge open. Trim the interfacing as close as possible to the stitching.

Grading the Seam

1. Trim the seam allowance of the collar to ¼" (0.5cm) along the sides and bottom edge.

2. Trim the seam allowance of the under collar to ⅛" (3mm) along the sides and bottom edge.

3. Clip the trimmed seam allowances of the bottom edge of the collar assembly at ½" (1.5cm) intervals.

TIP
When stitching across the collar point, stitch a single stitch across the point.

Completing the Collar

1. Turn the assembled collar right side out so that the interfacing lies between the collar and the undercollar, gently pushing out the points with closed scissors; pull the points out farther from the outside with a pin.

2. Open the collar assembly from the unstitched neck edge as far as possible and press the seams open from the inside.

3. Gently roll the outside of the collar seams between your fingers to bring the stitching out to the edge. Roll again lightly so that the seam stitching is turned 1⁄16" (2mm) onto the undercollar side and baste to hold in place. Press.

4. Make a line of edge stitching, topstitching, or both around the seamed edges if desired.

Interfacing the Neckband

1. Using the same steps for assembling the collar, pin and baste the neckband interfacing to the wrong side of the outer neckband, and trim the interfacing close to the basting along the straighter edge. For precision when sewing, make sure to transfer all markings to the band for exact placement and stitching.
2. Trim the outer neckband fabric along the straighter edge, ¼" (0.5cm) from the trimmed interfacing.
3. Turn up the straighter edge of the outer neckband along the seam line and baste it against the interfacing. Press.

Attaching the Outer Neckband to the Collar

1. With right sides together pin the collar band to the neck edge of your tailored shirt.
2. Begin pinning in the center of the band matching pattern notches and work toward each side. Baste and remove the pins. Press the seam allowance toward the collar band.

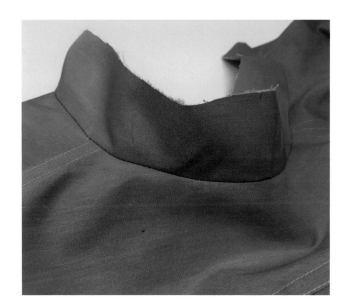

Attaching the Inner Neckband to the Collar

1. Place the finished collar on the top edge of the collar band with right sides together.
2. Pin and baste the curved-end edge of the inner neckband to the unstitched neck edge of the collar, matching the pattern markings. Remove the pins.
3. Machine stitch alongside the basting, then remove all bastings.

Completing the Collar and Neckband

1. Pin the neck edges of the collar facing to the inner neck band, having curved ends match pattern markings. Baste and remove the pins. Machine stitch alongside the basting, then remove all basting.
2. Trim the seam allowance of the interfacing close to the stitching line.
3. Trim the collar assembly seam allowances to ⅛" (3mm).
4. Trim the inner and outer neckband seam allowances to ¼" (0.5cm).
5. Clip all the trimmed seam allowances at ½" (1.5cm) intervals along the middle and notch at ½" (1.5cm) intervals along the ends where the curve is more pronounced.
6. Turn the neckband right side out and press seam allowance toward the collar band.

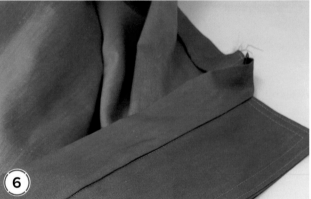

Sewing the Neckband to the Garment

1. Spread the neckband open. Pin the inner neckband to the wrong side of the garment's neck edge. Begin pinning on the center of the neckband and work toward each side, matching the pattern markings. Baste and remove the pins.
2. Machine stitch and remove the basting. Trim the inner neckband seam allowance to ⅛" (3mm).
3. Trim the garment neck edge seam allowance to ¼" (0.5cm).
4. Turn the garment right side out. Press the garment neck edge and inner neckband seam allowances inside the neckband up toward the collar.
5. Pin and baste the outer neckband to the garment, covering the stitches made above. Remove the pins.
6. Machine stitch as close to the bottom edges of the neckband as possible from one end to the other. Remove the basting.
7. Run a line of decorative edge stitching, topstitching, or both on the outer neckband if desired.

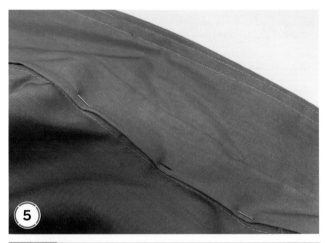

THE ROLLED COLLAR

Making the Collar

1. Make the convertible collar following the instructions for the shirt collar on page 242, omitting step 3 of Grading the Seam.
2. Clip into the neck edge seam allowance of the collar at each of the two shoulder markings (see pattern for markings).

Attaching the Collar to the Garment

1. Stay-stich and then clip the seam allowance around the neck edge of the garment at ½" (1.5cm) intervals, cutting close to the stay-stitching as shown in blue.
2. Pin the collar to the outside of the garment at the neck edge, matching center back, shoulder and center front markings. Begin pinning in the center of the undercollar and work toward each side.
3. Baste the collar to the neck edge from one edge to the other. At the clipped shoulder marking, you may pivot slightly to reposition and ease the collar into the neckline.
4. Fold both front facings of the garment back along the fold lines and pin and baste the facings to the collar, matching pattern markings. Remove the pins.
5. Machine stitch the entire length of the neck edge. Be sure not to catch the loose seam allowance of the collar when stitching between the shoulder seams. Remove the basting.
6. Spread apart the seam allowances of the facing and garment neck edge, then trim the collar assembly seam allowance to ⅛" (3mm). Be careful not to cut the folded down section of collar seam allowance.
7. Trim the facings and garment neck edge to ¼" (0.5cm).

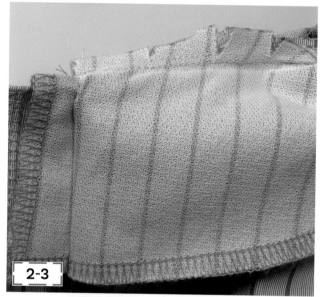

2-3

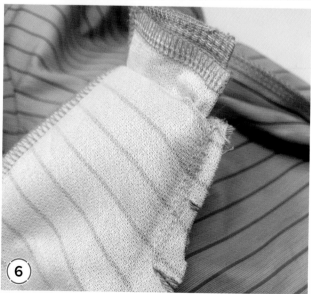

6

Finishing the Collar

1. Turn the facings right side out, pushing the points into shape with the points of closed scissors. Press.
2. Press the stitched seam allowance between the shoulders up toward the undercollar.
3. Turn under the trimmed seam allowance of the collar along its stitching line. Pin the collar over the trimmed neck edge seam allowance, just covering the stitches.
4. Baste, then remove the pins and slip stitch. Remove all bastings and press.

THE FLAT COLLAR

The flat collar is assembled in the same way as the rolled collar. Begin by interfacing and sewing the collar piece. Because the collar is flat, it is sewn right sides together to the garment neckline. The neckline edge is finished off with a facing (see page 256).

THE TAILORED JACKET COLLAR

Preparing the Undercollar

1. Assemble the undercollar in the same fashion as the shirt collar (see pages 242–243). Baste interfacing and trim next to the stitching line. For fusible interfacings, trim prior to fusing. In a true tailored jacket, the interfacing is pad stitched to the undercollar. Option: Hand baste a roll line.
2. Finish the collar in the same fashion as the shirt collar (see page 243). With right sides together, stitch the upper collar to the under collar, trim seam allowances, steam press the seam allowance, and trim the corners.

Finishing the Outer Seamed Edge

1. Turn the assembled collar right side out and pull out the corners.
2. Roll the seamed edges to bring the stitching out to the edge. Roll the seam again so that the stitching is turned ¹⁄₁₆" (2mm) toward the undercollar. To keep the seam rolled under, run a line of ¼" (0.5cm) basting stitches, which should not be removed until the jacket is completed, ¼" (0.5cm) from the edge.
3. Using a pressing cloth, steam press along the seamed edge.
4. Turn the collar assembly so that the undercollar is down. Fold under the neck edge along the roll line. Using a pressing cloth, steam press the assembled collar into a horseshoe shape or the amount of contour you desire.

Attaching the Collar

1. With right sides together, pin the undercollar to the neckline edge. Make sure to only catch the under collar. Baste just inside the stitching, easing the excess fabric on each side of the shoulder.
2. Machine stitch along the seam line, being careful not to catch the facing or the edge of the interfacings. Remove the basting.

Finishing the Neckline Seam

1. Turn the jacket wrong side up and spread it out flat. Clip the curved portions of the neckline seam allowance on the jacket.
2. Catch stitch the undercollar seam allowance to the undercollar, picking up only the interfacing fabric.
3. Catch stitch the jacket seam allowance to the jacket, again picking up only the interfacing fabric.
4. Align one of the shoulder seams lines on the back neck facing with the shoulder seam line on one of the front facings. Machine stitch along the seam line, holding other layers of fabric out of the way. Press open the seam.

Finishing the Neck Edge

1. Turn the back neck facing down, so that its wrong side is on the back interfacing.

2. Fold the collar and lapels along the roll lines. Optional: Holding the collar in a rounded shape, run a line of diagonal basting stitches along the collar roll line, keeping the grain of the fabric straight. Do not remove this basting until the jacket is completed.

3. Turn under the neck edge of the upper collar and align the fold with the neckline seam on the jacket. Match and pin the folded edge of the upper collar to the neckline seam as you did when attaching the undercollar.

4. Baste ¼" (0.5cm) from the folded edge, easing the excess collar fabric evenly on both sides of the shoulder seam markings. Remove the pins.

5. Turn under the edge of the front and back facings so that the fold is aligned with the bottom edge of the collar. Pin. Baste ¼" (0.5cm) from the folded edge and remove the pins.

6. Using tiny blind hemming stitches, hand sew the folded edge of the facings to the folded edge of the upper collar. Remove the bastings and the tailor tacks.

7. Catch stitch the lower edge of the back neck facing to the jacket back, picking up only the interfacing layer.

TIP

Basting is always optional; however, nothing provides more control and accuracy than hand stitches. Resist the urge to cut corners simply to speed up the process.

HEMS AND FACINGS

The hemline can make a garment scream home sewn or showcase the care and attention given to this detail that finishes off one of the most important edges of any garment.

Often the last step in creating a garment, the hem has its own sewing techniques that help lead to a look of professionalism and even elegance. Facings and hems finish and conceal raw edges by turning them inside the garment.

On most fitted to slightly flared dresses, a 2 ½" (6.5cm) hem is a good average. The heavier the fabric and the more flare to the skirt, the narrower the hem should be. If a skirt flares, the bottom raw edge will be wider than the hemline, which is 1"–1 ½" (2.5–4cm) above that edge. The raw edge must be reduced, or eased, to fit the circumference at the hemline rather than making little tucks.

Of course, creative variations, such as the scallop hem, can enhance a design and add interest. A garment that has been under-lined requires yet a different technique, and a hem with bias interfacing has been stiffened slightly to reinforce the shape at the hemline. These variations will be enhanced with a classic finish of the same material as the dress or its underlining.

HOW TO MARK A HEM

Ideally, it is best to have someone else mark the hem of your garment. Wear all the foundation garments you will wear under the finished garment. Different bras and briefs will change how the fabric hangs and falls off your unique body contours and make the garment hang longer or shorter. Marking the hem with the shoes you will wear with the garment is also important. The heel height of a shoe, whether high or low, will affect your posture and how the hem hangs on the body.

Marking a Skirt or Dress Hem

Measure from the floor up. Never measure from the waist down because you may have one side that is different than the other. Measuring from the floor up will ensure you have a perfectly straight hem. Ideally, use a powder chalk marker and make several chalk marks that will then be connected on the marking table. The fuller the hem, the more marks you will require, but a good guide is a mark every 2" (5cm).

Marking a Pant Hem

Pants are marked in a similar fashion as skirts and dresses. With the correct shoes on, stand legs knee width apart and take a deep breath and relax. Look straight ahead rather than looking down trying to see what is going on with the hem. This is the number one mistake in marking a hem. When you look down, it alters the angle of the hem, making the front too short and the back too long. Mark the pant leg on the back of the leg. Of course, there are different lengths of pants, but for a traditional trouser 1" (2.5cm) from the floor is a good guide to use. Each leg should be marked from the floor up.

> ## TIP
>
> *When marking the hem line, mark slightly below the hem line so the chalk is not right on the turned under edge. Use a marking chalk that will be erased with steam or water if your fabric will allow.*

To create an even hem, use a chalk marker that measures from the floor up. A level and parallel to the floor line will be created regardless of shoe height or body variations that would otherwise make an uneven hem when measuring from the waist down.

A chalk marker can also be used to mark the final placement on a pair of pants, especially when the pant is cropped or above the ankles. Unlike a skirt, where you will mark all around the hem, the center back is the correct placement for the pant hem. The pant can them be placed on the table and marked entirely with a ruler edge.

Garments for the upper body can be marked and measured from the top down or bottom up. The key is to make sure any hem or edge is parallel to the floor, unless a design uses a different angle. To even out a garment from left to right, it may be necessary to measure from the shoulder down. Make sure shoulders are level before you compare left to right.

Marking a Blouse or Jacket Hem

The upper body may have different measurements vertically in areas from the shoulder to hem or underarm to hem. Start by measuring the vertical length to the hem, but also make sure the hem hangs level and parallel to the floor. The hem should not angle to the front or back unless you have a creative reason, such as a handkerchief hemline. The hemline on the upper body should not cut the body in half. Use the rule of thirds with the upper body as one-third and the lower body two-thirds for a flattering finish.

With the garment on the body, the hem should look like it is hanging even all around. Keep in mind, when you take the garment off the body, it may not look straight on the hanger, which naturally it would not.

The chalk mark is the finished hem line. Connect the chalk marks and then determine what kind of hem finish you will use. Do not cut on this line. Use a hem gauge and mark an additional line evenly spaced from the hem line the width of the desired hem allowance. Trim off excess on this line.

THE NARROW ROLLED HEM

Shirts and Blouses

1. With the garment wrong sides facing up, trim the raw hem edge evenly along the cutting line.
2. Turn the hem edge up ¼" (0.5cm) and press flat.
3. Turn the hem up again ½" (1.5cm).
4. Pin the hem to the garment at 1" (2.5cm) intervals.
5. Machine stitch the hem to the garment close to the edge that is turned under. If a hand finish is desired, use a slip stitch for woven fabrics or a catch stitch for knits.
6. Adjust the width of the hem based on the fabric style and width of the hem.

The Pant Hem

1. Mark a 1½" (4cm) hem allowance to the pant.
2. Turn under ½" (1.5cm), then turn under 1" (2.5cm). Press and pin as needed.
3. Stitch the hem close to the edge that is turned under.

TIP

The jeans hem is created using a 1" (2.5cm) hem allowance that is first turned under ½" (1.5cm) and then turned again. Use a denim topstitching thread to recreate a professional jeans hem.

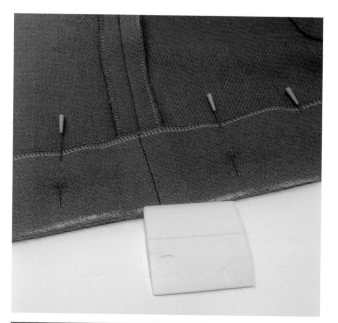

THE PLAIN HEM

Turning up the Hem

1. Turn the bottom edge up along the chalk-marked hemline.
2. Pin the hem to the garment, matching seams, at 1" (2.5cm) intervals close to the hem fold.
3. Try on the garment; adjust and re-pin the hemline if necessary.
4. If the garment is slightly flared, ease the excess fullness of the raw edge of the hem.

Finishing the Hem Edge

1. For woven fabrics, turn the garment right side out. Unfold and unpin the hem and pin seam tape to the hem edge so that the tape extends ¼" (0.5cm) beyond the raw edge of the hem. Stitch the hem tape to the hem allowance.
2. Re-pin the hem to the garment fabric, placing pins at 2" (5cm) intervals parallel to the finished edge.
3. Baste the hem to the garment and remove the pins.
4. Hand stitch the hem to the garment. Use a hemming stitch for woven fabrics or a catch stitch for knits. Remove bastings and press.

THE CLASSIC BIAS FINISH

Preparing to Make the Hem

1. Prepare the garment for hemming following the instructions for the plain hem steps 1–4.
2. Measure the circumference of the hem at the raw edge.
3. Cut strips of lining fabric on the bias 1" (2.5cm) wide and join the pieces to make a continuous circular strip the length of the circumference of the garment at the raw edge. Alternately, use double-fold bias tape pressed open.

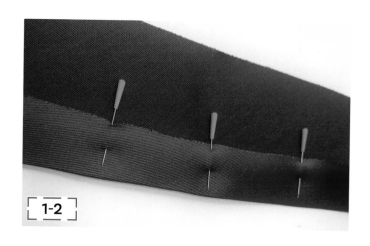

1-2

Attaching the Bias Strip

1. With the wrong side of the bias strip facing up, machine-stitch the strip to the hem ¼" (0.5cm) down from the raw edge.
2. Fold the strip over the raw edge of the hem far enough to cover the stitching line. Pin at 1" (2.5cm) intervals.

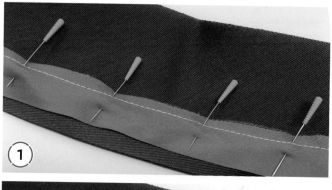

1

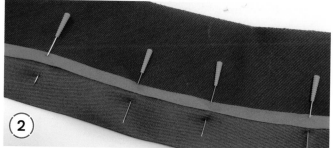

2

Completing the Hem

1. Hand-stitch the finished hem edge to the garment, with a blind hemming stitch.
2. Remove all bastings and press the hem on the wrong side.

THE BIAS-INTERFACED HEM

Using the same process for attaching a bias strip to the edge of the hem, the bias can be added to the edge of the garment so the bias is at the bottom edge. This is useful for lengthening a hem when there is not enough fabric to add to the hem.

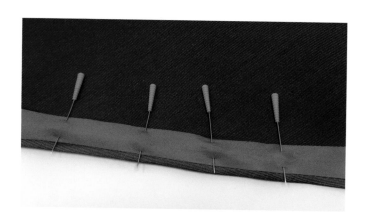

THE HORSEHAIR HEM

The horsehair hem beautifully adds body and shape to the edge of any fabric. It is visibly seen on a netted tulle skirt, adding dramatic flair, or it can add body to the edge of a taffeta skirt. There are a few variations on where you place the hem and how you attach it to the garment with machine and hand stitching. This method gives you an easy application, but experiment with how you use horsehair in your lined and unlined designs.

1. Select the width of horsehair braid for your design. Trim the hem allowance on the hem to ½" (1.5cm).

2. Place the horsehair on the right side of the hem overlapping the edge of the horsehair next to the raw edge of the hem allowance.

3. Stitch ¼" (0.5cm) from the raw edge.

4. Turn the horsehair to the inside on the ¼" (0.5cm) line of stitching. Press if needed. Turn the hem again an additional ¼" (0.5cm) with the horsehair encased in the edge of the fabric and the fabric now folded on the hem line.

5. Using a blind stitch, pin and stitch the top edge of the horsehair to the garment or lining.

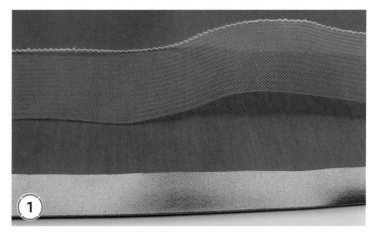

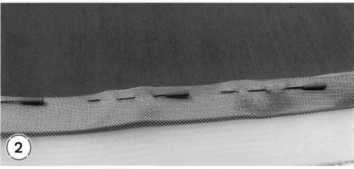

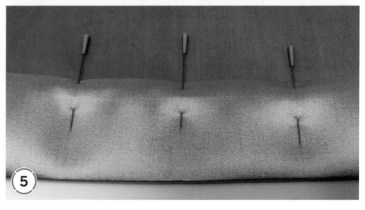

THE SCALLOPED HEM

Preparing to Make the Hem

1. Trim the raw edge of the garment evenly 1" (2.5cm) below the hemline marking.
2. Measure the circumference of the garment along the bottom raw edge.
3. Make a facing from 2 ½" (6.5cm) strips of the garment fabric cut on the lengthways grain and join the pieces to make a continuous circular strip 1" (2.5cm) longer than the circumference of the garment at the raw edge.
4. With right sides together, pin the facing to the bottom edge of the hem. Stitch through all layers of fabric, matching the seams in the facing to the side seams and other vertical seam intersections wherever possible. Baste the top edge of the facing to the garment ¼" (0.5cm) from the raw edge of the facing. Remove the pins.

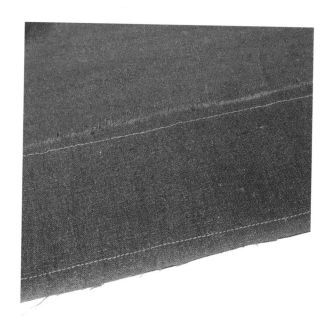

Making the Scallops

1. Pin and baste the actual tissue pattern for the scallops on to the facing. Place the curved bottom edges of the scallops on the hem line, marking and centering the garment's side seams and other vertical seam intersections over the scallop curves wherever possible.
2. Using a small machine stitch—15 to 20 stitches to 1" (2.5cm)—stitch around the curved edges of the scallops using the edge of the tissue pattern as your guide. Pivot the needle at each point between scallops by leaving the needle in the fabric, raising the presser foot, and turning the fabric underneath it; then, lower the foot again and proceed down the next scallop. Tear off the tissue pattern.
3. Trim the scallop edges to ⅜" (1cm). Cut notches around the scallop curves, and clip into the points, being careful to cut up to, but not into, the machine stitching.

Finishing the Scallops

1. Turn the facing to the wrong side, rolling the edges of the scallop between your fingers to bring the edges out.
2. On the wrong side of each scallop, make a line of small running stitches near the curved edge, catching the facing and the seam, but not the outer fabric of the garment.
3. Finish the raw edge of the facing with the classic bias finish and stitch the finished hem edge to the garment with a blind hemming stitch. Remove bastings, press.

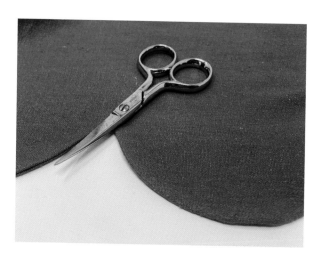

THE ARMHOLE AND NECKLINE FACING

Preparing the Facing

1. Cut and mark the front and back armhole facing pieces. Apply interfacing if needed and finish off the outer edge with a narrow-rolled hem, serging or making the desired finish.
2. With right sides together, pin the front and back facing pieces along the underarm and the shoulder seam markings. Stitch. Press open both seams and trim to ½" (1.5cm).

Attaching the Facing to the Garment

1. Turn the garment right side out and pin the facing, right sides together, matching the armhole seam markings. Pin. Baste and remove the pins.
2. Machine stitch along seam markings, beginning and ending at the intersection between the underarm and armhole seams. Remove the basting.
3. Trim the facing armhole seam allowance to ⅛" (3mm).
4. Trim the garment armhole seam allowance to ¼" (0.5cm).
5. Clip into both armhole seam allowances at ½" (1.5cm) intervals, cutting close to, but not into, the stitching.
6. Turn the garment wrong side out.
7. Turn the facing up so that it extends away from the garment and press the armhole seam allowances toward the facing.
8. Understitch the facing and seam allowances by topstitching the seam allowance to the facing ⅛" (3mm) next to the seam line.

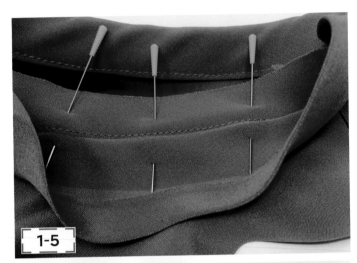

1-5

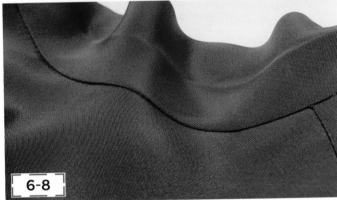

6-8

Hand Finishing the Facing

1. Turn the facing down over the wrong side of the garment and press flat.
2. Pin the facing to the garment at the shoulder and underarm seams as shown and attach the facing to those seam allowances with a slip stitch. Remove the pins and press.

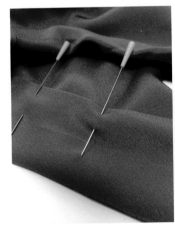

POCKETS

Pockets are a convenient place for an iPhone, credit card, and car keys. You may be surprised to learn that the original pocket began much differently than how they are purposed today. Pockets began to appear in waistcoats and trousers more than 500 years ago. However, it was much earlier in history when pockets for women were sewn as a separate garment tied on between the skirt and petticoat, and they held all sorts of necessities, such as a pincushion, spectacles, and snacks.

The Victorians adapted smaller waists and slimmer skirts in their fashions, so the pocket went out of fashion and the purse was adopted—but they did not stay out of fashion for long. Modern designers have incorporated pockets in many creative and decorative ways. As technology has gotten smaller, the demand for the functional pocket has grown so that it can hold the new, modern necessity—the cell phone. Even a wedding dress can be designed so that a bride can carry her phone in her pocket!

Two of the most common types of pockets are the patch and in-seam—one in plain view, the other concealed. Even though the patch pocket is the easiest to make, it requires care in positioning to make sure it is conveniently and attractively placed. The in-seam pocket is stitched, as its name implies, inside the garment seams. Additionally, the welt pocket is often seen as the most desired pocket sewing technique. Often seen in fine tailoring and couture sewing, any sewist can master this pocket by following a few steps to enhance any sewing design.

PATCH POCKETS

Preparing the Pocket Section

1. Run a basting stitch along the pattern markings for all the seam lines and the hem fold line.
2. Finish off the top edge of the hem with a narrow-rolled hem, serging or hand stitching.
3. Fold the hem along the fold line to the wrong side. Stitch across the hem. Press.

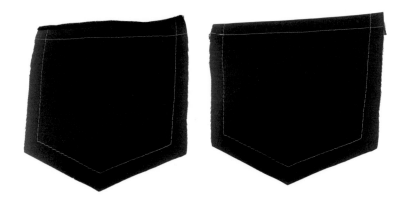

Completing Straight Pockets

1. On pockets with straight bottoms, turn the pocket section wrong side up, turn over the hem and press.
2. Fold in the side seam allowances just beyond the line of machine basting and press.
3. Fold up the bottom seam allowance and press.

Completing Pointed Pockets

1. On pockets with pointed bottoms, turn the pocket section wrong side up, turn over the hem, and press.
2. Fold up the two bottom seam allowances that form the point just beyond the line of machine basting.
3. Fold in the side seam allowances and press.

TIP

Cut the pocket pattern from oak tag, a manilla file folder, or cardstock. Remove the seam allowance. Use as a guide for turning under the edges by placing on the wrong side of the pocket and pressing under the seam allowance.

Completing Rounded Pockets

1. On pockets with rounded bottoms, turn the pocket section wrong side up, turn over the hem, and press.
2. Notch the curves at ½" (1.5cm) intervals.
3. Fold in the seam allowances just beyond the basting and press. Overlap the notched segments where necessary.

TIP

Use temporary spray adhesive to attach the pocket, eliminating the need for pinning.

Stitching the Pocket to the Garment

1. Place the pocket, wrong side down, on the right side of the garment—the side that will be visible when the garment is completed. Align the edges of the pocket with the basted placement lines on the garment that were made when the pattern was cut out.
2. Pin the pocket to the garment at each corner and at 1" (2.5cm) intervals.
3. Baste along the side and bottom edges of the pocket, ¼" (0.5cm) in from the edges. Remove the pins.

Making an Invisible Finish

For an invisible finish, hand stitch the pocket to the garment with a slip stitch next to the edge.

Making a Visible Finish

1. To add strength and give a visible finish, machine stitch the pocket to the garment close to the edge with a line of topstitching.
2. Add additional rows of topstitching for embellishment.

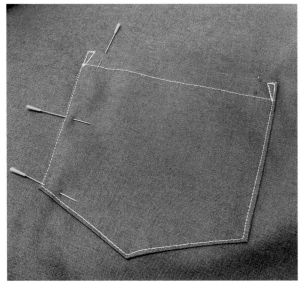

Stitching the Pocket to the Garment

IN-SEAM POCKETS

Preparing the Pocket Section

If any adjustments have been made to the side seam and hip area of the garment, those changes need to be transferred over to the corresponding pieces of the pocket so they fit the body correctly. This will eliminate any pulling in the side area due to differences in the contour of the pocket.

1. Cut pocket bag pieces from lining material and pocket facing from the fashion fabric.
2. Add interfacing to the wrong side of the facing. Transfer all marks from the pattern.
3. Edge finish the outer curved edge of the pocket facing.

Stitching the Facings to the Pocket

1. With wrong sides together, overlap outer pocket facing to the bottom pocket lining.
2. Topstitch in place ¼" (0.5cm) from the edge of the curve.
3. Repeat and position the inner pocket facing on top pocket lining. Stitch.

Sewing the Pocket

1. With wrong sides together, sew across the bottom edge of the pocket. Edge finish or serge.
2. Open the pocket bag. With right sides together, sew the slanted edge of the upper pocket facing to the slanted edge of the garment. Turn and press under.
3. Fold the pocket in half on the inside of the garment. Line up the top and side seam of the pocket with the garment.
4. Baste across the top and side just inside the seam allowance.

TIP

Stitch seam tape or twill tape to the slanted edge to reinforce and prevent stretching.

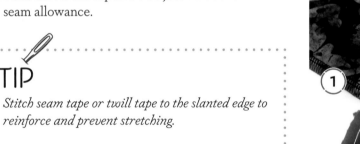

TIP

For fabrics such as twills, which have a more open weave, line the pocket prior to sewing for an additional finish inside the pocket.

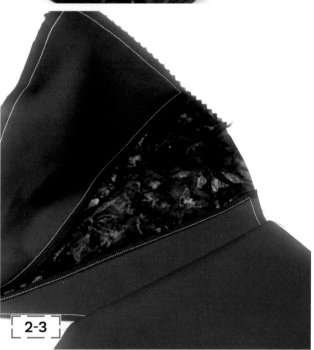

WELT POCKETS

The welt pocket is one of the more elegant variations on the essential pocket. All but the top edge, or welt, of the pocket is entirely hidden inside the garment. Welt pockets are best suited to garments made from a firmly woven fabric that does not fray easily. The pocket should be of lightweight fabric, and its color should harmonize with the garment, although contrasting fabric and unique shapes add much creativity to this technique. The welt itself is a straight strip of fabric sewn with precision and a pocket lining of matching or decorative fabric.

The well-made welt pocket should look crisp, and the welt should lie completely flat, like the one pictured above. To achieve this effect, take special care to match all pattern markings precisely and to cut and stitch accurately when making the little triangles at each end of the pocket opening. Take care to mark and cut with precision for beautiful results.

1. Stitch lines of basting stitches on the garment along the pattern markings for the stitching lines and the slash line for the pocket opening.

2. Cut the welt pocket from the fashion fabric and fuse interfacing to the wrong side. Optional: Fuse interfacing to the wrong side of the garment where the welt will be place if the garment is not already interfaced.

3. Finish the long edges of the welt piece.

4. Place the welt on the right side of the garment face down. The wider part of the welt will be on the lower side of the placement line. Line up the markings and baste in place.

5. On the wrong side of the garment, place the pocket lining centered on the welt. Pin or baste in place.

6. On the right side of the garment, stitch around the parameter of the welt using a shorter stitch length. Stitch through the lining on the wrong side. Back stitch to secure the welt. Press the long sides of the welt on the stitching line.

The welt pocket is often placed on the back of a trouser pant and may feature a button closure or contrasting fabric.

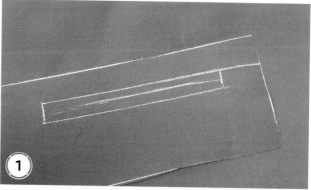

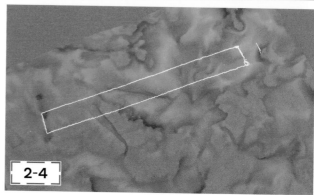

Attaching the Welt to the Garment

1. Cut through the center of the welt, stopping ½" (1.5cm) from the end. Clip at an angle to each corner, making sure not to cut through the stitching. This angle will create a triangle piece that will be later sewn.

2. Turn the welt to the inside of the garment and press flat around all sides.

3. On the lower, wider part of the welt, fold in half to make an accordion pleat. Baste in place along the seam allowance.

4. Flip to the right side and stitch in the ditch along the short edges.

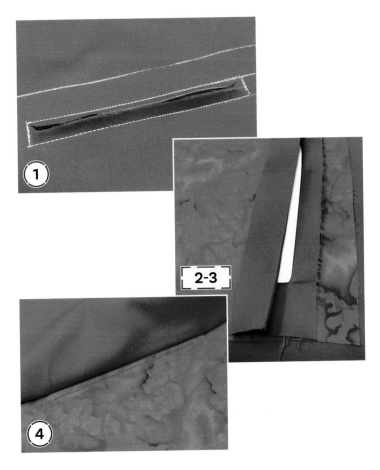

Lining the Pocket

1. Turn up the side edge of the welt and stitch the triangle made above to the welt seam allowance. Sew as close as possible. This will secure the side of the welt.

2. Fold the garment out of the way and pin the bottom edge of the welt to the lining.

3. Stitch the welt facing to the corresponding lining.

4. With right sides together, place the lining with the facing over the welt and welt lining making sure the facing lines up with the welt.

5. Stitch down both sides of the lining and edge finish.

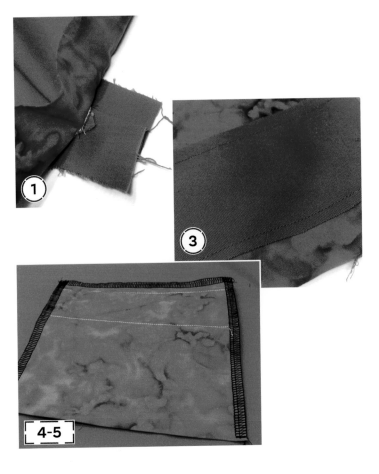

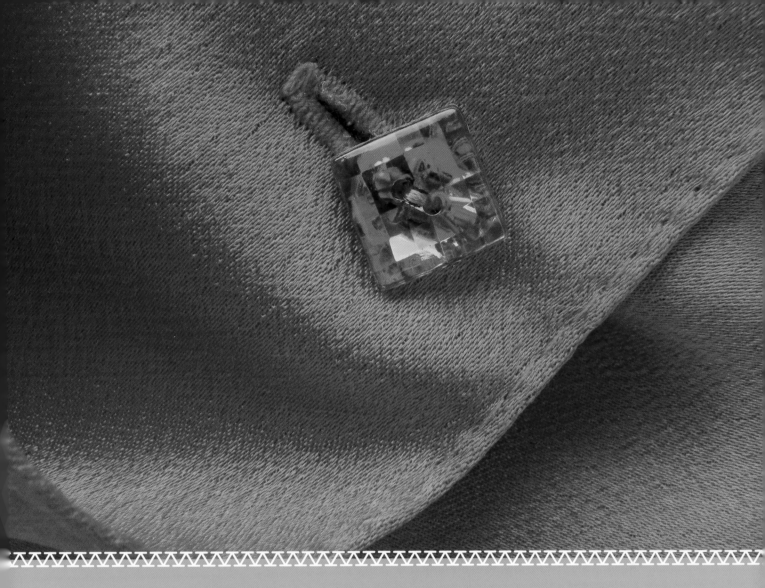

BUTTONHOLES AND CLOSURES

The tiniest details of bound buttonholes, buttons, snaps, hooks and eyes, and other closures are the final professional touch to be added only after a garment is otherwise finished. Buttons are decorative as well as functional; select them with an eye to the fabric as well as the size of the wearer. For example, small pearl buttons would be lost on a checked tweed dress, and large metallic buttons might overwhelm a tiny figure.

Horizontal buttonholes should be used on close-fitting garments where there is some stress. Vertical buttonholes should be used where there is less strain, such as on a shirt. The bound buttonhole adds a high-end effect to any garment.

Hooks and eyes are best used as hidden fasteners for overlapping edges, such as the waistbands of skirts or pants. Snaps have little holding power and are used to tack down edges invisibly in conjunction with other fasteners.

These instructions are intended for women's garments, which close with the right-hand side over the left. For men's garments, reverse the directions in the instructions.

THE BUTTON

Measuring a Button

To find the size of your buttonholes, measure the buttons to be attached. For a flat, thin button, measure its diameter and add ⅛" (3mm). For a thicker button, measure its diameter and add ¼" (0.5cm). For a mounded or ball button, place a thin strip of paper across the mound or ball, pin it tightly in place, slide the paper off, flatten it, then measure it and add ¼" (0.5cm).

Sewing on Buttons with Holes

1. Using a strand of knotted buttonhole twist, make a small stitch in the fabric at the point where the center of the button is to fall. Insert the needle through one of the holes on the underside of the button and pull the thread through.

2. Make two or three stitches; in the case of a four-hole button, make two rows of parallel stitches. Do not pull the thread too tightly. It should have some give for the shank. A throwback technique is to place a match across the button as a spacer.

3. Remove the match and pull the button up, away from the fabric to the top of the threads.

4. Wind the thread five or six times, tightly, around the loose threads below the button to create a thread shank.

5. End by pulling the needle through to the back side of the fabric and tie off.

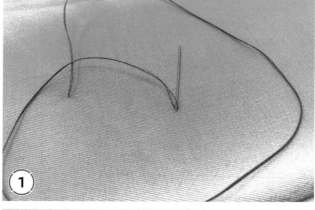

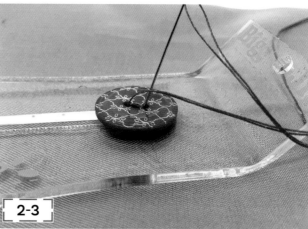

TIP

Using tailor's beeswax, thread the needle and then pull the thread through the wax to add a smooth coating, which will prevent tangling and will also strengthen the thread..

Sewing on Buttons with Shanks

1. If the button already has a shank base, begin the same as step 1 for a regular button.
2. Angle the button away from the fabric with your thumb and take two or three stitches through the fabric and button shank.
3. Wind the thread tightly five or six times around the thread shank.
4. End by pulling the needle through to the back side of the fabric and tie off. Even though the button has a shank, wrapping the thread will provide even more durability.

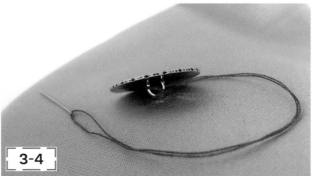

THE BUTTONHOLE

Determining Position

1. To determine the outer placement line for your horizontal buttonholes, run basting stitches parallel to and ⅛" (3mm) outside the center front line on the right front of the garment. Use thread of a different color to distinguish this placement line from other basted markings.
2. To determine the inner placement line for your buttonholes, measure in from the outside placement line a distance equal to the size of your buttonhole. Make a line of basting stitches parallel to the outer placement line. Space buttonholes according to the quantity of buttons, the size of the button, and the length of the garment.
3. To determine placement for vertical buttonholes, determine the distance from the edge of the fabric and baste a vertical line up the length of the opening.
4. To space vertical buttons, mark the location of the first button and measure down from the bottom of the first button to the next.

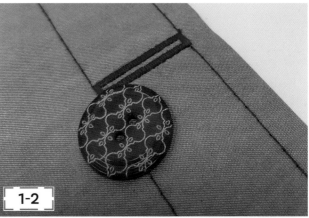

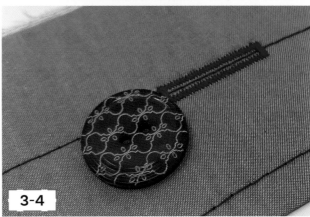

Making the Buttonhole

1. To make a buttonhole entirely by machine, follow the instructions provided with your specific model. To make the holes by hand, see the hand-worked buttonhole on page 267.
2. With a buttonhole blade or sharp pointed scissors, cut the buttonhole open.
3. Pin the right side of the garment over the left, matching the neck edges of both sides and lining up the basting stitches marking the center front lines.
4. To determine the correct position for the center of each button, insert a pin through each buttonhole at the center front line; the pin should continue through the center front line of the left side of the garment.
5. Mark the position with another pin.

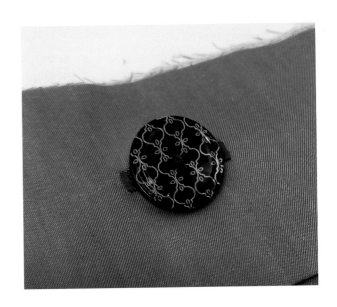

SEWING ON SNAPS

1. Place the half of the snap having a prong or ball in its center on the wrong side of the overlapping part of the garment.
2. Hold the pronged half in place by putting it at the point of closure and about ⅛" (3mm) from the edge to be held in place and inserting a straight pin through the tiny hole inside the prong.
3. Using a double strand of knotted thread, take a small stitch—catching only the inside layer of fabric—through one of the holes and then around the edge of the snap. Tuck the knot under the snap.
4. Take a second stitch at the first hole, then slide the needle under the snap and up through another hole. Repeat until all the holes are completed and end with two small fastening stitches at one edge under the snap.
5. Place the overlap so that the straight pin holding the pronged half in place goes through the underlap. Insert a second pin through the underlap to mark the spot pierced by the first pin.
6. Slide the socket half of the snap onto the second pin and sew it in place.

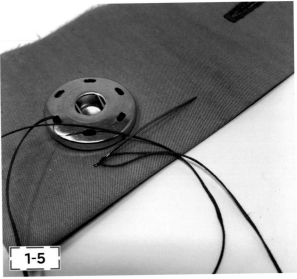

1-5

6

SEWING ON HOOKS

1. When edges meet on the back of garments, place the hook at the left-hand side of the closure, ⅛" (3mm) from the fabric edge. Using a double strand of knotted thread, stitch around each metal ring, catching only the inside fabric layer.

2. Continue by sliding the needle under the hook and take a few stitches over the hook and under the bend. End with a fastening stitch through the inside layer of fabric.

3. Place the round eye on the right-hand side of the closure so that it protrudes just beyond the edge and the garment edges meet exactly. Sew around each metal ring. End with a fastening stitch.

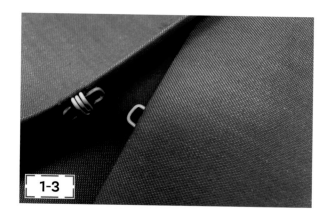

Working with Hooks with Straight Eyes

1. On garments where the edges overlap, attach the hook to the overlapping side of the closure, as in steps 1 and 2 for sewing snaps.

2. Place the overlap so that the bend of the hook falls where the straight eye is to be positioned. Sew the eye in place by stitching around the two metal rings, catching all layers of fabric.

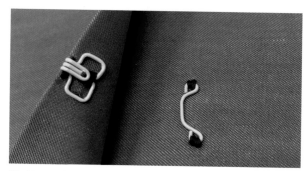

Working with Hooks with Straight Eyes

THE HAND-WORKED BUTTONHOLE

1. Determine the placement of the buttonhole (see page 265). Mark the opening with chalk and use tailor's tacks to mark the top and bottom of the buttonhole.

2. Working on one buttonhole at a time, cut with small-pointed scissors along the center line. Start in the middle and cut to the inner and outer placement lines.

3. To form an eyelet at the outer end of the buttonhole, first make two ¹⁄₁₆" (2mm) diagonal clips on one edge, starting both clips ¹⁄₁₆" (2mm) from the outer placement line. Make two similar diagonal clips on the other edge. Trim off the wedges by cutting around the outside of the clips with cuticle scissors.

4. To protect the edges of the buttonhole from fraying, sew around them with ¹⁄₁₆" (2mm) overcast stitches. As you sew, squeeze the garment and facing layers of fabric so that the interfacing, which is between the two layers, will not be visible when the buttonhole is finished.

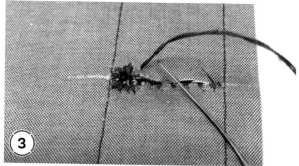

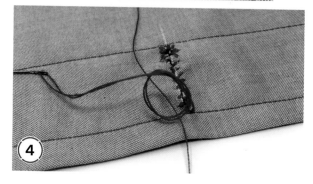

Stitching the Buttonhole

1. Thread your needle with an arm's length of knotted buttonhole twists the same color as the garment fabric and hold the jacket so that the eyelet is away from you. Insert the needle between the interfacing and the facing layers of fabric on the left edge of the buttonhole at the inner placement line. If you are left-handed, insert the needle on the right edge.

2. Bring the needle out ⅛" (3mm) beyond the edge, embedding the knot between the layers of fabric.

3. Take a ⅛" (3mm) buttonhole stitch, but do not tighten it.

4. Cut a piece of gimp or another piece of buttonhole twist that is equal in length to twice the length of the buttonhole plus 2" (5cm).

5. Lay the gimp or twist along the edge of the buttonhole and slip 1" (2.5cm) of it through the untightened buttonhole stitch.

6. To finish the stitch, first pull the thread firmly back toward you. Then pull the thread firmly forward and away from you.

7. Continue making buttonhole stitches along the edge, catching the gimp or twist in the stitches. Make stitches that fan around the eyelet. To tighten each stitch, pull the thread straight up.

8. At the inner placement line, finish the edge with a bar tack. After you have made the fastening stitches for the bar tack, cut away the loose ends of the gimp. Then finish making the bar tack.

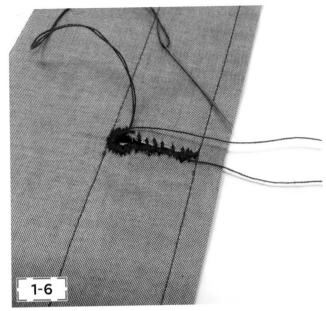

1-6

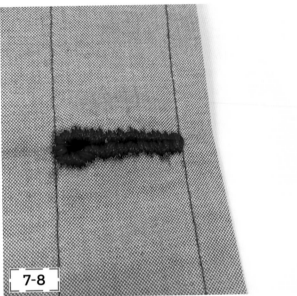

7-8

THE BOUND BUTTONHOLE

Bound buttonholes are created with a patch of fabric finishing the edges as opposed to hand or machine stitched buttonholes, which have edges finished formed with thread. If you have sewn a welt pocket, the bound buttonhole is created in a similar fashion. It is among the most intricate fastening elements to sew, involving careful stitching in a very small area. Its couture look, however, makes the effort worthwhile. The binding for the buttonholes may be made from the same fabric as the garment or, for a dramatic effect, from a contrasting fabric.

Before you begin the buttonholes, practice on spare pieces of all the materials involved, including the binding and garment fabric, interfacing, and lining or underlining. Then start on the garment itself with the buttonhole that will be least conspicuous. Once you master the basic bound buttonhole, you can create this closure in different shapes and sizes for added creativity.

Marking and Interfacing

1. Interface the areas of the garment that will hold the buttonhole. Baste the buttonhole markings on the garment.
2. To mark the location of the placement lines on the interfacing and the outside of the garment, use one thread color to baste along the inner, outer, and buttonhole placement lines. Use another thread color to baste along the center front line.

Marking and Interfacing

Preparing the Patch

1. For each buttonhole, make a binding patch that measures 2" (5cm) along the lengthways grain of the fabric and at least 1" (2.5cm) wider than the desired width of the finished buttonhole.
2. Fold each patch in half crossways with the wrong sides together and mark the center line of the patch with a row of basting stitches on the fold.
3. To mark the upper- and lower-fold lines of each patch, make a parallel row of basting stitches ¼" (0.5cm) above and another row ¼" (0.5cm) below the center line.
4. Fold the patch along the upper fold line, wrong sides together, and pin it.
5. Machine stitch halfway between the center line and the upper fold line. Stitch slowly, slipping out the pins as you go. The stitching must be straight and even to ensure a precision finish. Repeat on lower edge. These two rows of stitching, ¼" (0.5cm) apart by the upper- and lower-fold lines, will create two tucks that will form the visible bound edges of the finished buttonhole.
6. Remove the upper- and lower-fold line bastings, but leave in the basting stitches along the center of the patch.

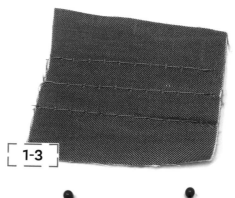

1-3

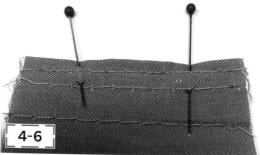

4-6

TIP

Use one color to baste the outer edge of the buttonhole and a contrasting color for the center marking.

Attaching the Patch to the Garment

1. On the right side of the garment, on one buttonhole placement, spread the patch open so that the basted center line is visible, and with right sides together, match the basting to the buttonhole placement line. Let the ends of the patch extend ½" (1.5cm) beyond the inner and outer placement lines.

2. Pin the patch to the garment, checking again to be sure that the center line on the patch exactly matches the buttonhole placement line.

3. Baste over the center line of the patch to fasten it to the interfacing and garment fabric. Remove pins.

4. Fold the top of the patch down so that the upper row of stitching is visible. Place a pin at each end of the patch inside the outer and inner placement lines.

5. Replace the presser foot on your machine with a zipper foot. Insert the machine needle at the inside edge of the pin at the outer placement line. Turn the machine wheel by hand to make one stitch backward over the pin. Remove the pin and stitch forward until you reach the second pin.

6. Turning the wheel again by hand, make one stitch over the second pin, slip it out, and secure the thread with two backstitches.

7. Fold the bottom of the patch up so that the lower row of stitching is visible. Pin and stitch as described above, sewing just outside the visible stitching, making sure not to catch the upper fold. Remove the bastings from the patch.

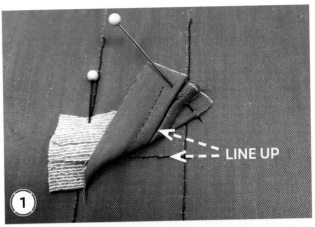

LINE UP

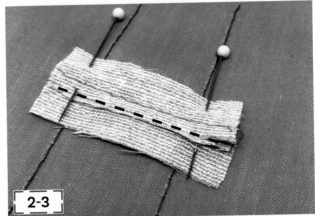

2-3

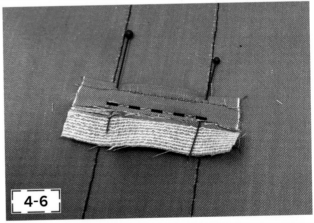

4-6

7

Opening the Buttonhole

1. Spread the patch open. Using the row of basting stitches on the buttonhole placement line as your guide, cut the patch in half with small, sharp-pointed scissors.

2. Turn the garment wrong side up. Make a ¼" (0.5cm) long cut at the center of the buttonhole, parallel to the visible rows of machine stitching on the front patch midway between them. Be sure to cut through the interfacing, lining or underlining, and garment fabric.

3. Make diagonal cuts through all the fabric layers from the center cut to each of the four corners of the buttonhole. Cut up to, but not through, the ends of the machine stitching. Keep the edges of the patch on the opposite side of the garment out of the way of the scissors.

4. Turn the garment wrong side down and, with your fingers, push the edges of the patch and the triangles of fabric at each end of the buttonhole through the opening to the wrong side of the garment.

5. Turn the garment to right side out and make sure that the little triangles formed by the diagonal cuts are pushed completely through the buttonhole opening. Press the edges of the patch flat with an iron.

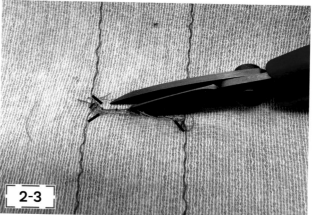

Completing the Buttonhole Patch

1. To hold the buttonhole in shape while you make the finishing stitches, on the right side baste the visible bound edges of the buttonhole together with diagonal basting stitches.
2. On the wrong side, fold the garment and interfacing back along the outer placement line so that the underside of the patch extends away from the folded garment.
3. Machine stitch parallel to the outer placement line from about ⅛" (3mm) above to ⅛" (3mm) below the two visible rows of stitching. Make sure to catch the little triangles.
4. Complete all the other buttonholes. Remove all basting stitches except those marking the center front line of the garment and those holding the edges of the buttonholes together.

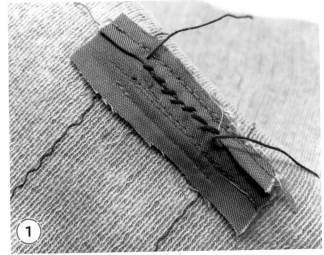

Finishing the Buttonhole

1. On the wrong side of the fabric, fold over the interfacing along the fold line or the seam line and pin it down.
2. Baste the facing to the garment around each buttonhole. Insert pins through the fabric at each corner and at the center of one buttonhole. Turn the garment wrong side up. Follow the pin markings and cut open the facing as above. Remove the pins.
3. Tuck under the top and bottom edges of the cut and the triangles at either side. Sew the edges with tiny hemming stitches.
4. Repeat at all other buttonholes and remove all bastings.

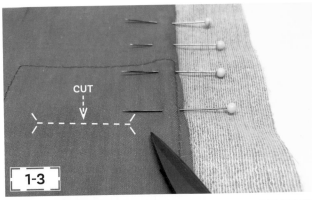

LININGS

Nothing sets apart a garment as professionally made more distinctly than a lining or an underlining.

An underlining, which gives support to the fabric, is cut in the shape of the main pieces of the garment from tightly woven fabric such as silk organza, interfacing, or broadcloth. The underlining is sewn to each piece of the garment, then the two layers are treated as one when the garment is constructed.

A lining is constructed independently of special lining fabric, such as rayon, polyester blends, or even silk. It is then installed inside the assembled garment as a layer to separate the garment from the body. This prevents the garment from clinging and allows it to retain its own shape. Lining also has other purposes that cannot be seen; they finish the garment as perfectly on the inside as on the outside and conceal construction details such as darts and seam allowances.

Choose a lining suitable for the fabric and garment to be made. The underlining will keep the garment in good shape and prevent it from stretching when worn.

LINING TIPS

1. Before constructing the garment, cut out the underlining from special underlining fabric, using the main pieces of your pattern, exactly as you cut out the garment fabric. Do not cut out underlining for garment pieces that will be interfaced or for those that will be on the underside of the garment, such as facings.

2. Transfer all pattern markings to either side of the underlining; do not transfer any pattern markings to the garment fabric pieces to be underlined.

3. Working on one section at a time, lay the underlining marked side down and cover it with the corresponding garment section wrong side down. Pin the two pieces of fabric together around all the edges, keeping them as flat as possible.

4. On large pattern pieces, run parallel rows of diagonal basting stitches about 3" (7.5cm) apart down the length of the section, smoothing the two fabrics as you go to eliminate puckers and creases.

5. Turn each section over so that the underlining faces up. Run hand bastings along all seam lines and pattern markings, stitching through both garment and underlining. Smooth the layers of fabric outwards from the diagonal bastings so that both layers lie as flat as possible. Start at one corner or seam intersection and stitch to the opposite corner; stop, leaving 2" or 3" (5 or 7.5cm) of thread loose. Begin again in the next direction with a new thread. Remove pins.

6. Check the underlining and garment fabric to be sure they are smooth. If either layer pulls or creases, clip the nearby bastings and re-baste.

7. Repeat steps 3–6 on all pattern pieces that are to be underlined.

8. Sew the garment, but do not remove the basting stitches holding the underlining to each section until the garment is completed.

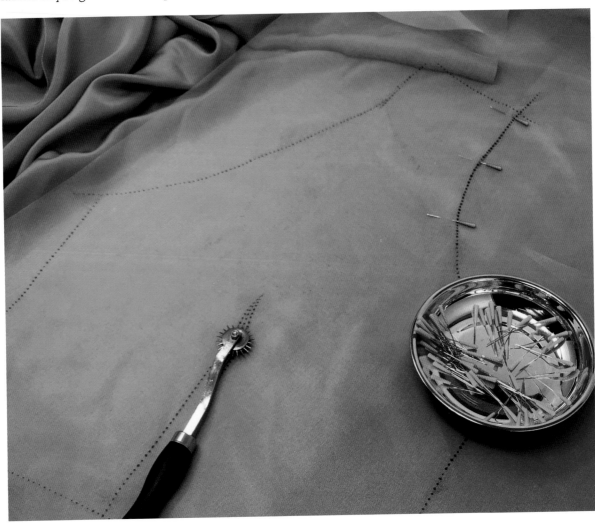

LINING FOR A DRESS WITHOUT FACINGS

1. If your pattern does not provide separate pattern pieces for the lining, cut out the lining fabric exactly as you did the garment fabric, using only the main pattern pieces.
2. Transfer the pattern markings to the wrong sides of the lining.
3. Machine stitch the darts and all the seams except the waistline seam and armhole seams to complete the lining for each section of the garment, making any fitting adjustments you made on the garment. Press the darts and seams.
4. Machine stitch along the neckline and armhole seam lines to prevent stretching. Also stitch along the waist seam line on the skirt.
5. Machine baste—at six stitches per 1" (1.5cm) two parallel lines ¼" (0.5cm) apart along the top of the sleeves and between the notches, leaving loose threads at both ends for easing.

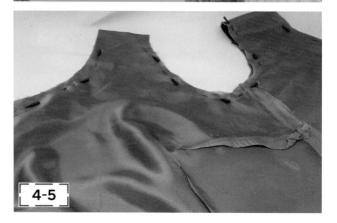

LINING FOR A DRESS WITH FACINGS

1. Cut out, mark, and machine stitch the lining as shown in steps 1–3 above.
2. Pin the patterns for the facings over the wrong side of the appropriate lining pieces, matching the seam lines at the edges.
3. Draw a line with chalk on the lining along the inside edge of each facing pattern. Remove the pins and pattern.
4. Run a line of machine stitching on the edge of the lining ⅝" (1.5cm) from the chalk line made above.
5. Trim the edge of the lining ⅝" (1.5cm) from the machine stitching; clip at ½" (1.5cm) intervals into the trimmed edge at the curves to within ⅛" (3mm) of the stitching line.

ATTACHING LINING TO A BODICE

Lining a Bodice without Facings

1. Turn the bodice wrong side out and tuck the sleeves inside the bodice armholes.

2. Place the bodice lining over the garment with the wrong sides together. Pin the lining to the garment around the armholes and neckline at 2" (5cm) intervals, matching seam lines and pattern markings.

3. Fold under the lining along the zipper opening so that the folded edge is ¼" (0.5cm) from the teeth of the zipper and pin.

4. Check to be sure the lining does not stretch or pull the garment fabric out of shape. If it does, re-pin, even if this means that the folded edge of the lining may have to be drawn back slightly from its original position.

5. Baste the garment and the lining together along the line of machine stitching at the neckline and armhole of the garment.

6. If no sleeve lining will finish off the armhole seam, then a bias binding created from the lining may be used to finish off the seam. Cut a rectangle of fabric on the bias the length of the arm opening by 2" (5cm) wide. Fold the bias band in half. Place the unfinished edge of the binding against the inside of the seam. Baste next to the seam line. Wrap around the seam allowance and continue with step 7.

7. Hand stitch a row of running stitches around the armholes, going through both lining and garment layers as closely as possible to the outside of the seam line of the armholes.

8. Slipstitch the folded edge of the lining to the zipper tape. Remove all pins.

9. Attach the collar, neckband, or other neckline finish as the pattern instructs.

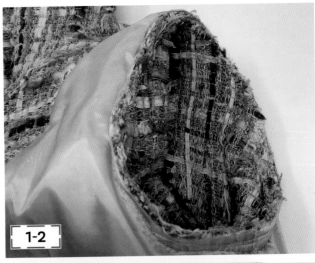

1-2

6

7

ATTACHING THE SKIRT LINING

1. Turn the garment wrong side out and fold the lined bodice down inside the skirt, leaving the waistline seam uppermost.
2. Place the skirt lining, wrong side in, over the skirt and pin the two together around the waistline, aligning the seam lines at the waist and matching all pattern markings.
3. If the garment opening has a zipper, fold under the seam allowances of the skirt lining along the opening so that the folded edges are ¼" (0.5cm) from the teeth of the zipper. Pin.
4. Attach the skirt lining to the garment along the waistline seam with a line of small running stitches, then slip stitch the lining to the zipper or facing at the opening. Remove the pins.

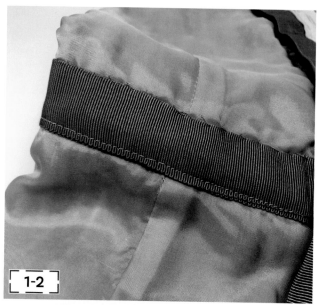

Attaching the Bodice Lining to the Skirt

1. With the dress wrong side out, smooth the bottom of the lining fabric up toward the shoulders about ¼" so that it blouses slightly, then pin the bodice lining to the bodice 1 ½" (4cm) above the waistline seam, matching the side seams of the lining and garment.
2. Fold under the bottom of the bodice lining so that the folded edge just covers the hand stitches made at the waistline seam and pin.
3. Slip stitch the bodice lining to the skirt lining. Remove the pins. The lining will blouse slightly over the waistline, creating wearing ease.

Preparing the Sleeve Lining

Gently pull the loose ends of the ease threads at the top of the sleeve lining, first at one side, then the other, to distribute the ease evenly.

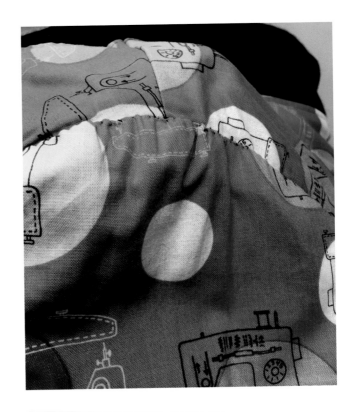

Attaching the Sleeve Lining to the Garment at the Shoulder

1. Put the dress on a hanger or dress form, lining side out. Tuck the sleeves of the dress inside the bodice and insert the sleeve linings into the sleeves, so that the wrong sides of sleeves and sleeve linings are together.

2. Fold under the seam allowance along the top of the sleeve lining so that the ease stitching is hidden.

3. Align the folded edge at the top of the sleeve lining with the armhole seam line of the garment and pin together at 1" (2.5cm) intervals, matching seam intersections and other pattern markings and distributing the easing evenly as you go. Do not be concerned if the lining puckers slightly at the upper edge of the sleeve cap; this allows for wearing ease.

4. Slipstitch the sleeve lining to the bodice lining; keep the stitches ¼" (0.5cm) apart under the armhole and ⅛" (3mm) apart on the top of the armhole. Remove the pins.

5. Repeat on the other sleeve.

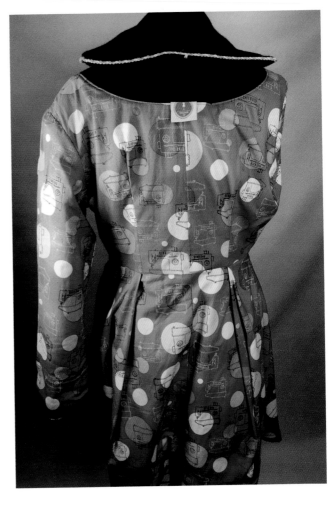

ATTACHING LINING TO A SLEEVE

1. Fold up the sleeve to the desired length and pin. Stitch the hem, using a blind hemming stitch Remove pins, press.

2. With the garment right side out, pull out the sleeve lining so that it hangs below the bottom of the sleeve.

3. Pin the sleeve to the lining 3" (7.5cm) above the bottom edge of the sleeve. Baste and remove the pins. Try on the garment. If the sleeve reaches below the elbow and the lining causes strain when the elbow is bent or if it causes the sleeve to ride up, clip the basting stitches, push the lining up slightly toward the shoulder, and re-baste.

4. Place the garment back on the hanger, lined side out. Do not be concerned if the lining blouses above the row of pins or the basting; this blousing provides wearing ease.

5. Trim each sleeve lining so that it is even with the bottom edge of the hemmed sleeve.

6. Turn under the sleeve lining so that the folded edge of the lining is ⅝" (1.5cm) from the bottom edge of the hemmed sleeve. Pin and hem with a blind hemming stitch.

7. Remove the pins and any basting stitches. The sleeve lining will drop slightly (almost to the sleeve edge) when released; this is necessary for wearing ease. Press lightly at the hem.

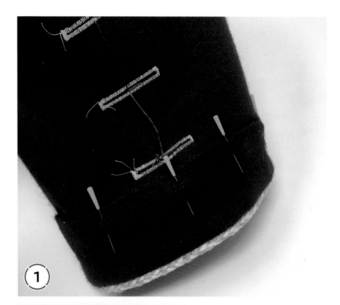

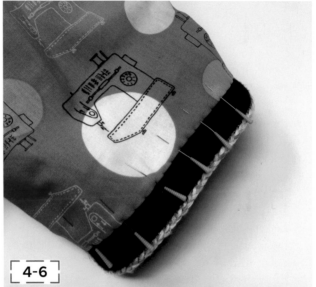

ATTACHING LINING TO THE HEM OF A GARMENT

Hemming the Lining

1. After the hem of the garment has been finished, place the garment on a dress form or hanger, lining side out. Trim the lining to the level of the bottom edge of the garment.
2. Fold the cut edge under ¼" (0.5cm) all around the bottom of the lining and pin. Baste the fold in place and remove the pins.
3. Turn the basted edge 1" (2.5cm) to the underside of the lining to make the hem and pin along the fold. Finish the hem with slip stitches; remove the pins and bastings. Press lightly.

Attaching the Lining to the Garment

1. Connect the hem of the lining to the hem of the garment at each vertical seam with a 1" (2.5cm) long chain of thread called a French tack. To make a French tack, begin by making a 1" (2.5cm) bar of thread between the lining and the garment hem. Using a doubled thread knotted at the end, make a stitch in the middle of the lining hem, then draw the needle through and pick up a few threads of the under layer of the garment hem. Repeat these two or three times in the same place, then end with a backstitch on the hem of the garment.
2. Make the chain part of the French tack by inserting the needle through the loops of thread, as in the blanket stitch, using the bar of thread as if it were a fabric edge.

Best wishes in your sewing adventures!
Designer Joi

GLOSSARY

Adjustment Line: A line printed on a pattern piece to indicate where it may be lengthened or shortened.

All-Purpose Foot: See **Presser Foot**.

Backstitch: A stitch used to reinforce the beginning or ending of a seam.

Bar Tack: A stitch used for reinforcing the ends of buttonholes and other openings.

Baste: To stitch to hold fabric pieces together temporarily, or to indicate pattern markings on both sides of the fabric. Basting stitches can be made by hand or by machine, generally at six stitches per inch.

Bias: A direction diagonal to the threads forming woven fabric—the warp and weft, or "grains." The true bias is at a 45° angle to the grains. Fabric is cut on a bias to make it drape in folds, as in a skirt, or to make it stretch slightly, as in a belt or binding.

Bias Tape: A strip of fabric, cut diagonally to the fabric threads— on the bias—so that it will stretch to cover curved edges of a garment piece. It is available in ¼" (0.5cm), ½" (1.3cm), and 1" (2.5cm) widths. The 1" (2.5cm) width has edges folded ¼" (0.5cm) to the wrong side. It may be single fold, with edges that are folded to the wrong side and meet in the center, or double fold, with an additional fold just off center.

Blanket Stitch: A hand stitch used for decoration and for protecting the raw edges of fabric.

Blind Hemming Stitch: A hand stitch used to create an almost invisible hem and to attach facings.

Bobbin: The spool holding the lower of the two threads a sewing machine locks together in a stitch.

Catch Stitch: A hand stitch used for hemming and attaching interfacings.

Chalk Marker: A gauge used to set skirt lengths. It consists of an adjustable stand holding a rubber bulb that, when squeezed, emits a puff of chalk to mark a hemline.

Clip: A short cut into the fabric outside a seam to help it lie flat around curves and corners.

Closure: The area on which fasteners—such as buttons or zippers—are placed to open and close a garment; also, the fasteners themselves.

Collar Interfacing: Stiff, firmly woven fabric that is sewn between the collar surface and the undercollar to help give shape to the collar.

Crosswise Grain: See **Grain**.

Cutting Line: A long, unbroken line printed on a pattern, often accompanied by a drawing of scissors, that indicates where it must be cut.

Dart: A stitched fabric fold, tapering to a point at one or both ends, that shapes fabric around curves.

Diagonal Basting Stitch: A hand stitch used to hold together layers of fabric such as underlinings and garment fabric during construction of the garment.

Dressmaker's Carbon: A marking paper, available in several colors and white, used with a tracing wheel to transfer construction lines from pattern to fabric.

Ease: The even distribution of fullness, without forming gathers or tucks, that enables one section of a garment to be smoothly joined to a slightly smaller section, as in the seam joining a sleeve to its armhole.

Ease Allowance: The extra material provided for in patterns beyond body measurement to give room in a garment for comfort and ease of movement.

Edge Stitch: Machine stitching on the visible side of the garment, close to the finished edges.

Facing: A piece of fabric, frequently the same as that used in the garment, that covers the raw fabric edge at openings such as necklines and armholes. It is sewn to the visible side of the opening, then turned to the inside so that the seam between it and the garment is enclosed.

Fastener: Any device that opens and closes a garment—button, hook and eye, snap, or zipper.

Fastening Stitch: A stitch used at the beginning or end of a row of hand sewing to hold the stitching securely.

Flat Felled Seam: A double-stitched seam for tailored shirts and slacks in which the seam allowance of one piece forming the seam is trimmed and the seam allowance of the other piece is turned in and stitched on top of the first to give a finished effect on both sides of the garment.

Foot: See **Presser Foot**.

French Tack: A chain of thread that connects the hem of a lining to the garment hem.

Gimp: Heavy cord made of silk, cotton, or wool strands with a metal wire core, used to reinforce the edges of hand-worked buttonholes.

Godet: A triangular piece sewn into a seam or into a slash cut up from a hemline to provide a flaring section.

Grading: Trimming each seam allowance within a multilayer seam—the fabric, facing, interfacing, etc.—to a different width to reduce bulk and make the seam lie flat.

Grain: The direction of threads in woven fabrics. The warp—the threads running parallel to the selvage—forms the lengthwise grain. The weft—the threads running across the lengthwise grain from one finished edge of the fabric to the other—forms the crosswise grain. Only if the two grains are at right angles to each other is the fabric aligned on the "true grain."

Grain-Line Arrow: The double-ended arrow printed on a pattern piece indicating how the piece is to be aligned with the threads of the fabric, its grains. The line between the arrow heads must be placed parallel to either the lengthwise or crosswise grain, as specified on the piece.

Guide Sheet: Instructions included with a pattern to provide specific directions for using the pattern pieces to make the garment.

Gusset: A diamond-shaped piece sewn between a sleeve underarm seam and a garment side seam to increase freedom of movement for the arm without causing the fabric to billow.

Haircloth: A wiry, extra-resilient interfacing fabric made from a mixture of strong cotton fibers and tough horsehair. It is sewn over the wool interfacing to reinforce the chest and shoulder areas of a man's jacket.

Half Backstitch: A hand stitch for strong seams in awkward places and for topstitching.

Hemming Stitch: A hand stitch for hemming bound or raw edges.

Interfacing: A special fabric sewn between two layers of garment fabric to stiffen, strengthen, and support parts of the garment. It is usually used around necklines, in collars, cuffs, pockets, or waistbands.

Interlining: A special fabric, sewn and shaped exactly like the garment and lining, placed in between to add warmth or shape.

Lap: To extend one piece of fabric over another, as at the connection of the ends of a belt.

Lapels: The portions of facings—turned to the outside of a garment—that run down the sides of the front opening from the end of the collar to the top button.

Lengthwise Grain: See **Grain**.

Lining: A fabric, usually lightweight, constructed in the shape of a garment to cover the inside of part or all of the garment. It can also stiffen and strengthen the garment.

Machine Baste: To insert temporary stitching for marking or preliminary seaming, working by machine rather than by hand. For basting, the machine is set at six stitches per inch.

Mercerizing: A chemical treatment for cotton fabric and thread to add strength and luster, and make the material more receptive to dye.

Muslin: An inexpensive cotton fabric used for making prototypes of garments—also called muslins—as

an aid to styling and fitting a design. A fitting muslin is a special snug, straight-skirted muslin "shell" used only to make accurate and detailed body measurements for cutting and fitting other garments. A design muslin is a preliminary muslin version of a garment made by a couturier as an aid to visualizing the garment while designing it. A dress muslin is a preliminary muslin version of an actual garment that is used to perfect the fit of the design to the wearer before the garment fabric is cut and assembled.

Nap: The short fibers on the surface of the fabric that have been drawn out and brushed in one direction, such as on velvet or corduroy.

Notch: A V- or diamond-shaped marking made on the edge of a garment piece as an alignment guide. It is meant to be matched with a similar notch or group of notches on another piece when the two pieces are joined.

Notions: Supplies used in sewing—needles, thread, pins, buttons, zippers, etc.

Overcast Stitch: A hand stitch used to finish raw seam edges.

Overlap: The part of the garment that extends over another part, as at the opening of a blouse, jacket, or waistband.

Pattern Layout and Cutting Guide: The instructions and diagrams showing how to place the pattern pieces on the fabric for cutting.

Pick Stitch: Also called prick stitch, a hand-sewing stitch used as topstitching for decorative purposes and also used for sewing zippers into position.

Pile: A surface of upright yarns found on fabrics such as corduroy, velvet, and terry cloth. The pile tends to lie in a preferred direction, so that the fabric's orientation affects its appearance. To determine the direction of the pile, brush the fabric lightly with your fingers; if the surface looks and feels smooth, you are brushing with the pile.

Pinking: A serrated edge at a seam, produced by special "pinking" shears to prevent woven fabrics from raveling.

Piping: In tailoring, a narrowly folded strip of garment fabric, generally used to finish the top and bottom edges of a pocket opening.

Pivot: A technique of machine sewing for making angular corners. The sewer stops the machine with the needle down at the apex of a corner, raises the presser foot, pivots the fabric, and then lowers the presser foot before continuing to stitch again.

Placement Line: A line printed on a pattern to indicate where buttonholes, pockets, trimming, and pleats are to be placed.

Placket: A garment opening with an overlapping edge covered by a visible strip of fabric running the length of the opening. It is used with openings that are equipped with fasteners.

Plain Weave: A weave in which the yarns are interlaced in a simple checkerboard fashion. Plain weave is one of the two basic weaves used in tailored fabrics (the other is twill weave).

Pleats: Folds of fabric used to control fullness or shape a design.

Point Presser (also called a seam or tailor's board): A narrow hardwood board mounted on its side and shaped into a fine point at one end; used for pressing open small seams in hard-to-reach places, and for pressing open regular seams on hard fabrics.

Preshrink: The process of treating fabric to shrink it to an irreducible size before cutting. Washable fabric can be preshrunk simply by immersing it in water and pressing it when almost dry. Non-washable fabric should be preshrunk by a dry cleaner.

Presser Foot: The part of a sewing machine that holds fabric steady at the point it is being advanced and the needle is stitching it. The "all-purpose," or general-purpose, foot has two prongs, or "toes," of equal length, and is used for most stitching.

The "straight-stitch" foot has one long and one short toe and can be used for straight stitching and stitching over fabrics of varying thicknesses. The "zipper" foot has only one toe and is used to stitch zippers and cording.

Pressing Cloth: A piece of fabric, preferably cotton drill cloth or organza, that is placed between the iron and the garment when pressing.

Press Mitt: A padded, thumbless mitten used to press small curved areas that do not fit over a tailor's ham or a regular ironing board. One side of the mitt should be covered with cotton drill cloth, the other with soft wool.

Reinforce: To strengthen an area that will be subjected to strain, such as the bottom of a pocket, with a small patch of fabric or extra stitches.

Roll: To manipulate fabric between the fingers, usually along a seam line, in order to bring the seam out to the edge—or beyond the edge to the wrong side—of the garment.

Running Stitch: A basic hand stitch that is made by weaving the needle and thread in and out of the fabric.

Saddle Stitch: A hand stitch used for bold decorative topstitching, using buttonhole twist thread or embroidery floss.

Seam: The joint between two or more pieces of fabric, or the line of stitching that makes a fold in a single piece of fabric, such as a dart.

Seam Allowance: The extra fabric—usually ⅝" (1.6cm)—that extends outside the seam line.

Seam Binding: Ribbon, ½" (1.3cm) or 1" (2.5cm) wide, of rayon, silk, or nylon, that is sewn over fabric edges to cover them, concealing their raw appearance and preventing raveling. Seam binding is also available cut diagonally to the fabric threads—on the bias—to sew over curved edges. See also **Bias Tape**.

Seam Finish: The treatment of raw seam edges to prevent fraying and raveling.

Seam Line (also called stitching line): The long broken line printed on a pattern to indicate where a seam must be stitched; it is usually ⅝" (1.6cm) inside the cutting line.

Selvage: The lengthwise finished edges on woven fabric.

Shank: The link between the button and the fabric to which it is sewn. The shank can be made with thread or it can be part of the button, but it must be long enough to allow for the thickness of the overlapping fabric.

Slash: A long, straight cut to make a garment opening or to open a fold of fabric so that it will lie flat, reducing bulkiness.

Sleeve Board: Two small ironing boards of different widths, connected at one end, for pressing garment areas (such as sleeves) that will not fit over a regular ironing board.

Slip Stitch: An invisible hand-sewing stitch.

Stay Stitch: A line of machine stitches sewn at 12 stitches per inch on the seam line of a garment piece before the seam is stitched. Stay-stitching is used as a reinforcement to prevent curved edges from stretching, and as a guide for folding an edge accurately.

Stitching Line: See **Seam Line**.

Straight-Stitch Foot: See **Presser Foot**.

Synthetic Fibers: Man-made fibers produced by forming filaments from chemical solutions; examples include polyester, nylon, and acrylic.

Tack: Several stitches made in the same place to reinforce a point of strain, hold garment parts permanently in position, or finish the ends of pockets, pleats, and buttonholes securely. Also a synonym for a quick, temporary "stitch" in certain instances.

Tailor's Bodkin: A slender, 4" (10cm)–long ivory stick, pointed at one end and rounded at the other, used to pull out basting threads and to round out the eyelets of hand-worked buttonholes.

Tailor's Chalk: Flat squares made of wax, stone, or clay, used to transfer pattern markings or adjustments onto fabric.

Tailor's Clapper (also called beater, striker, or pounding block): An oblong or rectangular piece of hardwood which is wielded like a paddle to flatten parts of a garment, typically the edges of collars, hems and lapels, trouser creases, and pleats or to smooth and reduce the bulk of seams.

Tailor's Ham: A firm, ham-shaped cushion with built-in curves that conform to various contours of the body; used for pressing areas that require shaping. One half of a ham is covered with cotton drill cloth for general pressing, the other half with soft wool—which is used when pressing woolen fabric to prevent shine.

Tailor's Sleeve Cushion: A long, flat pad with a sleevelike silhouette; inserted into a completed sleeve when pressing to prevent wrinkling the underside or forming undesirable creases.

Tailor's Thimble: An especially sturdy metal thimble that is open at the top.

Take-Up Lever: The lever on the sewing machine that raises and lowers the presser foot.

Tension: The degree of tightness of the two threads forming machine stitches. Unless tension is properly adjusted in each, the threads will not lock evenly together in the stitch.

Thread: Twisted strands of fibers wound on a spool used for sewing.

Throat Plate: A flat metal piece with a hole through which the needle passes as it stitches. A general-purpose throat plate has a wide hole to accommodate sideways motion of the needle; many machines also have a second throat plate with a small hole, to prevent soft fabrics and knits from being pulled down into the machine and puckering during stitching. Throat plates have guide lines on the left and right sides to help you sew a straight seam.

Topstitch: A line of machine stitching on the visible side of the garment parallel to a seam.

Tracing Wheel: A small wheel attached to a handle, used in conjunction with dressmaker's carbon to transfer markings from pattern pieces to fabric. Tracing wheels with serrated edges are used for most fabrics, but plain edges are preferred for knits to avoid snagging the material.

Trim: To cut away excess fabric in the seam allowance after the seam has been stitched. Also, a strip of fabric—such as braid or ribbon—used to decorate a garment.

Twill Tape (also called stay tape): A thin, extra-strong tape of twilled linen or cotton fabric that is sewed along the lapel edges and roll line of a jacket as reinforcement, and to prevent stretching.

Twill Weave: A weave in which the yarns interlace in a steplike formation to create a diagonal rib on the surface of the fabric. The rib may slant to the right or to the left, or it may zigzag in alternating directions, as in herringbone twill (sometimes called chevron or broken twill).

Underlap: A part of a garment that extends under another part, as at the connection at the ends of a belt.

Underlining: A tightly woven fabric cut in the shapes of the main pieces of a garment and attached to these pieces before the garment is sewed together. Used only for women's garments to stabilize shape in stretchy woven fabrics and to conceal construction details like seam allowances in lightweight woven fabrics.

Understitching: Sewing into the seam allowance just outside a line of machine stitching, to prevent a facing from rolling out.

Vent: A slit in the skirt of a tailored jacket which keeps the hem line from binding when the wearer bends or reaches into a pants pocket.

Welt Pocket: An interior pocket that opens to the outside, finished with a horizontal band of garment fabric that covers the opening.

Welt Seam: A seam that is finished by stitching fabric and seam allowances together parallel to the original seam. Welt seams are used to accent the structure of a dress. A double welt seam is made with two parallel rows of stitching.

With Nap: A cutting direction on patterns to indicate how the pattern is to be aligned with fabrics that, because of their surface, napped weave or printed design, change in appearance with the direction in which they are set. When such fabrics are used, all pattern pieces must be laid and cut out in one direction—with the nap.

Zigzag Stitch: A serrated line of machine stitching used as decoration or to prevent raveling of raw edges, particularly on knits.

Zipper: A mechanical fastener consisting of two tapes holding parallel lines of teeth or coils that can be interlocked by a sliding bracket, or slider. The zipper generally has a top stop, a small metal bracket or bit of stitching at the top to prevent the slider from running off the tapes; a guide line, a raised line woven into the tapes to show where they are to be stitched to the garment; and a bottom stop, a bracket at the bottom against which the slider rests when the zipper is open.

Zipper Foot: See **Presser Foot**.

ABOUT THE AUTHOR

Joi Mahon is the founder of Dress Forms Design Studio, LLC, owner of The Sewing Factory Design Studio, an award-winning designer, an expert in fit, and a fashion entrepreneur with a wide array of sewing interests and endeavors. She is a McCall Licensed Pattern Designer, Craftsy instructor, and creator of Designer Joi's Perfect Pattern and Fit Club, a private membership program on Facebook. She is also a brand ambassador for Baby Lock Sewing Machines & Mettler Thread, and the founding instructor for the 2021 Nancy's Notions Wardrobe Builder Fashion Sewing Program on YouTube. Joi is deeply involved in the industry and attends several trade shows each year, with her specialty being fitting solutions. With a passion to convey real sewing and fitting solutions, Joi teaches what really works for the individual body based on her real-life fitting experiences. *Ultimate Illustrated Guide to Sewing Clothes* is Joi's third book, with her previous publications being *Create the Perfect Fit* and *Designer Joi's Fashion Sewing Workshop*. To learn more about Joi and see her work, visit her website (*www.designerjoi.com*) or her Facebook (@DesignerJoiMahon).

ACKNOWLEDGMENTS

I want to extend a special thanks to my family for their support and allowing me all the time to work on this in-depth project. A giant thanks to my big sis Joni for doing pre-editing and my students for their eagerness to learn. Thanks to Rhonda from Schmetz for always being willing to provide solid needle knowledge and Dr. Sara Kadolph, one of my professors from ISU, for an early edit of my textile science content. Lastly, thanks to my two furry friends who sat on my lap and kept me company for every book typing session.

It is interesting to think back to individual times when I learned a new skill or had a fresh sewing experience. They were not always successful, but each experience would lead to a better understanding and more confidence when a new project popped up.

The first time I read about sewing was when I mailed cash and coins through snail mail to get a subscription to *Sew News Magazine*. I was nine. Then in high school, I learned about *Threads Magazine*. I would never have dreamt that I would have an article on the cover some day.

The one and only how-to-sew class that I ever took was taught by a 4-H mom. She was the type that made you sew and rip to perfection. She is also the reason I try to teach friendly, recognize mistakes and encourage the joy of sewing before the perfection of sewing.

My first paid project was making hand puppets that looked like diverse people for a charity to use with counseling young children when I was thirteen.

I learned to run a tailoring business all through high school, and the reason I could start a business right after college was a result of all those experiences.

I taught my first sewing class when I was thirteen years old. When my home ec teacher was absent, I taught the class under the supervision of the substitute. This was the launching off point for teaching students all over the world both live and online.

My first mass produced project was making baby bibs for our hospital nursery as a 4-H project. That was my foundation for working with large corporations on freelance projects today.

I designed my first pattern when I was fifteen for 4-H and the judges hated it! But that was also the reason I worked even harder to master my pattern making and design skills.

Sewing is a lot like learning to play the piano — you certainly are not a maestro after one lesson or project, and you don't skip the intermediate recital just because you have not mastered the Concerto in D Minor. Today, in our instant society, it's easy to lose patience if we don't master a technique at first try. STOP THAT! When you experience something both successfully and unsuccessfully, that is when you gain mastery and confidence. I encourage my students to LOVE sewing first and then focus on the mastery because skill takes time.

INDEX

PHOTO CREDITS

All photos by the author unless otherwise noted here.

Images are credited to their respective creators: 40–41 (all images and text): SCHMETZ; 49 middle: photo courtesy Mettler; 52 top: Fotolia/Adobe Stock; 60 top: Fotolia/Adobe Stock; 60 bottom: Fotolia/Adobe Stock; 61 top: Fotolia/Adobe Stock; 61 bottom: Fotolia/Adobe Stock; 65 top: Fotolia/Adobe Stock; 124 bottom: photo courtesy McCall's Patterns; 135: photo courtesy Nancy's Notions & sewn by Audra Hoy Chaimson; 182: Fotolia/Adobe Stock; 190 bottom: photo courtesy Mike Yamin for *Threads* magazine; 191 bottom: Fotolia/Adobe Stock; 201: photo courtesy Mike Yamin for *Threads* magazine

The following images are credited to Shutterstock.com and their respective creators: front cover top: Elnur; front cover bottom middle: Elnur; front cover bottom left: Bushmanov Vladimir; back cover: almaje; 1 top left: garetsworkshop; 1 top middle: Normano1; 1 top right top: Kuzina Natali; 1 top right bottom: Bonita R. Cheshier; 1 middle left: CandyBox Images; 1 middle right: Africa Studio; 1 bottom: UfaBizPhoto; 18: Syda Productions; 35: New Africa; 39: Evgeniya369; 43: violetblue; 47 middle right: BearFotos; 48: Africa Studio; 50: BearFotos; 55: Studio Romantic; 63: mavo; 65 bottom: FotoDuets; 69 top left: luanateutzi; 69 top middle: Flas100; 69 top right: Flas100; 69 bottom left: Flas100; 69 bottom middle: Flas100; 69 bottom right: Manamigraphic; 117: Okrasiuk; 122 bottom: Chadchai Krisadapong; 123: studioloco; 126: elladoro; 146: Aleksei Isachenko; 153: Oksana Shufrych; 179: indira's work; 180: Lazuin; 181: Rawpixel.com; 183: LightField Studios; 184: Monkey Business Images; 195: Africa Studio; 215: Evgeniya369; 218: Katerina Ulyanova; 232: apazuhanich; 241: Okrasiuk; 251 bottom: Roman Samsonov; 257: vvoe; 263: Denis Pogostin